To MY friend
PauL Hebert
enjoy the

HER NAME IS AMERICA

A MEMOIR BY SABAH TOMA
AS TOLD TO BOB CANAAN

WESTBOW
PRESS®
A DIVISION OF THOMAS NELSON
& ZONDERVAN

WestBow Press books may be ordered through booksellers or by contacting:

WestBow Press
A Division of Thomas Nelson & Zondervan
1663 Liberty Drive
Bloomington, IN 47403
www.westbowpress.com
1 (866) 928-1240

ISBN: 978-1-5127-9326-0 (sc)
ISBN: 978-1-5127-9327-7 (hc)
ISBN: 978-1-5127-9325-3 (e)

Library of Congress Control Number: 2017910682

Print information available on the last page.

WestBow Press rev. date: 07/25/2017

PART I

THE IMMIGRANT

CHAPTER ONE

★ ★ ★

Strangers In the Al Batiwen Tea House

★ ★ ★

Frustrated and nearly frantic, Sabah knew he would need to run the entire three miles between his new home and Mutanabbi Street. Why did the move have to be *today*? All morning he'd been helping his family move their few meager possessions. Moving was nothing new for the Toma family; this was the fourth time they'd done so in Sabah's fourteen years. By now the process was efficient and routine, for which Sabah was especially grateful today.

He did his duty quickly and quietly, seldom speaking to his seven brothers and sisters as they unpacked. As he worked, hurried calculations filled his mind: times, distances, bus schedules. It was Wednesday, nearly four in the afternoon. Finding a bus at this time of day would be unlikely. Yes, he would have to run.

This decided, Sabah paused to study the dimensions of the single room his family would now be calling home. It was a ten foot by thirty foot room, nearly windowless with a smooth, concrete floor and plaster walls that were nothing more than rough pattern of patches. In his hands, Sabah held his most valued possession, a small red and white Webcor carrying case. He scanned the room, searching for the perfect place to hide it, but nowhere seemed safe enough. His fingers tightened possessively around the case. Only the safest possible place would do.

The case held exactly three doMen 45 rpm records. Sabah had spent years purchasing them, one by one with his scant savings. The Beatles,

1

Tom Jones, James Brown, Englebert Humperdink … In 1968, this was not a typical record collection for a fourteen-year-old boy in Baghdad.

In the end, he placed the record case gently in a corner and covered it with the rolled up mattress that was his bed. When he turned to look at his father, he found his father's eyes already upon him.

Was there more work to do? Of course, but Mr. Toma had asked enough of his son already. Older than his years, Mr. Toma had struggled nearly every day of his life to feed the eight children he had brought into the world. His eyes were tired, but not without humor. Deeper within those eyes, Sabah saw a flash of something more. Was it envy mixed with wistfulness? Whatever it was, Mr. Toma's face reflected an emotion so distinct and unfamiliar that, for an instant, Sabah entirely forgot his own urgent mission.

"Go on," his father said with the slightest nod toward the door.

"Are you sure?" Sabah asked. "Don't you need—?"

"Go on, before I change my mind." His eyes were smiling more than his lips. "Everything else can wait."

Without another word, Sabah was out the door, sprinting toward Mutanabbi Street. The district appealed to Sabah and he went there often. It was an area of book stores and knowledge, of educated people with interesting ideas. The Al Batiwen Tea House had long been a gathering place for people of this sort, but the tea house would serve a much more important purpose today.

Today, the Al Batiwen Tea House was one of the few public gathering places in Baghdad that would be showing the European Football Championship game live from London—and in color! Sabah had never seen a championship game or a color TV set before, and the thought of those two wonders made the three-mile run infinitely more bearable.

Perspiring and gasping for breath, he skidded into the tea house only minutes after the game had begun. Inside the darkened room, his eyes were immediately drawn to the television, which was mounted high on a far wall. Sabah moved toward the flickering color images like a moth toward a flame, hypnotized both by the miraculous technology and the event it was conveying.

As he moved, he was only vaguely aware of the commotion in the room around him. The noise was a seamless and logical part of the experience.

Football fans, even those as sophisticated and cultured as those who frequented the Al Batiwen, were known for their rabid loyalty, which often led to rowdiness and occasional quarrels with opposing fans. Even though Iraq's team wasn't in this match, a certain degree of bantering and sparring among opposing fans was natural for a contest of this importance. As Sabah drew closer to the television, however, he realized that something more was going on than mere fan fanaticism.

For the first time, he glanced around the dim, crowded, smoke-filled room. The scene didn't appear to be unusual. It was the typical gathering of mostly men, eclectic in their style, culture, and appearance. The tea house was, after all, an open forum for men with open minds, and it attracted a diverse group. This was what had drawn Sabah to the Al Batiwen in the first place.

But there was something different about the crowd today, and it had nothing to do with the soccer match. In the corner of the room, Sabah noticed a particularly loud, agitated group. They seemed to be a combination of students and professional people, some younger, some older, some with traditional dishdashas, some with western slacks and dress shirts. Several of the men were wide eyed, some gesturing wildly, others standing, others pointing. None of them seemed remotely aware of the television or the match being played on it.

This kind of agitation among the tea house patrons was not entirely unusual. Sabah had been here many times before, eavesdropping on intellectuals and world travelers. He had listened to them discussing politics, economics, or history at a level he could never comprehend, but it was like listening to one of his American records. He might not understand the words, but he could still enjoy the rhythm and melody of the music.

The passions and convictions of these scholars and world travelers would often erupt into very heated debates. Sabah would watch and listen as though a great theatrical pageant or spectacle were being performed just for him.

But it was different this time. Some line had been crossed between reason and rage, civility and brutality. Like dark clouds gathering before a torrential downpour, there was an ugliness and imminent sense of danger about this group.

A deafening burst of cheers erupted from the television as Manchester

3

United scored their first goal. Sabah's head jerked away from the group, while many of the tea house patrons reacted to the goal with either cheers or groans.

At that very moment, above the collective noise of the room, Sabah could hear one man's voice. He was yelling. Sabah's head jerked back to the group of men in the corner of the room. One of the younger men, dressed in more contemporary, western-style clothing, was standing almost nose to nose with an older man, pointing a finger at the man's chest.

"Total disaster! Complete, total disaster! Iraq needs al-Bakr the way Germany needed Hitler! The man is a bully and a thug. And a coward!"

On the television, the action continued fast and furious with the announcer yelling as loudly as the fans in the stadium. Sabah was momentarily torn between the two crescendos, but then a glint of metal from the group of men caught his eye. He sucked in a breath and took an instinctive step backwards.

The older man was holding a hand gun. Before Sabah could blink, the gun was held, point blank, against the younger man's forehead. Sabah would never know if the entire room actually went silent at that moment. But it had for Sabah.

The television was turned off and the tea house manager—a thin, balding old man with a neatly-trimmed moustache—spoke up from the opposite side of the room.

"Please," he said urgently, his eyes wide with alarm. "Please, no. Please."

"Do you love Iraq?" The older man's eyes were bulging now. He yelled again, "Do you love your country?"

He was holding the younger man by the throat with one hand, his gun still inches away in the other.

"Yes," the young man said softly. To Sabah, he looked both terrified and humiliated.

The older man's eyes flared. "What?" he bellowed.

"I said yes!" the younger man said, his words quivering with terror. "Of course I do!"

By now, three other men from the group had positioned themselves behind the man holding the knife, fanning out around the young man, surrounding him with such eerie synchroniMation it seemed almost rehearsed or choreographed.

"I don't think you do," the older man said. "In fact, you know what I think? I think you're a communist!"

The tea house manager, nearly hysterical now, moved closer to the group, his trembling hands clenched in front of him.

"Please, sir" he begged, the word a near whimper, "we are peaceful here, sir. Please."

From somewhere in the complete stillness of the room, a voice rang out sharply: "Call the police!"

The man holding the gun spun around, seeming to scan every person in the room at the same instant. No one moved. There was no sound but the hum of electric motors and worn, squeaky rubber belts slowly turning ceiling fans.

Gazing out at the crowd, his hand still wrapped around his victim's throat, the man gave a faint smile, as if appreciating some private joke only he could understand.

Finally, he pulled the gun away from the young man's head and slipped it into his jacket pocket. With a nod at his partners, he led the way toward the exit of the tea house.

At the exit door, he turned one last time. He took several long moments, staring at each person in the room, including Sabah. It seemed to Sabah the man was concentrating intently, as though he wanted to memorize every face he was seeing at this very moment. Then he spoke. Cold, metallic words rang out into the stillness of the room, seeming much louder than they actually were: "We *are* the police."

The four men vanished outside. For a long moment no one said a word.

Conversation filtered slowly back into the room, first in hushed whispers and then in louder, more confident voices as the mood began to relax. The television was turned back on. The frenMied fans of the soccer match could be clearly heard once again. The danger was over—time to get back to the business of enjoying their evenings.

For Sabah, though, there could be no enjoyment. Everything about the scene he'd just witnessed was incomprehensible to him. He had never seen this kind of savagery. He felt physically weak and sat down on a bench along one of the tea house walls. It was as though he were an infant again, able to see but unable to interpret the objects and actions around him.

There was no context for this event, nowhere to place it in his experience. What had just happened?

He looked toward the television and the now-silent soccer match, though his gaze wandered, his eyes unable to fix on the screen. Sabah then noticed two men seated at a table close by. They were speaking in hoarse, subdued whispers, leaning in close to each other. The only person in the room close enough to overhear them was Sabah, though he didn't turn to listen, instead keeping his eyes fixed safely on the television.

"What were you thinking?" one of the men was whispering. "He could have killed you. He could have killed you both!"

"What was I supposed to do? Sit here? Watch a man killed in front of me? Hama, no. No, not that."

There was silence for a moment. Then the first man spoke as Hama, his lips taut, slowly continued to shake his head. "You don't know who they are do you?" Hama's friend asked suddenly.

"Do you, Hama?" Slightly irritated by his friend's persistence, Hama said nothing for a moment then blurted, "Who knows? Crazy people? Drunks? Does it matter?" Ali studiedd his friend and waited for their eyes to meet before he spoke.

"Baathists," Ali said wearily, as though the very word exhausted him.

Sabah allowed himself to turn now and steal a glance at the two men beside him. They were ordinary working men, like his father. He'd seen men like them in every neighborhood he'd ever lived in. With their threadbare clothing, unpolished shoes, and piercing eyes, they were familiar to Sabah even though he'd never seen them before. As he glanced at them, he was just in time to see a look of understanding and despair fill Ali's eyes.

Ali simply pressed his lips together and slowly nodded his head. "Baathists," he said again.

For several long moments, the two men sat quiet and still, trapped in their own thoughts.

Finally, Hama looked at his friend. "What can we do?" he said softly.

Ali sighed. "What can we do? Get used to it. Just get used to it."

Baathist. Sabah had never heard the word before. What did it mean?

It reminded him of a time, not long before, when, in the middle of the night screams had come from the next door neighbor's house.

"Thief! Thief!" *a woman cried out, and Sabah's father was up before the screams ended, on his way to help if he could. Sabah jumped up off his mattress and chased after him.*

"Take me! Please, I want to see what a thief looks like."

"Come on, then; hurry," *his father answered, and they were both out the door in seconds.*

Sabah was thirteen, no longer a boy but not yet a man. Even so, in the same way small children believe in a boogeyman, Sabah honestly believed, even at this age, that a thief was not a human being but a creature closer to something he had seen years before in an American black and white horror movie. What had been the title? Oh, yes: The Creature From the Black Lagoon. *A thief must look something like that, he thought; a slithering, scale-covered monster.*

Was it surprising naiveté in a boy Sabah's age? Or was it the prevailing decency and high moral standards of his world that made meeting a thief as remote and unlikely as meeting Pele or an American astronaut?

Either way, Sabah was surprised, but not disappointed, when he and his father rounded the corner of the neighbor's house and saw a very ordinary, somewhat overweight middle-aged man wedged in a small bathroom window, halfway in and halfway out. Only at that moment did Sabah realiMe that a thief, after all, was just an ordinary man.

So this person Sabah had just seen in the Al Batiwen Tea House, this barbaric, savage person who had treated another man with more cruelty than Sabah had ever seen, was a Baathist. Yet his childlike imaginations of what a thief might look like instantly and forever disappeared when he actually saw one. Just the opposite was true of the Baathist, a person he had never heard of but who would come back, again and again and in ever growing numbers, each one more hideous and frightening than the one before.

CHAPTER TWO

★ ★ ★

Mr. Toma's Decision

★ ★ ★

Sabah walked home slowly, hardly aware of his surroundings which, under normal circumstances, were a constant source of interest. He loved Mutanabbi Street and the surrounding neighborhood. He loved walking by the cafés and hearing the sounds of silverware clattering against real china, the distinct chime of arak and beer glasses tapping against each other in a toast. He loved the feeling of life these sights and sounds produced, even if it was a life he could only dream of. He loved the sound of full and real laughter. He was even amused by the merchants haggling with their customers over the price of their goods. But tonight the world around him, usually so vivid and vibrant, couldn't penetrate his feelings. It was as though someone else were watching the world through his eyes.

Growing up in various neighborhoods within Baghdad, Sabah had found a common thread throughout each home. Wherever his family moved, their neighbors generally respected—or even cared about—each other, living together in comparative peace. Sabah had been blessed to live in a relatively protected and cloistered world, but now his idealized view of that world seemed to be cracking around the edges.

Those glaring, inhuman eyes, the glistening knife blade held against the young man's throat ... Those sights had created a new kind of fear in him, the very adult suspicion that there *were* monsters in the world, and they were all too human.

He began the journey home, walking slowly along the busy streets which seemed to have lost their familiarity. In a real way, on this day, one world had ended for Sabah and another had begun.

It was nearly 8 P.M. Gabir, the yogurt and date peddler, was finishing his day at his usual sidewalk location, which happened to be on Sabah's daily route to and from school. Gabir, a simple, uneducated man in his late twenties, was also a quiet and gentle soul, qualities almost infinitely magnified by his unusually large size. He was nearly six and half feet tall, a weightlifter, and seemed to Sabah to be the strongest man in Baghdad.

The two knew each other by name. Gabir liked Sabah, as almost everyone did. And Sabah liked Gabir. When he had first seen Gabir, he had been seized by the initial jolt of instinctive apprehension we sometimes feel toward those who, by size alone, can so quickly and easily overpower us. Very soon this gave way to a respect for the soft-spoken, gentle nature of such a physically powerful man. Finally, the equilibrium of familiarity and trust displaced both feelings. Now, when Sabah passed Gabir and his handmade wooden cart, he saw only a fellow human being and friend.

For his part, Gabir was partial to Sabah over many of the other school kids who passed along the same route each day. Gabir knew that, unlike some of his schoolmates, Sabah would never pocket any of the dates without paying for them. Sabah was honest, always polite, and never asked for more than he could afford. Though they were years apart, they shared a mutual recognition of one another's basic kindness. There was, between them, a simple, unspoken trust and respect.

The routine was nearly the same each day. The cart stood on the sidewalk near an athletic store, with Gabir standing on the street side of the cart, facing the sidewalk and the constant stream of people moving along it. Almost every day, as Sabah passed by on his way to or from school, he would stop at the window of the athletic store.

Many times, Gabir had noticed Sabah leaning up against the plate glass window, his palms pressed on the glass. A stack of new, all white Adidas Santiago soccer balls, still in their boxes, had been in the shop window for months. It was one of the few stores in Baghdad that carried them. Sabah would spend a few moments looking at them and then, almost invariably, would turn to look at Gabir. The two would nod to each other and Sabah would approach the cart. Sabah took his date inspection very seriously, which always amused Gabir.

Often, Gabir would notice Sabah pull a few coins from his pocket, shift them in his small palm, carefully count them, and then put them back again before continuing his date surveillance.

Eventually Sabah would make his selection. He would hold up several dates in one hand and present his coins in the other.

"Is this enough?" Sabah would ask.

"For you, it's OK," Gabir would answer, and Sabah would smile.

From time to time, Gabir would say to Sabah, "Hey, take another two or three, I got too much today."

Sabah would look at him appraisingly, as if wondering if he were telling the truth or just being nice. "Really?"

"Really," Gabir would answer, giving a mock-irritated sigh. "I don't wanna push this heavy cart all the way home today. It's a pain in the back."

Sabah didn't believe it for a minute. Gabir could have carried the cart on his shoulders if he wanted to. But Sabah would smile and take the extra dates.

Tonight, as Sabah came into view on the sidewalk, Gabir immediately noticed something different about him. It was an unusual time of day to be seeing Sabah, but it wasn't just the hour. There was something distracted, even absent, about Sabah. Gabir was slightly surprised when his friend continued past the athletic store window without even glancing at the soccer balls, even though the store lights were on and the shop was still open.

Concerned, Gabir watched as Sabah drew closer—and then walked right past the date cart without a word.

"Hey!" Gabir said, in a voice a little louder and sharper than he usually used.

Sabah stopped and turned around. His eyes focused, at last, on Gabir.

With a simultaneous movement of his arms, hands, and shoulders, Gabir offered a quizzical gesture that conveyed the clear, unspoken message, *What's up?*

Sabah gave a small tilt of his head and a faint smile as he approached the cart. "Aren't you working late?" he asked.

Gabir shrugged. "Not really, depends on the day. What are you doing?"

"I saw the European Final at Al Batiwen."

"Who won?"

"Manchester," Sabah said flatly.

Gabir grinned. "I told you."

"You did," Sabah said, glancing at the dates.

Gabir knew now that something was definitely wrong. Yet along with their mutual respect, the two young men understood the clear boundaries of their relationship. Neither was the sort to pry or push, and so Gabir said nothing for the moment.

"Gabir," Sabah said finally, without looking at Gabir but, instead, holding up a date and examining it in the dim overhead street light, "do you know what a Baathist is?"

The question surprised Gabir, but he instinctively felt he should keep his surprise well concealed. "I know them," he said carefully.

"Do you know any ... yourself?"

"No, I just know about them. Why? Did you see one?"

Sabah looked away and gave a faint nod. There was something in his mood and manner that told Gabir not to force anything.

"Sabah," Gabir said after a moment. "All you need to know about them is that you don't need to know anything about them. You leave them alone, they'll leave you alone."

Sabah gave another distracted nod. "Okay."

There was silence between them for a few moments.

"Hey," Gabir said, "you gonna pay for that date?"

"I don't have any money right now."

"Welcome to the club," Gabir said, smiling. "Go ahead, take a couple."

This seemed to penetrate Sabah's fog, and he met his friend's eyes. "Really?"

"Sure, but next time you either bring some money or you push my cart back home for me."

"Deal," Sabah said, and actually smiled.

As Gabir watched his friend walk away, his own words seemed to echo in his ears: *You leave them alone, they'll leave you alone.*

He only hoped it was true.

★ ★ ★

It had been almost two months since Mr. Toma had first discussed the move with his cousin, Gilyanna. Four years earlier, through a persistence and determination not uncommon within the Chaldean community, Gilyanna had obtained the lease on a large new home in one of the more affluent neighborhoods in Baghdad. Mr. Toma had congratulated his cousin on his good fortune and success, but he had known that there were many other blood relations closer to Gilyanna who would move into the home long before his own family.

From the very first day, five families—either blood relations or in-laws to Gilyanna—had occupied five rooms within the house. Gilyanna had taken two rooms for himself and his own family on the bottom floor of the house, which, even by wealthy American standards, was large and well-appointed. Since the day of their arrival four years earlier, no one had left.

But then two months earlier, Gilyanna had called Mr. Toma to say that one of the families was moving. Both the husband and wife had found employment at a new hotel that was opening near Lake Dokan, a beautiful resort town in northern Iraq. The night Mr. Toma received the news, his joy was tempered by the sober realization of a new responsibility.

Living strictly in his own apartment, Mr. Toma was obligated only to the owner of that building. Mr. Toma was an honest man, and a man of integrity. He took great pride in never being late on his rent, and in providing for his family in every way. But he knew from past experience that circumstances beyond his control could occur. This might make paying rent on time each month difficult or even impossible.

This new arrangement, living in a kind of communal collective, meant that Mr. Toma could never be late on his rent, not even once. The honor and reputation of his cousin, as well as the security of the four other families in the building, would depend on it.

Even so, whatever additional pressure this awareness may have created for Mr. Toma was heavily offset by the quality of the home itself, as well as the neighborhood it was in. There was never a question in response to Gilyanna's invitation. It was a thrilling opportunity and Mr. Toma said yes immediately.

He shared the news with his wife and she was as happy as he was. In a hundred little ways, the new home would improve the quality of life for the Toma family. There would be shorter walks to food markets and shops, more convenient access to public transportation, better schools for the children, and even just the simple pleasure of living each day in a prettier neighborhood. Mrs. Toma saw only good things in the move, and Mr. Toma was inclined to agree with her.

★ ★ ★

The morning after the incident in the Al Batiwen Tea House, Mr. Toma woke up well before sunrise and set off for work. He was a janitor for Swiss Airlines. As usual, he went to the bus stop carrying his bagged lunch, carefully packed by his wife. Waiting at the bus stop, a thought breezed through his mind: he would need to change his bus route when the family moved. It would be a slightly longer trip, but it hardly mattered. The extra ten or fifteen minutes of travel was nothing compared to what the family would gain.

The thought came and went, leaving Mr. Toma in an airy, hopeful mood. He saw the headlights of the oncoming bus and stepped into the line that was already forming alongside the street. As the bus slowed to a stop, he heard the usual rumbling and rattling, the squeak of air brakes— and then nothing more, only blackness.

There was no warning, no nausea or headache, no vertigo or pain in his arms or limbs. It felt like a heavy hammer had slammed somewhere in the center of his right temple. Mr. Toma fell to the ground.

★ ★ ★

Mr. Toma regained consciousness later that afternoon in a Baghdad hospital. Before he asked a single question, before he had time to react to the fear in his wife's eyes, he said these words:

"Don't tell Gilyanna."

He tried to repeat himself, but his wife, sitting only inches away from him at the side of his bed, held a finger to his lips to shush him.

"I understand," she whispered. "I understand."

Mrs. Toma immediately recognized the relief in her husband's eyes, then the subtlest shift and refocusing. After twenty-five years, she knew the man's face and his thoughts as well as her own. She answered the question before he asked it.

"It was a heart attack. They found the problem. They fixed it."

The words came out of her mouth with a calm, matter-of-fact, almost

13

journalistic precision. They were exactly the words Mr. Toma needed to hear and exactly how he needed to hear them.

Another wave of relief washed over Mr. Toma's face, and his gaze shifted to his hand, which was currently being held very firmly by his wife. Her thumb was entwined around his, her fingers pressing tightly on the back of his lifted hand.

His expression softened, then, and as his fingers tightened reassuringly around hers, Mrs. Toma knew that her husband understood her as well as she understood him.

He's here, she thought, and couldn't hold back the tear that trailed down her cheek. *He's still here.*

It would be a week before Mr. Toma left the hospital and returned home. By then, all the children had visited him, but only after the sternest warning from Mrs. Toma: no talk of this to anyone, anywhere, at any time. The family would be moving in two months and nothing would interfere with that. Did they all understand? Yes, they all answered, though she didn't expect the youngest of her children to grasp what they'd agreed to. At the same time, she was satisfied, by virtue of their young age and limited social contacts, that word would not spread outside their neighborhood and across the city to the ears of their kind cousin, Gilyanna.

Before he left the hospital, Mr. Toma received a notice from his employer. He was being placed on a medical leave of absence, at a rate of half his monthly salary, for the next three months. The rent for the room in the new home was slightly higher than his current apartment. Even before his heart attack, almost immediately after receiving the invitation from his cousin, Mr. Toma had been thinking about how he would make up the income difference. Now, home from the hospital, stronger and able to move about again but no longer able to receive his full salary, that mild dilemma had now grown into a dark and looming obstacle.

Mrs. Toma understood the problem and began hand washing clothes to earn extra money for the family. Despite his wife's constant reassurance, Mr. Toma could not help worrying about his decreased income at such an important time of transition. Extra money had to be brought in. Late nights before the move, after the children were all asleep, Mr. and Mrs. Toma would consider their options together.

Then, about a week before the move, Mrs. Toma came home with good news. Next door to where Mrs. Toma worked washing clothes, a seamstress woman, who was also a friend of Mrs. Toma, had a small store. The woman was aware of the Tomas' financial dilemma and had offered a small space in her store for Mrs. Toma to sell simple, home-cooked meals during the busy lunch hour.

The sewing shop was located in a dense and busy business district, and so was the perfect location for selling cheap, hot meals. Best of all, the district was closer to their new house and thus would be close enough for Mr. Toma to ride his bike to every day.

All they needed was just a little bit of time and money, Mr. Toma thought. He could work selling his wife's meals for now, and then would be back to work full-time a month after they moved into their new house, receiving his full salary again. Things would be more stable then.

"One thing," Mrs. Toma said, and her husband braced himself. He knew from her tone that something he might not want to hear was coming.

"You can't do it alone," she said, softly but firmly.

"It's not much," he said. "We can both carry what we need when you—"

"No. Please. You need help. Not much. Just one. That's all. Please."

It wasn't an order. It was a request. There was no wheedling, no harping, no anger, just a wife softly, urgently pleading with her husband because she loved him.

There was no more discussion. Mr. Toma nodded and soon his wife was asleep beside him. Mr. Toma lay awake a while longer, staring into the darkness, listening to the sounds of his family sleeping.

One other, but which one? Which of his children would be right for this?

Mr. Toma lay on his back, fingers clasped behind his head. He had done his best. He had worked nearly every day for his entire life, sometimes juggling two or three jobs at once. But he knew he was not a businessman. He had no feeling for entrepreneurial enterprises of any kind, but the future stability and happiness of his family relied on this business venture going well. And for it to go well, he would need to choose an assistant from among his children. He thought about each of them in turn, seeing their faces before him, each as precious and unique as the one before.

He tried to picture the work in the most practical terms. He himself would have to be sitting in the back when the food was being sold. There was no question about that. He would heat the pre-made meals and sandwiches. He would collect the money and keep it safe. There would be room for several small café tables in the shop, enough to seat twelve or fifteen people if they used a portion of the sidewalk outside, too.

Whichever of the children worked with him would be the person actually serving the meals, ferrying the food from the back room to the tables. That child would be directly interacting with the customers, greeting them, chatting with them, bidding them a friendly goodbye when they had finished. The more he pictured a typical day—a bustling, busy, hungry crowd of people with little time to eat—the more he tried to imagine who could best draw that crowd in, give them a good reason to sit at one of the few café tables.

Mr. Toma knew there could be only one choice: Sabah.

CHAPTER THREE

★ ★ ★

The Section Leader And the Oldest Brother

★ ★ ★

The Toma family had just enough time to settle into their new home at Gilyanna's house before summer break ended and the new school year began. For all the Toma children it meant redistricting and entering new schools. For Sabah, it would not only be a new school; it would be the first day of high school. He had just turned fifteen and, like most young people his age, regardless of their country or culture, high school meant that the unknown loomed ahead of him.

Like his other classmates, he would abruptly leave the top of one social order and arrive at the bottom of another. In a single day, ironically without the benefit of any school course that could prepare him, he would be transformed from established and dominant to unknown and insignificant. For some, the transition was nothing less than traumatic. For Sabah, it was just another adventure he couldn't wait to begin.

From elementary to middle school, and now from middle school to high school, Sabah anticipated each promotion the way children in America might look forward to going to Disneyland. For Sabah, the world was one big adventure, one endless amusement park. There was nothing he valued more than something new. Whether it was an idea, a song, a hairstyle, or a school, he embraced them all with a curiosity and wonder undiminished since his infancy.

It was the fall of 1968 and Sabah's smooth black hair had grown long during the summer. Neatly trimmed, it fully covered his ears and, not coincidentally, looked very much like Paul McCartney's hair on the cover of "Sergeant Pepper's Lonely Hearts Club Band." His haircut, along with the used denim jeans he'd found in his favorite second-hand store, made him look almost like any American teenaged boy, and that was just the way Sabah liked it.

Aran Neifeh was a man who also valued fashion but with very different tastes than Sabah. At thirty-four, Mr. Neifeh carried himself with a calm bearing and dignity usually found in much older men. For standard work attire, he preferred dark, striped, double-breasted suits and silk ties with subtle, understated patterns and colors. His wavy hair and thick moustache, both already streaked with the first few strands of gray, were so carefully groomed they looked nearly molded rather combed and trimmed.

On this particular morning, Mr. Naifeh arrived at Al MarqaMeea High School very early and planted himself firmly at the center of the steps leading into the school's main entrance. As the school's Vice Principal, Mr. Naifeh was the administrator responsible for maintaining discipline and order. Today he had every intention, as he did from the first day of each new school year, of establishing both his position and the tone of his supervision. He would be friendly but firm, inviting—but only to a point—and above all, he would make sure that every student entering his school knew that they could never, not even once, get anything past him.

But new eras and transitions are not exclusively for students. Mr. Naifeh understood this better than anyone. For Mr. Naifeh the summer had not been, as it was for most educators, a relatively uneventful and leisurely hiatus. On the contrary, it had been busier than the school year itself. As the last school year was ending, he had been called to a special meeting. Just as students learn, grow, and graduate from grade to grade, level to level, Mr. Naifeh had also been promoted. After five years of membership in the Baath party, he had been made Section Commander. Throughout the entire summer, he had been directly responsible for seven divisions, thirty-seven cells, fourteen supporter cells, and one-hundred fifty-four members or candidate members. Nearly one tenth of the city of Baghdad was under his direct control.

His position within the Baath party was well known by his colleagues. After all, he'd been at the school longer than he'd been with the Baathists. Throughout the years, even before Mr. Naifeh had joined the staff in 1962, there had been a kind of unspoken, slightly uneasy truce and co-existence between the school and the Baath Party. The rule had always been to walk softly and avoid direct discussions of differences. The relationship was based on avoidance, denial, and a lack of communication, similar to some family relationships. Contemporary counselors or therapists might describe it as "dysfunctional," but whatever else it was, relations were maintained at a relatively peaceful status quo over the years of Mr. Naifeh's tenure.

Now, however, changes were coming to his high school, and he would be the instrument of that change. Mr. Naifeh had known, even before the school district, that a Student Baath Party office, for the first time, was going to be created this year at Al MarqaMeea High School.

Several other high schools in Baghdad already had Baath Student Service offices on campus, but even knowing this, Mr. Naifeh had never aggressively pushed for such an office in his own school. He believed that power, real power, always came from the top down. This understanding largely accounted for his rapid ascent within the party. He had been promoted four times in five years while raising a minimum amount of distrust or animosity among his non-Baathist friends, neighbors, and co-workers. He was, in fact, admired and popular with most who knew him, though he was quickly becoming equally feared.

Passing Mr. Naifeh on the first day of school—seeing his strong gaze and solid stance, as though he were the very gatekeeper of the school—had become a minor tradition for the students. Most of the returning students made it a point to greet him and pay their respects. To his credit, Mr. Naifeh knew most of them by name.

As the crowd of students streamed past, one caught Mr. Naifeh's attention. He assumed, correctly, that the boy was a freshman because he had never seen him before. For Mr. Naifeh, the overall image wasn't particularly appealing. The boy was too contemporary, too liberal, too western—too much! Yet, as the boy came closer, unaware of the Vice Principal's gaze, Mr. Naifeh couldn't help noticing a particularly bright, inquisitive, and humble face. He didn't know whether to welcome him or warn him, so he did a little of both.

"Hey, rock star," Mr. Naifeh said as Sabah moved to walk past him.

Sabah looked up at the large and confident man staring down at him. "Me, sir?"

"I don't see anyone else who looks like the Beatles."

Sabah offered a sheepish smile. He felt off balance. He was both flattered, embarrassed, and a bit apprehensive, not sure how to interpret the comparison.

Mr. Naifeh noted the discomfort and let Sabah remain in it for a moment.

"You're new?" Mr. Naifeh asked at last.

"Yes, sir, I'm a freshman."

Mr. Naifeh said nothing but sized the boy up for another moment. "You're not a troublemaker, are you?"

"Oh, no, not at all," Sabah said, shaking his head emphatically.

"That's good. You know why?"

"No, I don't."

"Because trouble makers don't do well in this school."

Sabah said nothing. He merely looked calmly and evenly into Mr. Naifeh's eyes, somehow without a single trace of disrespect or impudence. Mr. Naifeh chuckled and surprised himself by extending his hand to Sabah, not a typical gesture toward any student, particularly a new one.

"I'm Mr. Naifeh, Vice Principal."

Sabah took the man's hand and did something his father had taught him to do when meeting an elder. He neither pressed too firmly or too softly, but returned the same grip he received.

"Sabah Toma. Pleased to meet you, sir. Thank you."

Mr. Naifeh gave the boy a quick shake of his head, as if to say, "on your way," and with that, Sabah continued into the school building. Mr. Naifeh stared after him, a faint smile on his lips.

This kind of effect was precisely why Mr. Toma had selected Sabah to assist him in the café. Mr. Toma had seen the same situation many, many times. In one minute, Mr. Naifeh had made a decision and his decision was that he liked Sabah.

Sabah entered the school and was immediately engulfed in a swirling chaos. Hundreds of students shuffled and circled in random patterns, eventually coalescing into a dozen parallel lines leading to a long row of temporary folding tables. School officials sitting behind the tables shuffled through cardboard file boxes. The administrators and teachers were pulling papers, presenting them, answering or asking questions, then moving on to the next student as quickly as possible. Nearly any kind of group activity shared by human beings was of interest to Sabah. He fed off the energy of any crowd and this one was no exception.

He stepped into a line with a sign above it that read "R - T" and waited his turn. As he stood in line, his eyes were scanning the perimeter of the large open space where he and his fellow students were being processed. It was a large quadrant, bordered on all four sides by rows of classrooms and offices. A bank of windows covered the wall closest to Sabah. Inside, he could see secretaries, cubicles, and office equipment. He gathered that these were the school administration offices. He made a mental note to avoid being sent there and continued his rapid but thorough visual surveillance.

Right next to the administration offices was another school room that didn't quite look ready for the school year. Painters and other construction workers were carrying building materials in and out of the door. The room appeared slightly out of place to Sabah, as everything and everyone else in this school seemed completely prepared to receive and process this swarm of young people. Standing just outside the door of the room was Mr. Naifeh. He was speaking with three or four young people who looked, to Sabah, like fellow students.

They were about Sabah's age, maybe a year or two older. They were dressed like students. They wouldn't have attracted Sabah's interest for any particular reason except one: each of the young people surrounding Mr. Naifeh wore a thick black leather holster, and in each holster was a handgun. It was a peculiar sight, but seen in the context of an already unfamiliar environment, it didn't command his full and instant attention. Sabah simply thought they must be a gun club or even a security team for the school. It wouldn't be long before he knew exactly who they were.

The worst kind of tyranny comes quietly to a people. History is full of cases of revolution and spectacular violence, but in all ages, cultures, and for all races where freedom is lost by a people, tyranny often comes undisguised and unnoticed before it's too late. What is a coup d'état, after all, to someone naked and starving? Is it a rumor, a headline, a distant cry muffled in the wind? How can a people, for whom living means simply staying alive, see above the mundane confines of a family, a shop, a cart to peddle from, a handful of streets, or a room called home?

The simple act of survival, repeated day in and day out for years or decades, dampens and blurs a larger view of forces gathering and seizing power. Societies, nations, and cultures are often unaware of the actual moment the seismic shift occurs They only feel the new force, power, or regime reaching down to them with all the subtlety of a mist or fog, until it completely envelops and strangles every part of a struggling and starving people.

This lack of awareness was certainly true in the Toma family, with the possible exception of Sabah's oldest brother, George, who was the only college graduate in the family. Baghdad University, in the early and mid-1960's, was not unlike many other colleges in the world. It was a place that nurtured thought and ideas. This was where the veil was lifted and awareness was found in countless ways.

George was exposed to the shifts in Iraq's political landscape, not so much from his classes, but from informal late-night discussions, from parties in dorm rooms or arguments in cafés. His suspicion that the country was on the cusp of another major revolution had been culled, not from his teachers, but from other students whose ways of thinking had been forever changed by those teachers.

Only months out of college and already hired by one of the largest electrical contractors in Baghdad, George was told to get his passport in order and pack his suitcase. The company had received a large contract and George would be taking a trip with his boss and a dozen of his co-workers. This team would be traveling to another country and staying in three or four cities over the next several months. And the country was not just any country. The country was America.

When George received the news, he didn't call his parents on the landline phone he had purchased for them with his first paycheck. instead, he came home from his office to tell them in person.

It was early in the evening, but George knew his mother would already be cooking, preparing meals to be sold by her husband the next day at the market. And sure enough, when he entered the kitchen, he saw her stirring rice in a fifteen gallon kettle, his father standing next to her peeling and slicing vegetables. Sabah was sitting at a table near them. He'd arrived only minutes before and was busy rattling off the details of his first day in high school.

His parents were listening to him, appearing tired as they usually did, but somehow managing to work and ask questions at the same time. It was an image George had seen his entire life, his parents showing unwavering interest in all their children and at all times, regardless of the weight they carried each day for the family's very survival.

George watched them for a moment, standing unnoticed behind them in the doorway. An overwhelming feeling of love tore through him with an unexpected, almost violent intensity. He had to lean against the door frame for a moment to regain his equilibrium.

Finally, he stepped forward and announced himself. His father greeted him, as he always did, with a kiss on the cheek. As he embraced his mother, George lowered his head so she could give him the usual kiss on the forehead. Years later it would be the gestures and expressions of his parents, more than their words, that George would remember about this evening. He would always remember exactly what each of them had done when he told them he was traveling to America.

His mother, in the first instant after the news was related, simply stared at him as though he were speaking in a foreign, completely incomprehensible language. Then, without changing her expression, her eyes still fixed on his, she crossed herself, pulled a silver crucifix from under her soiled blouse, and kissed it. She shuffled toward him and placed one palm on each of his cheeks.

"God bless you, God bless you," she said, her eyes shining with a deep joy far removed from the lines of care and worry that lightly etched her face. She drew his head downward and kissed his forehead again.

Mr. Toma approached with an even greater somberness and sobriety.

"My son, my first son ... You have done well."

He placed both arms around his son and held him, for a much longer time than he usually did. As the embrace continued, George knew that his father was crying, yet was unwilling to make his son uncomfortable with such a dramatic show of emotion. George held his father just as tightly and, after a few long moments, the men separated. Mr. Toma drew a deep breath and brushed a tear from his eye.

"America," he said, and shook his head in disbelief. "America."

Sabah remained at the table. He had only been halfway through the recounting of his school day when George had come in. Sabah was, at first, slightly irritated by the interruption. He liked to tell a good story and had just been getting to the part about the boys with pistols when his parents greeted his brother. Even the fact that his brother would be traveling did not seem, to Sabah, *that* much more interesting than a first day in high school.

But when his brother said the word "America," Sabah, even more than his parents, was engulfed by something surreal and dreamlike. Could he really be hearing this? Could this really be possible?

The news prompted something far more than simple happiness or excitement in Mr. and Mrs. Toma; it was almost as though George would be meeting God Himself. Sabah had similar feelings but, for Sabah, God wasn't America, no more than America was God. If, however, God did live on Earth now, at this moment, during Sabah's life, God would certainly live there. If a better world really existed, somewhere, if life was lived the way God intended it to be, if there was a paradise on Earth, it was in this place. It was in America, and George, Sabah's own brother, was really, actually going there.

As happy as his parents were, George could not share their exact feelings, nor could he explain why his own were slightly different. Something in his college experience, something to do with his understanding of his country and the imminent tumult looming just beyond the horizon, didn't allow for simple excitement. In the first moment George was informed of his travel assignment to America, his most powerful emotion wasn't happiness. His awareness of this, even now at this moment as he held his parents and rejoiced with them, created the smallest twinge of guilt. No, the news of his trip hadn't filled George with happiness; it had filled him with relief.

CHAPTER FOUR

★ ★ ★

Warnings and Invitations

★ ★ ★

iving in a 3,500 square foot home with thirty-eight other people didn't seem unusual to Sabah. It seemed perfectly normal—in fact, better than normal. It was the best home his family had ever lived in. Sabah had a vague sense that this house was different, and not simply because of its size or neighborhood location. He understood that his father's cousin lived on the bottom floor with his family. He also knew that there were three other families in the home, not including his.

The circumstances were familiar, if on a slightly larger scale. Finding space in densely populated environments with his own family, relatives, and neighbors was the only life Sabah had ever known.

Perhaps his fascination with the walls began on his walks to school. Or was it during the mile-long rides he took, sitting on the metal frame of his father's bike? Sabah would hold onto the handlebars as his father peddled to the café, the bike weighed down by two huge kettles and several baskets of bread, strapped to a rack specially built by Mr. Toma. During his first excursions through his new neighborhood, Sabah noticed the high brick or concrete walls blocking his view of the homes beyond. Not every home had a wall and gate, but enough did that his curiosity was constantly engaged. What were the houses like behind these walls?

Occasionally, a gate would seem to open by itself. His father, seeing Sabah's amazement, told his son this was something called "remote control." The people who lived here had a little box they carried in their car. They could actually press a button on the box that would open the gate. To Sabah, this was like something out of a science fiction story.

Though his father didn't seem particularly interested, when a gate would open Sabah's eyes would focus, unblinking, on the fleeting views of these homes as the bicycle rolled steadily by.

He caught glimpses of towering shade and fruit trees, fountains with water spouting up and cascading down in a fine mist. There were pillars and front entry doors two-stories tall, with massive, gleaming gold fixtures. He saw statues and finely mowed, lush green lawns. Parked on long, winding driveways were shiny cars he had never seen before but would later recognize as Mercedes-Benzes, BMWs, Porsches and even Cadillacs. It was like a vision of another planet.

For Mr. Toma, this was just the way the world was. In this man's heart and soul, there was no jealousy or petty coveting. He understood that there were people in the world who had many things he would never have. He knew that these people had existed from the beginning of the world, and would always remain relatively few in number. Despite this, Mr. Toma did not think of the world, or even of his country, as being unfair or unjust. For Mr. Toma, the wealthy were simply not part of a reality he knew of or understood in any practical way. The aura and mystique of the very wealthy had no power over him. He was exposed to them, even directly interacted with them on rare occasions, but his manner never changed. Mr. Toma, like all men of integrity, always remained who he was regardless of who he was with.

As for Sabah, he had always only been able to see people as people. The same part of him that saw a thief as a monster viewed a rich person as nothing more than, at most, a more sanitized version of himself.

Also, importantly, after several weeks in his new home, Sabah knew most of the other tenants by name. Faces, families, and relationships gradually fell into place. Gilyanna's family, his own, and the other families in the large house all belonged to the local Chaldean congregation. Sabah's world though impoverished, had always been complete. The love of his family, the comfort of his faith, these threads constantly crossed and crisscrossed in a living fabric, not of gold but of steel. It is not easy for a happy person to be envious. And if Sabah was, and always had been, anything, he was happy.

Though he was transfixed by brief images of pristine, manicured landscapes, lush green lawns and a self contained world of flawless order and perfection, he did not and could not make a connection between what he was seeing and the possibility that these people were, in any important way, different from himself. More than anything, he simply felt happy and grateful to live in such a pretty neighborhood. As far as Sabah was concerned, it sure beat life in the tenements.

In his first week of school, Sabah met Kasim. After that, the boys regularly walked to or from school together. Kasim was one grade ahead of Sabah and so was able to give him a few pointers on the in's and outs of the school, all the information not covered in student manuals or orientation classes which, of course, was always the most valuable.

Kasim was also a reservoir of information on the neighborhood. He knew where the prettiest girls lived, and, most interestingly, who some of the people were behind those high walls. Finally, Kasim was a soccer fanatic. There was no question that the two would become the closest of friends.

Sabah was not only grateful, but in a way, flattered by the confidential admonitions he received from Kasim. He accepted Kasim's opinions and interpretations of their little part of the world almost without question, not because he was unable to think for himself, but because Kasim was his friend and Sabah trusted his friends. However, there was one point in The World According To Kasim manual on which Sabah did not fully comply. It was the issue of Rukia.

Rukia was a neighbor who lived next door to Gilyanna's house. She lived with her family and three other siblings. She was sixteen and just beginning her junior year at Sabah's high school. She was also very pretty. Though petite, she was curvy and had a modern, short hair cut. Sabah noticed right away that she was more fashionable than the average Baghdad high school girl.

One afternoon, as the boys walked home from school, Rukia was walking with another boy directly across the street from them. They'd only been walking on these parallel paths for a few minutes, but within this time, Rukia had already glanced in their direction several times.

"Don't look at her," Kasim said tersely after her second glance.

"Why not?" Sabah asked.

"Because she wants us to."

"So, what's wrong with that?"

Sabah was not at all convinced that she was looking at both of them. In fact, he had the distinct, exhilarating impression that her eyes were only on his own.

"Because that's what she does! Her whole purpose in life is to tease you to death!"

Right off hand, Sabah could think of worse things, but he didn't raise any immediate objections. Kasim continued.

"She's always been like that. She's an attention monster. She doesn't want a boyfriend. She wants *everyone* to be her boyfriend. Just look at her. Actually, *don't* look at her! Really, who cares, do what you want!"

Actually, Sabah was having some trouble following Kasim, but his well-mannered, instinctively diplomatic nature prevented him from direct confrontation with his friend, despite feeling his heart beating faster after each shared glance with Rukia.

"It's pathetic," Kasim was saying. "She's a junior and she's looking at *us*? I mean, I'm a sophomore you're only a freshman. Give me a break. I mean, nothing personal, but guys like us don't even exist to girls in her grade."

As with most conversations, Sabah was listening to how the words were being said nearly as much as the words themselves. There was a slightly shrill and unfamiliar intensity in Kasim's voice. The boys walked a few more steps.

"Did you ever go out with her?" Sabah asked quietly.

For several moments, there was what seemed to Sabah to be a slightly awkward pause. Then Kasim spoke.

"I wanted to, once … before. That's why I'm telling you. Boys are just a big game for her."

She'd hurt him and Sabah knew it. Just how much, he didn't know, but it had been enough. Sabah was sure of that.

He glanced across the street one more time. Rukia was still looking at him, this time offering the faintest smile. How could such a sweet face be so cruel? It didn't make sense, but Sabah gave it no more thought because, at that exact moment, something far more interesting happened.

A glistening white Adidas Santiago soccer ball came rolling up the sidewalk directly toward Kasim and Sabah. Kasim, perhaps distracted by his own thoughts, didn't notice the ball as quickly as Sabah did. It rolled directly to Sabah, almost as though it were a friendly puppy, wagging its tail and coming to say hello.

Sabah extended his right foot and, with a single flick, sent the ball ninety degrees straight up to his forehead where he bounced the ball several times, up and down, in a perfectly controlled, nearly acrobatic display of soccer skill. He was introducing himself to the ball, as the ball had introduced itself to him. It was the first time he had felt the leather or sensed the exact inflation and weight of the ball he had always only seen through glass. It was even finer and more responsive than he'd thought it would be.

Kasim was looking at the ball and, much like Sabah, wondering if this was Manna from Heaven. Sabah held the ball in his hands as if it were solid gold. Both boys studied it closely. It might have been the most beautiful thing they'd ever seen. It looked brand new. It had no scuffs or scrapes on it and their first thought was, what was it doing *here*? This ball was worthy of the best stadium in Iraq, and not just a dirt field but a real grass field that has been carefully mowed and precisely chalked. What in the world was it doing bouncing and rolling along the asphalt streets of their neighborhood?

"Nice header," came a voice from nearby.

Kasim and Sabah both jerked their heads up at the same moment. Standing a few feet away was a boy, close to their age, who was smiling at them. He was good looking, well groomed and with perfectly white, straight teeth. He wore what looked like an authentic, professional soccer jersey. Sabah had seen similar ones in stores but never worn by a person and never this close. Kasim and Sabah were so stunned by this unexpected sequence of events that they couldn't make an immediate connection between the ball and the person standing in front of them.

"May I ... have my ball please?" the boy said, looking amused at their blank expressions.

"The ball, yes, sorry, of course. Sorry." Sabah dropped the ball and, swiping at it with the side of his foot, gave it a gentle kick that sent it sailing through the air to land softly in the arms of the waiting boy.

The boy gave him an impressed look. "You've played some soccer."

"Yes, a bit." He glanced at Kasim. "We both have."

"I can see that," the boy answered. "I'm Milad."

The boys introduced themselves, and Milad, a confident and direct young man, wasted no time.

"Do you live in the neighborhood?" he asked.

"Just a few blocks down, yes. We both do," Kasim answered.

"Some friends and I play every day about this time. You're welcome to drop by if you like."

"Where do you play?" Sabah asked.

"Just over there, at my house." Milad gestured toward one of the high walls Sabah had passed so many times on his father's bicycle.

"You play in your house?" Sabah asked, imagining for a moment that the boy lived in some huge indoor sports arena.

Milad laughed warmly. "No, in the yard. The front yard."

Kasim and Sabah both nodded slowly, trying to balance their imaginations with their understanding.

"You have a full soccer field in your front yard?" Sabah asked finally.

"Well, no, not quite. But almost." This last was said without a trace of arrogance or boasting.

"It's grass?" Kasim added quickly.

"Grass?" Milad echoed. "The yard, you mean?"

"Yes, the yard."

"Well, yes." He gave a friendly smile that was completely free of condescension. "Yards usually are made of grass, aren't they?"

Suddenly, Kasim felt foolish and slightly embarrassed, though he had no reason to. The fact was, he had never seen a yard and so had no idea what they were made of. Neither, for that matter, did Sabah.

"Tomorrow then?" Milad said.

Kasim and Sabah traded a glance, then looked back at Milad and nodded.

"Good, see you then." He turned to go—then quickly turned back again.

"Hey!" He threw the soccer ball to Sabah. "Here, keep it. For the days you can't make it over." He turned to go again, apparently not even expecting a reply.

"Milad!" Sabah called after him, nearly in a state of shock. "You don't want to keep your ball?"

"Nah, I've got five more just like it. See you tomorrow!"

Sabah and Kasim watched him go, then turned to each other with identical expressions of shock on their faces. They continued their walk home in a daze, trying to process the events of the last few minutes. In their amazement and joy, neither of them noticed Rukia moving past and away from them, sending several backward glances toward Sabah as she went.

CHAPTER FIVE

★ ★ ★

The Man Who was the Beginning of Everything

★ ★ ★

I n fact, Sabah's heart had sunk the moment Milad offered his invitation. He knew he'd be working with his father at the little café and wouldn't have time for the game, but declining might have meant that Kasim wouldn't be able go either.

"We can go another time, when you're not working," Kasim said as they approached their street.

Sabah's voice was firm. "No, definitely not."

"But it wouldn't be even. He needs two of us to—"

"Kasim," Sabah cut in, "you have to go. I'll get there sometime, for sure. You have to go and tell him that."

"Sabah, I've lived in this neighborhood four years and no one's ever asked me to come over to their house like he did. It just doesn't happen. Not to me. Maybe to you; that's why you need to go, too."

"Listen," Sabah said, growing a little impatient with his friend, "he's just a guy, like you and me. He likes soccer and he wants us both to play. That's all. And you know what? He's probably not half as good as you. But maybe you shouldn't him let him know that. We might not get invited back."

Kasim's expression shifted from somber self-preoccupation to a smile. The comment had achieved its desired goal.

"That's true," Kasim said.

"Of course," Sabah said, confident the subject was closed.

The next day after school, Sabah went directly to the café where his father was already working. Two months after his heart attack, Mr. Toma was now nearly back to full strength. Still, he'd asked Sabah to stay and help, at least for part of the day, for just a week or two longer. As Mr. Toma watched Sabah deliver plates of rice and hot okra soup to their customers, he could tell that his son was distracted. Between customers, he wasn't in his usual place on the sidewalk, smiling, waving, and saying hello to passersby, inviting them to have a seat. He wasn't especially talkative to the customers who did sit down.

Sabah seemed to be having a small disagreement with one man who had approached him but had not taken a seat. After a moment, Sabah turned and looked at his father. Mr. Toma remained on his stool behind the small stove and kettle, farther back in the shadows of the tiny shop. He'd been watching the conversation. He kept his eyes on Sabah and jerked his chin up as if to say, *What?*

Sabah approached his father. The customer remained fixed in the spot where they'd been talking.

"He's only got ten phillas," Sabah said.

Mr. Toma gave a brief nod. "That's okay."

"Mom said she wanted fifty."

"Ah, well, you know, some pay a little less, some pay a little more. It all works out."

"I've seen the less, but where's the more?" Sabah asked.

"You'll see, you'll see," his father answered with a faint smile.

The only thing Sabah was seeing, at that exact moment, was a mansion with a quarter acre of green grass where a dozen boys were kicking a perfect soccer ball.

Mr. Toma watched as Sabah returned to the customer, pulled out a small, flimsy folding chair beneath a wobbly café table, and held it for the man. The man bowed his head and took the seat, his left profile visible to Mr. Toma.

Only then was Mr. Toma struck by something peculiar about this man. First, he didn't look, in any way, like the kind of man who only had ten phillas. He was wearing a very clean, very white starched dress shirt with the top button fastened. His suit might have been black, except the late afternoon sun was just catching his shoulders so Mr. Toma could tell that it was navy blue, with the sheen of a fine wool blend. The crisp white cuffs of his shirt extended out only an inch or two from the fringe of the jacket sleeve.

As the man rested one arm on the café table, Mr. Toma could clearly see a gold cufflink sparkling on the starched band of cotton covering his wrist. His gaze moved down the man's legs, one draped closely over the other, to his finely creased pant cuffs and then further to the highly polished black wing tip shoes.

Mr. Toma considered this for a moment. This man had asked for a discount and was wearing cuff links worth more than Mr. Toma made in a month. Many men might, at the very least, have taken umbrage to these circumstances. Mr. Toma's only reaction was curiosity.

It was unusual for Sabah to be less than fully engaged in any activity he was involved in. Whether it was work, play or school, Sabah had a natural, childlike affinity for tightly closing the blinds on future and past events. Most of his life was spent in one eternal present. Though few actually analyzed what it was that made Sabah so likable, if pressed, most might say the same thing: when Sabah was with you, he was *with* you. Sabah completely saw and heard a person, whatever he was doing and wherever he happened to be.

But on rare occasions, when circumstances converged and collided in the most precise and unfortunate way, Sabah would find himself in one place while he dreamed of being somewhere else.

It was much more than the soccer game, though this was his favorite activity in the world. He wondered who Milad was, what his life was like, who the other boys would be. Sabah tried to console himself. There would be other opportunities, after all. But when? Between school and work, he'd had no free time for over two months. At this moment, Sabah was on the verge of feeling something so foreign to himself he could not have defined or named it. Sabah was close to feeling self-pity.

Exactly because of this, he failed to notice the unusual attire of the man sitting at his café table. On any other day, under any other circumstances, this was exactly the kind of man Sabah would have been most intrigued by: a refined Iraqi gentleman with a distinctly western appearance.

The gentleman, however, was not unaware of the preoccupation of his young server. As he'd been eating, he'd noticed Sabah sweeping, straightening, cleaning, and constantly primping the tiny serving space. This activity had recently come to a standstill, however, and the boy was now standing with his back against a wall, absently holding a broom while he stared off into space.

"Excuse me, Ringo?" the man said.

At the sound of these words, the boy blinked and seemed to break out of his reverie.

"Me, sir?"

The man smiled and gestured for Sabah to come to his table. Only at this late moment, after the man had been there nearly ten minutes, did Sabah notice how refined and well-appointed this customer was.

"Ringo Starr, right?" the man asked, smiling.

"Oh, I don't know," Sabah said, flattered he'd been observed this closely by someone who seemed so accomplished, if not important.

"Or maybe it's the other one, the good looking one. What's his name?"

"Paul ... Paul McCartney."

"That's the one," the man said, watching a blushing grin transform the young man's face. "Don't know how I could have gotten you confused." He looked down at his empty bowl. "Who made the soup?"

"My mother," Sabah said proudly.

"Well, you tell your mother I said this is the best okra soup in Baghdad."

Sabah was fairly convinced of this but had no doubt that if anyone knew, with absolute certainty, what the best okra soup in Baghdad was, it was this man.

"I will, sir. I promise."

As Sabah picked up the empty plate and bowl, the man nodded in Mr. Toma's direction. "This is your father?"

Sabah nodded and watched the man dab the corners of his mouth with a paper napkin. It was a refined, dainty, but not effeminate gesture. It was also consistent with everything else about the man. He was not part of any world Sabah was familiar with.

As Sabah watched, the man pulled a black, rectangular leather box from beneath the table. Sabah had not noticed it until now. In fact, Sabah had never seen one before but would discover later that it was called a briefcase.

The man placed the briefcase on the table and pressed his two thumbs on either side. The polished brass clasps flew open with a suddenness that startled Sabah. The man opened the case and looked inside.

"You know, I apologize, but I made a mistake," he said. "I thought I'd left my wallet in my office, but it was with me all the time."

He took the wallet out of the briefcase, unfolded it, and pulled a bill out. He handed it to Sabah.

"You tell your father I am grateful for his kindness. But I am also glad he has a son who wants to protect him."

Sabah looked at the bill. It was a five dinar note. It was as much as Sabah and his father would make in three days of work.

"Please give that to your father and tell him to keep it with my thanks. And please, keep this for yourself."

The man handed Sabah a business card. Sabah looked at both the card and note but said nothing.

"I have a little shop, too, not far from here. If your father allows, and if you like, perhaps you will think about working in my shop."

Sabah read the card. The man's name was Abdul YaMen Moghadam, the owner of Tokalon Hair Salon. Sabah recognized the name of the street it was on. It was the street that bordered the Tigris in the nicest neighborhood of Baghdad.

"You're a hairdresser?" Sabah asked, looking up sharply from his careful review of the card.

The man smiled. "No, I just own the shop. My work is the law. I'm an attorney."

"I see," Sabah said, though he actually saw nothing at all. He didn't have the vaguest idea what an attorney was. Mr. Moghadam was the first attorney Sabah had ever met.

That night, as Sabah drifted to sleep on his thin floor mattress, the last two things he saw on the shelf beside him were a soccer ball and a business card. How strange and mysterious, he thought, that these two things should be with him now when he'd had neither just two days before. Even more strange and surprising to Sabah was that, of the two, the business card was far more precious. The ball had been a dream for as long as he could remember, but the business card … That was something else entirely. It might as well have been Aladdin's magic carpet.

Sabah knew it meant opportunity, even if he didn't fully understand what opportunity meant. Intuitively, very near that region of his heart and soul that had forever been a shrine to his faith in God and goodness, Sabah felt and understood his life was about to change.

★ ★ ★

CHAPTER SIX

Changing Days, Changing Ways

★ ★ ★

After only a few months at his new school, Sabah had already become a popular, well-known figure on campus. This was partially because his long hair and fashionable appearance existed in a place where both were virtually unknown. Second, Sabah treated every person he met—whether teachers, older students, friends, or strangers—with the same amount of consideration and respect.

One morning, Sabah was preparing for school when he noticed a postcard on the family table. The picture was face-up and he knew, even from fifteen feet away, that he hadn't seen it before. He'd memorized the seven other cards already. He was so familiar with the broad outlines, shapes, colors, and details of each card that he knew instantly this one was new.

At least once a week since he'd left, George had been sending glossy, richly hued cards from America, each one with an image more fantastic than the one before. There was a dam that looked like it held mountains together. There was a golden-orange bridge a mile long, floating in the sky high above a busy harbor. There were letters, each bigger than a house, on the side of a mountain. The word they spelled was nearly sacred to Sabah: "H-O-L-L-Y-W-O-O-D."

There was even one picture Sabah had already seen. He'd clipped the same image out of a magazine, years before. It was a tall, round building. Sabah knew the building had something do with the Beatles. When he was younger, he'd thought it might be one of their houses, but he had long since discarded that theory. Looking back on that idea now, he was amused by his youthful naïveté. Whatever the connection between this building and his idols, Sabah sensed it was important. He'd placed the postcard next to his magazine clipping and had spent almost an entire hour looking closely at one, then the other, then back again, comparing every minute detail.

But this new one … This one was the most incredible of them all. This one was, quite literally, unbelievable.

George had spent most of his business trip in California and, Sabah knew, was now in a city called San Francisco. The image on the card was of a tall building, maybe twenty or thirty stories, surrounded by other tall buildings. On the back of the card, his brother's writing explained that the building was a hotel he'd been staying at for over a week. In the photo, clearly visible on top of the building, was a swimming pool.

This could not be true. Though it was past the time for Sabah to be out the front door and on his way to school, he could not take his eyes off the picture. It had to be a trick. But his brother's note said that he'd actually *swum* in the pool! There were no swimming pools thirty stories above the ground! Not even in America.

"Mom," Sabah said.

His mother sat on the other side of the table, repairing a tear in her husband's sock. She glanced up at him as he held up the postcard.

"May I take this to school? I'll bring it back home today. I have to show this to someone."

His mother seemed to consider for a moment, then nodded and returned to her stitching. "All right, but be careful with it. They all go in the scrapbook."

"I know. I will. Thanks, Mom."

And with a quick kiss to his mother's forehead, Sabah pocketed the postcard and hurried out the door.

Sabah only had one friend at school who had been to America. His name was Jamir, and he was a friend of Milad's. In the first few months since meeting Milad, over a few very memorable soccer matches inside the cloistered walls of Milad's home, Jamir and Sabah had become good friends. If anyone had ever seen such a thing as this swimming pool, it would be Jamir.

Sabah arrived at school about ten minutes before the first class was scheduled to begin. Hundreds of students were already assembled. They loitered and wandered in clusters within the school quad, doing what students do everywhere. They joked, jostled, poked, laughed, shrieked, and chased one another, unable to control the raging glandular forces working endlessly within their volatile community.

Scanning and passing through the crowd, Sabah was greeted and called out to by name. Returning the greetings with polite smiles, nods, and waves, he continued toward his destination at the far end of the quad.

There was a group of six or seven students standing there, among them Milad, Kasim, and Jamir. Like all the other groups and cliques knotted together on the quad that morning, Sabah's friends were joking and playing with each other as he approached them.

He had already taken the postcard out of his bag and was holding it in his hand as he approached the group.

"You guys, you have to look at this," he said. "Jamir, I just got this. It's from my brother in America."

"What is it?" Milad asked as the others pulled in closer to Sabah.

"Jamir, you've been to America? To California, right?"

"Yes, I have," Jamir said, stepping closer. Of all Sabah's friends, Jamir was the most sophisticated. Though physically slight and unimpressive, he had a certain quality unique in boys his age. Sabah didn't have a name for it but, in a word, Jamir was suave.

"Did you ever see this, or anything like this?"

Sabah handed the card to Jamir, who held it up to the light as the group craned and twisted their heads, all of them trying to see the small picture at the same time.

"That's … a swimming pool?" Kasim said. "On a roof!"

"Yes!" Sabah said, nodding vehemently. "Can you believe it?"

"Sure," Jamir said casually. "That's San Francisco. I've stayed there."

All the boys turned to stare at him, sharing the same expression of wide-eyed astonishment.

"You were in *this* pool?" Sabah said, moving quickly from amazement to awe.

Before Jamir could answer, a voice broke in: "Hey, Milad, how's it going?"

Distracted by the photo, the group hadn't noticed the arrival of three other students. The three had positioned themselves in strategic positions around the group, quietly herding and confining them. Sabah had never spoken with them but he recognized them immediately. Each of them wore a holster and each carried a gun.

"Hey, good morning," Milad answered. Sabah immediately noticed the tension in Milad's voice, all the more disturbing because it was so foreign in such a relaxed, fun-loving person.

The boy speaking to Milad was probably the same age, but his bearing was that of a much older person. He stood directly across from Milad, his boots planted firmly on the ground. He and his colleagues each wore matching green military jackets and red berets. The boy addressing Milad was Ali Ramsi.

Sabah assumed, correctly, that he was the highest ranking member of his group, not simply because he was the one speaking, but because he alone had a golden pin attached to his red beret. Even in these unusual and unsettling circumstances, Sabah's attention to detail was unwavering. He didn't know what the pin meant and he didn't have time to consider it, as Ali had just taken a step closer to Milad. He was standing too close. What little movement there was among Sabah's group of friends came to a complete stop. With that single step, the group had become a breathless tableau.

"We didn't see you last night," Ali said.

"I know," Milad said. "I'm sorry. I had to help my Dad with a few things around the house."

"Help your Dad? Your Dad doesn't have enough help without you?"

The question drew some chuckles from Ali's friends. Ali turned and grinned at them, acknowledging their appreciation of his clever repartee. Before Milad could answer, Ali spoke again.

"What's this?" he said, and snatched the postcard out of Jamir's hand.

"It's just a—" Milad began.

"It's mine," Sabah said, knowing even as he said the words that they would make him a target.

Ali examined the postcard with all the officiousness of a passport inspector at a border checkpoint.

"What is it?" he said, flipping the card over and reading the note on the back.

"It's from my brother. It's a hotel. He's working in America."

"America? You mean the head of the snake, where the women are tramps and the men are sheep?"

Ali's friends laughed more loudly this time. Ali smiled with them for a moment, then his expression suddenly changed, going hard and cold. His voice was deadly quiet.

"So this is what, the playground of the infidels? This is where they prove to themselves, to each other, to *us,* how important they are? Well, you know what?" Then, dramatically pausing between each gutteral, word, he tore the post card into ever smaller pieces. "The … infidels … can … die." He smiled and, with outstreched arms, let the pieces of paper fall like tiny leaves to the ground.

As every boy in the group, stiffened by shock and horror, stared at the remains of the postcard, Ali lurched forward and grabbed Milad by the collar of his shirt, dragging him forward so they were nose to nose.

"Listen to me," he hissed. "We don't care who your Daddy is, Milad. We don't care who he knows or how much money he has or who his famous friends are. We don't give invitations. We give orders. When we tell you to go to a meeting, you go to the meeting. Do you understand? You've been selected. And when you're selected, you participate. So next week, you tell your daddy you're busy. Okay, Milad?"

Sabah felt the same overwhelming sense of nausea he'd experienced at the Al Batiwen Tea House, but it far more poignant and painful now. This time, the subject of humiliation was his friend, someone he personally admired.

How could this be? Sabah had felt honored, even flattered, just to be in the same place as Milad. This child of privilege and opportunity, this cultured and enlightened boy who had befriended him, this wonderful person who had pleaded with his parents to allow him to attend a public school rather than a private one as his brothers and sisters did. That this person should be humiliated by these animals, unworthy of him in every way, tore at the very fabric of Sabah's world.

Sabah was witnessing a great wrong. Moments earlier he had been surrounded by friends, mingling in a world of light and warmth. Now all of them were alone, separated from one another in their own solitary, darkened worlds, filled only with their own thoughts, unable to comprehend what they were seeing.

"Do you understand me, Milad?" Ali asked again.

Milad's eyes were fixed on Ali's, his face utterly calm. "I understand you perfectly," he said, and Ali shoved him away.

"Good," Ali said. He looked at his two friends, gave a quick tilt of his head, and the three of them started to walk away. Before they'd gone more than a few steps, however, Ali stopped and looked back at the boys with a friendly smile, as though the ugly scene of a few moments earlier had never occurred.

"Oh, and Milad, feel free to invite your friends," he said, and for a moment his eyes locked on Sabah's.

With that, Ali gave one final smirk and turned again to go—and Sabah, filled with a rage unlike anything he had ever felt before, took an angry step forward. Jamir and Kasim reached out for him, trying to pull him back into the safety of the group, but Sabah pushed their hands away.

"And what if *I* don't accept the invitation?" he called out.

The three uniformed boys stopped dead, then slowly turned around to look at him. Ali watched Sabah for a few moments with a look of remote indifference on his face, then grinned and glanced at his friends.

He stepped toward Sabah. "The new boy."

Sabah said nothing. Ali took a step closer, but Sabah did not move.

"Yes," Ali continued softly, "we know who you are. Sabah."

At the sound of his own name, Sabah felt a chill go through his entire body. Ali saw the fear. Like a fighter who knows his opponent is stunned and hurt, he immediately followed up one painful blow with another.

"Do you know where people go when they go missing, Sabah?"

Sabah didn't answer, and Ali let the question hang between them for several seconds before continuing.

"I didn't think so." He gave a slow, predatory smile. "You know what? We don't either."

He laughed, and so did his friends, and at last they turned and swaggered off.

The boys stared after them, confusion and anxiety hanging like thick fog in the air between them. After a moment, Kasim knelt down and started picking up the fragments of the postcard, piling them carefully in his palm.

Everyone in the group was wondering the same thing, but it was Jamir who finally posed the question out loud.

"How did he know your name?" he asked Sabah, quietly.

Sabah just shook his head and watched the three red berets vanish into the crowd.

CHAPTER SEVEN

★ ★ ★

Moghadam's Heaven

★ ★ ★

A bdul Moghadam was a lawyer who had never loved the law. The son of an upper class family, he had been raised in Mosul, Iraq, and both his father and grandfather had been lawyers before him. Throughout his entire life, Abdul had been exposed to the double-edged sword of lineage. Opportunity had been balanced with responsibility, financial advantage with diminished choice, and most of all, personal interests and passions sacrificed in the name of family duty. It was a story often told within wealthy families, and nearly always among those of noble birth.

His gratitude for the advantages and opportunities his family had given him was constantly, and increasingly, offset by his guilt. As far back as high school, Abdul had known that his life path would radically detour from the one so carefully planned for him. He'd held this secret for years, waiting for the right time and place to surprise his family. On his graduation from law school at the University of Baghdad, Abdul had announced that he would not be returning to Mosul, and instead would be settling permanently in Baghdad.

There were many reasons for his decision. First, it was close enough to his family to still be a part of them, but far enough away that he could live outside their control. More than that, however, was the fact that from the very first moment he'd arrived in Baghdad, he'd sensed this was a place where he could succeed in his own way and on his own terms. This was a place where a man with limited vision and talent, but with one good idea, could go a long way.

What impressed Abdul the most, from his earliest days in Baghdad, was how completely void the city was of fashion or anything that might be called personal style. It was an ancient city, rich with history and culture, which made it all the more surprising that it appeared to be nothing more than an outpost.

Yet these were mere clinical impressions, resulting from an active and analytical mind. Abdul was a product of his upbringing and a beneficiary of a strong family with devoted, nurturing parents. The predictable conclusion was a man who judged rarely, and only when necessary. He did not look down on the residents of his new community. He only saw an opportunity to be of service to them and to himself. The real Abdul, the Abdul he'd always wanted to be, was a businessman and entrepreneur. More than anything else in his life, he wanted to start a business and make it successful.

But if Abdul had learned anything from his family, it was to approach life's big decisions only after careful deliberation and with an equal amount of preparation. This was not a hasty, impulsive, or impatient young man. He would work as an attorney as long as it would take to make his business dreams come true. And, in 1959, after nine years in Baghdad, that was exactly what he did.

Over the years, despite the initial disappointment in their son's quest for an independent life, Abdul's parents maintained warm and cordial relations with him. Often he would vacation with them in Europe and abroad, sometimes in the United States. A man of great taste and impeccable style, Abdul wore suits made in the Knightsbridge district of London or on their famous Seville Row. For something a bit more daring, yet equally understated, he would wear shirts, shoes, and accessories from Galeries Lafayette in Paris or the season's offerings from Milan.

Wherever he went in Baghdad, he was noticed. He was tall, 6'2, and had the dark brown complexion, dark eyes, coarse black hair, and moustache of a Middle Eastern man, yet he dressed like Cary Grant or David Niven. His jackets featured neatly pressed white handkerchiefs with embroidered initials. He wore twenty-four carat gold cufflinks with matching tie clasps. He carried monogrammed silver cigarette cases. He was, in a word, elegant. He was also friendly, outgoing and likeable, all important qualities in the world of business.

He could have quit the law firm and started his business long before he actually did, but it had seemed an unnecessary risk. All he needed was one partner, one right person he could trust his business with. That final ingredient and catalyst came in the form of Baligh, a very young man who did what many men did in Baghdad, but in a way very few of them did it. Baligh cut hair, but he was not an ordinary barber. He was a dresser, stylist, and artist, similar to those Abdul had seen on his travels abroad. He was Lebanese and his own fashion sense, though not identical to Abdul's, was equally refined and pronounced. A bit more flamboyant and flashy, perhaps, but just right for the role Abdul had in mind.

Finding a salon-level hairstylist in Baghdad in 1959 wasn't an easy task. But neither was Abdul's business goal. His vision was to create a salon that would not only be chic; it would introduce the concept of chic to a fashion wasteland. This was why, for several years, Abdul never had his hair cut twice by the same barber. Somewhere in this arid style vacuum, there had to be at least one person who shared Abdul's sensibilities and vision for a different kind of Baghdad. There had to be one responsible, talented person who believed, as he did, that fashion was a powerful gateway to the present and that the present was the very place Baghdad most needed to be.

One day, Abdul sat in Baligh's barber chair. He had just started his standard pre-haircut instructions speech when Baligh interrupted him with a wave of his hand.

"Will you trust me?" Baligh said.

Abdul looked at the man before him, who was barely twenty years old, and was amused more than offended by his arrogance. "Is there any particular reason I should?"

"Well, I'm the best hairstylist in Baghdad. Is that good enough?"

Abdul laughed out loud. The man was confident, if nothing else, and the fact that he used the term "hairstylist" rather than "barber" was encouraging.

"Proceed, sir," Abdul said.

He started to lean back, but before his skull reached the headrest, the entire chair reclined. Abdul found himself looking at the ceiling, his head tilted backwards over a sink. In seconds, he was being shampooed. This had happened to him only once before, in a salon near Paris. It was the last thing Abdul expected in Baghdad, particularly in a barber space designed for one person and roughly the size of a closet. Though surprised, Abdul said nothing and simply the let the man go about his work.

Something about the speed and precision with which Baligh worked immediately impressed Abdul. So much so that, despite his typical audition approach and his generally silent critique of a barber's performance, Abdul soon found himself easily and comfortably chatting with Baligh.

Seated upright again, Abdul studied Baligh's face in the large mirror. The man's expression could not have been any more focused had he been a master jeweler making the first incision in a rough diamond. The intensity was almost comical, nearly a parody of a hairstylist, as though Baligh were a character in a Marx Brothers movie. Despite himself, Abdul chuckled slightly and the reaction was not unnoticed by Baligh.

"What's funny?" Baligh asked.

"Nothing," Abdul said, still smiling. Not wanting to offend Baligh but feeling the need to say something, Abdul continued. "Not too many barbers shampoo hair."

Baligh stopped clipping and lowered his arms. Abdul saw, through the mirror reflection, Baligh take two steps to the side of the barber chair, where he paused and waited for Abdul to turn and look at him. Baligh took a moment to collect the full measure of his dignity. Then he spoke.

"First of all, as I mentioned, I am a hairstylist."

"Pardon me," Abdul said, trying not to smile even as he felt himself tickled by a giddy optimism.

"Second, there is no haircut without a shampoo. Haircut, shampoo. Shampoo, haircut. They go together. You see?"

"I think I follow you."

"Thank you," Baligh said, and immediately returned to his surgical task.

In one moment, Abdul made his decision. After many years and a hundred barbers, Abdul had found his man. He didn't even have to see what his haircut would look like. He already knew it would be perfect.

"I apologize, again" he said. "I should have introduced myself. My name is Abdul Khalik Moghadam."

"Baligh. Baligh Sirra."

Strangely, though his search had taken years, Abdul had never considered what he would actually say to the person who would become the face of his salon. Only at this moment did it occur to Abdul that the person he had chosen for the position may not actually want it. The realization made him a bit nervous, an emotion he was unaccustomed to. He sat for several minutes, rehearsing his next words very carefully.

Even in this concentrated mental process, Abdul could not help noticing Baligh's silence. Despite this man's colossal self-confidence, Baligh seemed to understand the first law of customer service: never speak more to your customer than your customer speaks to you. Considering the kind of clientele Abdul expected his salon to attract, this skill would be vital.

Abdul had two options. He could carefully wade into his offer through a series of questions carefully selected to determine Baligh's level of interest. Or, he could just put his cards on the table. Abdul opted for the latter.

"Baligh, what would you say if I made you a business offer?"

"I'd say I'm expensive."

Abdul laughed and wasted no more time. He unfolded his vision of the spa and hair salon. He told Baligh he'd even found a perfect location, a corner spot for lease in the Al Ilwya district. He asked Baligh if he'd like to see it at the end of his work day.

Just at that moment, Baligh finished cutting Abdul's hair. He pulled the sheet away and carefully brushed away the few remaining hairs on his customer's shoulders. Then, without another word, Baligh went to the shop door, turned the open/closed sign to "closed," then stood in the doorway looking at Abdul expectantly, waiting for him to lead the way.

Before he left the small shop, Abdul glanced at his reflection in the mirror. Just as he'd thought; his hair was perfect.

★ ★ ★

Within weeks of meeting Mr. Moghadam at the family café, Sabah was an employee of Tokalon Hair Salon. It was, without question, Baghdad's finest beauty salon. It was an easy transition from his father's small café. With his father's full support and encouragement, though with some slight trepidation from Mrs. Toma, Sabah began what would be far more than a new job. It would, in every way, be a new life.

By now the shop had been operating for almost ten years. Mr. Moghadam had long since stopped his active law practice and had become, through profits from the salon and subsequent real estate investments, a well-to-do man about town and gentleman of leisure.

The salon itself featured six full-time hairstylists, a masseuse, a hair colorist, a manicurist, and a makeup artist. Reigning over the operation, and loving every minute of it, was Baligh. Not yet thirty years old, he was the salon's star stylist and one of the best known bachelors in Baghdad. For anyone other than the wife of an ambassador, daughter of a cabinet member, or any female member of the Hussein family, average advance appointments with Mr. B, as he was now known, were measured in months.

Sabah had never seen the salon before but sensed, just based on Mr. Moghadam's demeanor and appearance, that he should make himself as presentable as he possibly could. His appearance had always been important to Sabah, something measured, considered, coordinated, and often adjusted. He would study himself in the mirror each day before making his appearance in the world. He would do this not because he was vain, but because he took pride in being the best he could be. His commitment to quality in his life extended to tempermant, knowledge, character and faith, as much as fashion.

At this point in his life, assembling his daily fashion statement was so routine it required very little thought or energy, but today was different. Usually an unselfconscious, nearly effortless task, today nothing seemed right. He changed in and out of pants, shoes, and shirts as though playing a game of musical clothing. Growing increasingly anxious, his indecision began to creep into, and then beyond, the time he should have already left.

When facing a very tight deadline, as he was now, Sabah resorted to a trusted strategy. He would focus on one element of his ensemble and select everything else based on that. He chose the British-made "Mascot" black leather motorcycle jacket with the chest fringe. He'd found it under a small mountain of clothing at a street bazaar a year earlier. A bright yellow dress shirt with a collar wide enough to extend over the jacket, dark blue jeans, and his black Chelsea boots would complete the image. He looked like he was ready for Carnaby Street, even if he didn't know what Carnaby Street was.

Baligh was standing at the reception desk inside the salon when Sabah came in. Abdul had told him that a new boy would be coming in for training. Baligh had assigned Melody, the shop manicurist, training duties for the new boy. Having just completed her first year with the salon, and being recently promoted to manicurist, Melody was highly qualified to show Sabah each of the most menial tasks of the shop.

As Sabah approached, Baligh could see that the boy's age was as described, but Abdul hadn't told him anything more than that. Baligh scanned Sabah from head to toe in less than a second and smiled.

On every choice Abdul ever made, from the salon design and décor to the marketing, promotion, services, standards, and even the combs and scissors they used in the shop, Baligh always found himself agreeing wholeheartedly with Abdul's decisions. And here, he knew with a single glance that Abdul had done it again. It was completely clear to Baligh, from the moment Sabah stepped through the front door, that he belonged in this place.

CHAPTER EIGHT

★ ★ ★

The Trapeze's First Bar

★ ★ ★

After a full day of sweeping up hair clippings, taking out trash, cleaning bathrooms, and running errands for shop clients, Sabah had never been happier in his life. On the way home, he passed Gabir's cart and stopped to survey the day's offerings.

"You're looking sharp, my friend," Gabir said with a grin.

Holding a date in one hand and looking at it closely, Sabah reached into his pocket and pulled out two dinar bills.

"Whoa! Look at this rich guy!" Gabir said.

Only then did Sabah look up from the date and flash Gabir a beaming, radiant smile.

"Tips!" he said. "I got them today at my new job!"

"Good for you, Sabah!" Gabir said, and he seemed honestly happy for his friend. "Good for you!"

They spoke for a few minutes about the details of the job, Gabir listening closely and nodding at the appropriate times.

"And how's business?" Sabah asked.

"Oh, you know, hanging in there. They're putting up all these new street lights and changing the sidewalks. Makes getting around with the cart a lot harder. But I can't complain, even though I do." Gabir gave a tired smile.

Sabah nodded. It was true. He'd seen it for himself: little things, new rules and restrictions. In his mind, Sabah saw Gabir walking those extra blocks, each step an effort, because some bureaucrat had put in a new sign or sidewalk. They'd taken away a well-worn route he'd walked for years.

Even if this man was the strongest in Baghdad, it didn't seem right that his life should be made any more difficult than it already was.

A wave of compassion swept through Sabah, but as was his practice with this particular friend, he said nothing that might divulge the true depth of his feeling. Somehow, it didn't seem appropriate to express sentiment toward such a towering hulk of a man, someone so incredibly strong in every way.

Sabah purchased a small bag of dates, more than his usual handful, and with a simple goodnight continued on his way home.

★ ★ ★

It is a workplace truism that attitude often determines altitude. This never applied to anyone more than to Sabah in the Tokalon Spa. It was a place he would have gladly paid to work in, for many reasons.

First, there was the building itself. It was like working in a palace; the white Italian marble floors were so polished he could nearly see his own reflection. Every wall was either covered with floor to ceiling mirrors or else decorated with paintings, most of which featured odd geometric patterns and colors unlike any Sabah had ever seen, even in the art galleries on Mutanabbi Street. Later, Sabah would discover that these were original works by artists with strange names like Willem de Kooning, Caziel, and Van Hoeydonck.

Chandeliers hung from the ceilings throughout the salon. They were made not of crystal but of textured paper and plastic, in bold primary colors of blue, red and yellow. They looked like intricate mobiles, slowly turning in response to the slightest breeze.

It was completely unlike any place Sabah had ever seen or been in, including the tea house. Despite the many pleasant times he'd had at the Al Batiwen, Sabah couldn't help feeling that this place was better in every way, brighter and happier. The social energy he constantly fed off wherever he went was at a non-stop crescendo in the salon. It was peak level, maximum volume, full tilt action, from the moment he started work to the moment he finished. Often, Sabah would leave work feeling more energized than when he'd arrived.

Then, of course, there were the women. At fifteen, Sabah was on the cusp of his re-introduction to women. He had arrived, as both genders do, at the second meeting point of the sexes. This place is not at all like the first realm of contact. It is no haven blessed with childhood innocence and all the freedom ignorance brings. In mid-adolescence, after the initial shock of puberty with its related trauma, we cross that relatively short bridge of just a few years. Then, we instantly enter a completely foreign world.

During our separation, we retreat to our respective camps, girl and boy. We huddle together, we the beginnings of women and men. We study the other camp from afar. We counsel with each other on who or what these alien creatures are and on the best course of action in dealing with them. Then, eventually, inevitably, with the full force of nature in all her power and glory, we begin our initial forays into terra incognita.

That, in itself, is a beautiful, terrifying, and fantastic journey for any teenager. But that this particular teenager should be working in this exact place, at this moment in his life, was the difference between driving a four cylinder Fiat and a dragster loaded with nitro methane. Not only had girls become a huge blip on Sabah's radar, they were standing in line to get inside his work place. And not just any women—these were the most beautiful women in Baghdad.

Far more important than his exotic workplace, with all the euphoria it induced, and even more significant than the women who formed a ceaseless parade of living sculpture, were his co-workers. Sabah had never known men like this, let alone the privilege of daily contact with them. In a fundamental way, these men would alter the course of Sabah's life and his destiny. And if they didn't alter it directly, they provided the foundation and support on which Sabah's dreams and direction would be firmly built.

For all these reasons, Sabah was thrilled to go to work. That, on top of his already cheerful, polite, and generous disposition, made for an exceptional and very well-liked employee. Baligh, ordinarily preoccupied with his own daily duties and extracurricular interests related to clients, rarely took an active interest in new salon employees. He made an exception in Sabah's case, however, and immediately took him under his wing, watching out for him and caring for him almost like a little brother.

The two female hairdressers found Sabah so adorable that they actually fought with each other over who would manage the boy's long, shiny mane. Both had a vision for its design and Sabah was more than happy to let them perform their radical experiments on his hair.

By the end of his first month, it was clear to his co-workers and the salon customers: Sabah was a vital part of the salon's delicate alchemy. Though he did little more than sweep and clean, he approached his work with tail-wagging joy and enthusiasm.

In fact, the lady customers thought he was as cute as a black Labrador puppy and treated him that same way. They fawned over him, oohing and aahing, petting his long hair and extending treats on occasion, all of which Sabah was both flattered by and grateful for.

Life had never been better for Sabah. Between school, his friends, and work, he was home only once a day, just long enough to sleep and start all over again. The moments of his life were connected with perfect fluidity and precision, events and activities interfacing like the gears and sprockets of a fine Swiss watch. Perhaps because of this effortless, constant upbeat tempo, Sabah was least prepared for what he saw when he entered his classroom a few minutes before the first bell of the day.

There, standing over Sabah's open desk, was Ali Ramsi.

At the sight, Sabah froze in the doorway to the classroom, not knowing whether he should go in or walk away. Ali was holding what appeared to be a newspaper, and he and his two regular cronies were closely examining the publication.

Unmoving and barely breathing in the doorway, Sabah tried to piece together the reason for this sudden inspection of his desk. It was election week at school and Ali was running for student body president—could it have something to do with that?

Did it matter? Ali and his friends were thugs, and it was probably better to avoid a confrontation with them. He tensed his muscles to go—but at that moment, Ali glanced up and looked directly at him. And with that, Sabah knew it was too late; he'd waited too long. Leaving was no longer an option.

"Hey, Sabah," Ali called. He summoned Sabah with a few flicks of his index finger.

Sabah approached the desk even as other students in the immediate vicinity quietly got up from their desks and moved away. Sabah was afraid, but he did his best not to show it as he stopped in front of the three boys.

"What is this?" Ali said, tossing the newspaper at Sabah.

Sabah caught the paper and looked at it. It seemed to be just an ordinary newspaper, the kind for sale on any street corner. What was it? What did Ali mean? Sabah was confused and the moment was quickly becoming surreal.

"I don't know. I've never seen it before."

"Never seen it? It was in your desk."

"Well, I didn't put it there. It's not mine."

"Then why was it in your desk?"

"I don't know!" Sabah said, his voice going shrill. "I don't even know what it is!"

Ali gave him a cold, dangerous look. "You're a communist, aren't you?"

Sabah's fear was rapidly moving toward terror, and he was all too aware of the gun in Ali's holster. "No, sir, I am not," he said. "I've told you before, I'm not political. I'm not involved in politics at all, ever."

"This is a communist newspaper."

"Okay," Sabah said.

"And it was in your desk."

"I told you, I don't know how it got there!"

Ali glanced at his friends and one of them spoke.

"Ali, maybe he can run against you as the communist candidate."

Ali smirked. "Good idea; I like that. What do you say, Sabah? You're a popular guy, right? People like you, right? I mean, you've got lots of friends. You could be a good student body president. Don't you think so?"

"I don't want to run for—"

"Even if you are a communist. I mean, what's the difference, right?"

Sabah was trembling now, a cold feeling of dread and helplessness in the pit of his stomach. "What do you want, Ali?" he said.

Ali was silent for a moment, and then took three steps around the desk until he was only inches away from Sabah. His entire face seemed to be pinched and pursed, focused on a single purpose.

"Two things, but I'll let you choose. You can join us, like your rich friend Milad, or you can be classified as a communist."

Sabah knew this much about these dark, twisted animals: they had nothing but contempt for anyone who didn't belong to their group, but they particularly hated communists. Sabah also knew, as did everyone else in his school, that a self-proclaimed communist student had been missing for two weeks. It was rumored that he was dead, but his body hadn't been found. Sabah had never known fear in his life like he knew it at this moment.

"Okay," he said, the word tasting faintly bitter on his tongue. "Meetings are Thursdays after school, right?"

"Very good," Ali said, and smiled. "See you then, Sabah."

As the three started to walk away, Ali called back over his shoulder. "I hope you'll remember me on Election Day. I'd really appreciate your vote."

By now, the teacher had long been standing in front of the class, watching the scene at Sabah's desk unfold. He knew better than to interfere and so pretended to be busy organizing papers, avoiding eye contact with the Baathists as they walked out the door. Only when they were gone did the teacher look up at Sabah, who was now sitting at his desk, his eyes dazed and empty.

The day before the Baathist Student Association meeting, Sabah was at work, more quiet and withdrawn than usual. Despite the dark event looming, he managed to do his duties without making his co-workers suspect that something was wrong. By now Sabah knew, along with his entire country, that this was not a problem that could be solved. There was no one who could help. No friend, no matter how close; no co-worker, no matter how smart; no family member, no matter how loyal; not even a man with the strength of Gabir could make this go away.

Sabah stood near the front window of the salon. It was an unusual posture and demeanor for him. He rarely stayed in one place for more than few moments when at work. With broom in hand, he gazed idly out into the busy street, at nothing in particular but at the entire scene as a whole. Everything appeared less inviting, somehow, more distant, as though he was being torn away from one world and forced into another.

At that moment, a car pulled up and stopped directly in front of the salon.

It wasn't unusual to see beautiful cars arriving at the salon. In fact, it was the rule rather than the exception. He'd seen them all: Mercedes, Jaguars and Cadillacs. A beautiful woman usually stepped out of each car. Cars would gracefully glide to the curb, pausing only for a door to open and cue a delicate departure. He saw the same scene every day at work. It was a connection that would stay with Sabah for the rest of his life.

A beautiful car, a wealthy man, and a beautiful woman; the three went together with strength and permanence, like a perfect triangle.

The red car stopped and the man driving immediately got out. He walked around the car and opened the passenger door. He was wearing a tailored suit. The woman was Iraqi but had honey blonde hair. She wore a light, flowing outfit that was a combination of a dress and pants. It had a bright, multi-colored floral pattern. Sabah had been around the shop long enough, had heard enough conversations and asked enough of his own questions, to know that her clothing was Italian. Though he didn't know the designer, Emilio Pucci, he knew that what she was wearing cost more than he would make in six months.

The man turned and escorted the woman toward the front door of the shop. Only at that moment did Sabah recognize him. It was Mr. Naifeh, the Vice Principal of his school. The broom dropped from his hands and Sabah was at the front door almost before it hit the floor.

"Hello, ma'am!" Sabah said, holding open the door. "Hello, sir! Hello! Welcome!"

The woman walked by him. If she smiled, it was so faint that Sabah couldn't be sure. Mr. Naifeh was a different matter.

"I know you," Mr. Naifeh said, smiling and looking both surprised and pleased.

"Yes, yes, of course. I'm Sabah. How are you, Mr. Naifeh, sir?"

"I'm fine," Naifeh said, still possessing his authoritarian demeanor even in this completely foreign setting. "What are you doing here?"

"I work here, sir!"

"You do?"

"Yes!" Sabah said, reading the surprise in Mr. Naifeh's face and delighting in it.

There was something more, though, in Mr. Naifeh's eyes. There was a certain confirmation of inevitability.

Mr. Naifeh had encountered this young man several times in the short time since Sabah had arrived at the high school. Each time, he'd been wearing some outlandish outfit or hairstyle, yet his manner had been so humble and unassuming. In everything Mr. Naifeh saw Sabah do, in the countless ways he interacted with his fellow students and friends, Mr. Naifeh saw only generosity and kindness.

It was, to Mr. Naifeh, a pleasant paradox. Friendliness and fashion did not mix very well, in his view, but this boy was a clear exception to that rule. He liked him, and in the brief encounters they had at school, Mr. Naifeh always had a kind word or inquiry as to how things were going in Sabah's life. Sabah always kept his answers short but honest, direct but respectful, keenly aware of Mr. Naifeh's importance. Mr. Naifeh was curious about the boy and had hoped to get to know him better, but hadn't made the time. Sabah was, after all, only one of nearly 1,300 students in the school.

Seeing Sabah in this place didn't exactly surprise Mr. Naifeh. It was somehow predictable. It simply made sense.

Sabah glanced over at the reception area where the woman Mr. Naifeh had brought was being welcomed by Baligh. As was his custom with most of his female clients, Baligh greeted the lady with a peck on each cheek, so light that Sabah wondered if his lips ever actually made contact. It was a practice Sabah wasn't particularly fond of, but the mannerism—or affectation, as some might say—barely diminished Sabah's idolatry of the man.

"So, Sabah, tell me," Mr. Naifeh said as he took a seat in one of the oversized yellow leather chairs, "how are things at school?"

"Good," Sabah said, the slightest hesitation in his voice. "I like the school very much."

Perhaps Mr. Naifeh caught the hesitation or perhaps habit compelled him to assert his position. Either way, he asked another question.

"Anybody giving you problems? Causing trouble for you?"

Sabah went silent. He looked away for a moment, not sure what he should say, or how much. He glanced around the salon, nervously. He partly felt guilty for spending too much time talking to a customer when he should be working, and he also felt afraid, knowing who Mr. Naifeh was. He was completely unsure how to proceed.

"What is it?" Mr. Naifeh said, but not with the impatience of a vice principal whose time is being wasted in his office. It was the voice of a friend. It was Milad's voice. It was Kasim's voice. It was his father's voice.

Sabah looked at him, trembling. "Please, sir, I don't want trouble. I don't."

"Tell me, Sabah," Mr. Naifeh said gently.

With a strange combination of dread and relief, Sabah told the story of Ali Ramsi, how the newspaper had been placed in his desk. He described Ali's veiled but deadly threats as to what would happen if he didn't attend the this week's meeting. Mr. Naifeh listened carefully and said nothing, but trimmed a cigar and lit it as Sabah spoke. When Sabah finished, Mr. Naifeh sat thoughtfully, smoking his cigar for a few moments.

"Before you go to that meeting, you come to my office. OK?," he said finally. "You hear me?"

"Yes, sir," Sabah said. He didn't know why Mr. Naifeh would want him to come to his office but he was far too frightened to ask questions.

"You see the woman I brought with me today?" Mr. Naifeh said.

"Yes, sir, certainly."

"You take care of her. You make sure she's happy. Okay?"

"Of course, no problem. We'll take good care of her."

"Good. I'll see you tomorrow."

★ ★ ★

Sabah arrived at Mr. Naifeh's office exactly ten minutes before the scheduled meeting time of five P.M. Mr. Naifeh was reading reports, and after telling Sabah to have a seat, he went back to the pile of papers as if there had been no interruption. He was shuffling through the reports and making notes at his desk until it was five minutes after the scheduled meeting time. Only then did he stack his report sheets and close his binders.

"Come with me," Mr. Naifeh said, and led the way to the office door.

Confused, Sabah stood and followed him. Mr. Naifeh walked so quickly through the hallways of the school that Sabah found himself nearly skipping beside him to keep up.

"Ali said not to be late," Sabah said as they moved. "He said they locked the doors right at five. He said if I was late he would ..."

At this exact moment, Mr. Naifeh arrived at the front door of the Baath Party student office and kicked the door in. Sabah stopped dead in his tracks and watched every head in the room turn at once toward Mr. Naifeh. For a moment, no one moved, including Mr. Naifeh. He studied the room and every person in it. There were about twenty people in the room, including Milad, Ali and his two henchmen.

Without a word, Mr. Naifeh walked directly toward Ali, his path as straight and true as a bullet. Sabah, standing in the doorway, felt suddenly dizzy; he held onto the doorframe to catch his balance.

"Hey! Punk!" Mr. Naifeh shouted, his voice like a thunder crack in the silence of the room. "You little punk!"

He grabbed Ali by the front of his shirt and slammed his head into the blackboard, so hard that the board actually cracked under the impact.

"I want you to see something. You see that guy? You see that guy over there?"

Mr. Naifeh was pinning Ali against the blackboard with one hand and pointing to where Sabah stood with the other.

"Do you?"

Ali's voice was muffled and shaky. "Yes, sir, I do."

"You … do not … fool with that guy. Ever. You understand me?"

Ali did not immediately respond, consumed by as much surprise as everyone else in the room.

"Do..you..understand..me?!" Mr. Naifeh screamed, whipping Ali's head into the chalkboard once more.

"Yes, sir, I understand," Ali said, but so softly Sabah could barely hear him.

"Say it again. Say it so everybody hears it."

"I said yes, sir!" Ali said, so loudly this time that it could have been heard from across the school parking lot. "Yes, sir, I understand!"

Sabah didn't know whether to laugh or cry, be relieved or terrified. For a moment, he was paralyzed with emotional cross-currents so strong he could hardly breathe. He certainly couldn't move.

Mr. Naifeh let go of Ali, pushing him away as though he were some contaminated rag. Mr. Naifeh wiped his hands, straightened his tie, and pulled his jacket sleeves in place before he spoke again. Now his voice was even and perfectly modulated, as though he were among colleagues at a staff luncheon. The transition was eerie and somehow horrifying.

"You cause any trouble for that guy, or his friends, you give them one bit of trouble and I swear to Allah himself, Ali, I will put a bullet straight through your head."

Everyone in the room knew who Mr. Naifeh was. Everyone knew that he could, with complete impunity, do exactly what he threatened to do.

The power of that simple truth resonated through every inch of the room in a breathless silence. At that moment, the horror in Ali's face was so alien, Sabah almost didn't recognize him. He saw Ali nodding and trying to speak but the words wouldn't form properly.

Mr. Naifeh walked out of the room. As he passed Sabah, he simply said, "Let's go." Sabah was so disoriented he either didn't hear the words or couldn't react to them. He stared at Mr. Naifeh. Mr. Naifeh stopped and turned toward Sabah. He sighed and seemed to offer the suggestion of smile.

"It's OK Sabah. It's OK now. Come on."

Sabah nodded and followed him out the door without a glance back, even as he was thinking, "This is the way God works. This is the way God works"

CHAPTER NINE

★ ★ ★

The Lengthening Shadow of Abu Tobar

★ ★ ★

D ays after the event, Sabah continued to wonder why. Why had Mr. Naifeh done that? Why had he gotten that angry?

Why did he do that for me?

For a week afterward, he was enveloped by a warm, murky afterglow of relief and confusion. To protect Sabah, this man had turned on one of his own with all the viciousness of those wild pack dogs that constantly roamed the city. At his most raw, visceral level, Sabah found himself more grateful to Mr. Naifeh than he had ever been to anyone. Yet this man was one of *them*. He was a Baathist. The more Sabah thought about it, the less sense it made.

There would be many other incidents ahead for Sabah involving these creatures, growing ever larger and more prominent with each passing day. But never again, not once, did the group bother him at school. Sabah walked through the campus halls and classes with a new calm. His sense of security and peace was so strong it emanated from him like a nimbus from a holy man in an ancient portrait.

Word of the incident spread quickly through the school. If Sabah had already attracted people with his warmth, sincerity, and non-judgmental disposition, now he was something of a phenomenon. Milad was more impressed than anyone, as he was the most direct and significant beneficiary of these recent events. His friendship with Sabah grew even closer and Sabah found himself, more and more often, at Milad's house or at the houses of one of his new friends in the neighborhood.

It was as if the one dark storm cloud looming over Sabah's life had burst with a sudden heavy downpour, leaving nothing but sparkling vistas and clean, fresh air. Nothing encumbered him. He was ready to devote his full, undivided attention to something—which happened to be, at this time, his introduction to an entirely new world.

★ ★ ★

In his first few months at the Tokalon Salon, Sabah was vaguely aware that his reputation was transforming. He was embraced by his co-workers and the clientele from his very first day, well-liked and even doted upon, but they seemed to think of him more as a mascot or a pet than a fully functioning human being. It didn't particularly bother him, however—he was simply grateful for the job, and threw himself fully into his work. He remained absolutely focused on his duties, committing himself each day, with near-religious Meal, to doing a better job than he had the day before.

As time went on, he began to be seen and treated differently. His sense of fashion became more refined and worldly, yet in a completely organic way, void of all self-consciousness. Sabah had always coordinated his clothing with care and precision. Now, with ongoing guidance and assistance from the stylists—especially Mazhar, who often brought back trunks of up-to-the-second global fashions from Lebanon—Sabah was actually becoming sophisticated.

That a young man of Sabah's age should have the kind of job he did may not seem unusual, today, to many people in many parts of the world. But in Sabah's world, at this time, it was a job that carried extremely high status and prestige. After all, in Baghdad in the late '60s, what were most fifteen-year-old boys doing for work, if they worked at all? Selling candy on a street corner? Shining shoes, perhaps? During this period in Baghdad, the social status and desirability of a hairdresser was somewhere near a rock star and, perhaps, just below a member of the royal family. Based solely on how women related to his co-workers, Sabah recognized and understood this implicitly from his first week at the salon.

This knowledge was exponentially reinforced by how others began to treat him. He had always been popular and well-liked, but now girls he'd never met or spoken with randomly approached him at school or on the street. Sabah had always been, and would always be, ambitious. He was also just young and vain enough to tell what he considered a harmless white lie.

"You really work at the Tokalon Salon?" the girls would ask, wide eyed and incredulous.

"I do, yes," he would answer, striving to sound cool and casual.

"You're an actual hairdresser at the Tokalon?"

A twinge of guilt would mix with the euphoric exhilaration, but he would always answer, "Yes, I am."

He couldn't help himself. Seeing those lovely young faces marked by awe and desire was just too tempting. But Sabah knew the lie would eventually catch up with him. He needed to make sure it didn't.

As with almost every other aspect of Iraqi life at this time, there were no regulations, prescribed training, certifications, or licenses associated with hairstyling or hairdressing. Baghdad was a city where anyone could do anything, anywhere, at any time. They could call themselves anything they desired, impose the title of their choice, offer a service or product without restrictions, knowledge, or expertise. Before long, many residents of the city would look back fondly and nostalgically on this way of life. They viewed this disappearing world as though they were, at one time, happy adolescents temporarily left unattended at home, free from parental supervision and control.

As the 1970s approached, there seemed to be new rules and regulations everywhere, and they were expanding all the time. A new order was coming and they called it progress. Perhaps there would be a time, in the not so distant future, when licenses, degrees, certifications, and credentials would be required, like they were in the West, for anything from personal training to selling hot dogs, but that time was not now, not yet. If one wanted to be a hairdresser at this time, one taught oneself, which was exactly what Sabah did.

Of course, he received tips and pointers from time to time at the salon. But the salon was not a school and nor would Mr. Moghadam allow it to be. First, it was not in keeping with the service standards of the salon. It simply wasn't good form for a lady of high society to have a spectator, trainee or not, hovering nearby, watching her hair being done.

That wouldn't do at all. Aside from that, Mr. Moghadam had made it clear that Sabah's employment was based on one condition, and one condition only: that Sabah would always remain in school for as long as he worked at the Tokalon.

Initially, Sabah could not understand Mr. Moghadam's adamancy on the rule. After all, if making a career as a hairdresser was good enough for Baligh, Mazhar, Faraj, Rashid, and others in the salon, it was certainly good enough for Sabah. Only after many years and a lifetime away from the innocence of his youth in Baghdad would Sabah understand the wisdom in Mr. Moghadam's guidance.

Even so, Sabah's commitment to his formal education wouldn't prevent him from becoming like his idols in the salon. After consulting with Mazhar, Sabah bought his first pair of haircutting shears. The preferred scissors of his salon mentors were the highest quality Japanese shears, forged from tempered steel in the tradition of samurai swords. These were far too expensive for Sabah, however, and so under Mazhar's supervision, he bought a second-hand pair of lower quality and took them home, cradled in the blue velvet of their black leather case.

Along with the Adidas soccer ball given to him by Milad and his collection of forty-five rpm records, the scissors instantly became one of Sabah's treasured possessions. It was strange, but owning the scissors made him feel differently about himself. He wasn't just Sabah anymore; he was a person who owned professional haircutting scissors. Somehow, the acquisition had altered his dimensions. He wasn't bigger or better, necessarily, but he was different.

Armed with a growing confidence supported by so many inquiries and expressions of interest, Sabah offered his professional services to his sisters. He could have used a hundred sisters but only had five.

To one he offered a dramatic mini-bouffant. Another received an illustrious beehive, another an adorable pageboy, and each artistic effort was a greater disaster than the one before. The willing support and participation of his sisters was not entirely related to moral support, familial loyalty, or even affection. It was, in fact, a choice driven by equal parts vanity and economic reality. None of his sisters had ever been to a beauty salon and had almost no hope of going to one anytime soon.

On the other hand, they were young girls who were willing to try or risk almost anything to look as good as they could. This included a possible mutilation at the hands of their brother. Mrs. Toma saw her daughters periodically slink into the house, meekly appear at a meal table, or even run past her screaming in horror, having been transformed into something almost unrecognizable from the person she had brought into the world.

Each time this happened, Mrs. Toma's first impulse was to go to church and light a candle. But, she reminded herself, it was only hair. It would be grow back eventually and, in the meantime, perhaps her son might be learning something of value.

One night, long after the initial trauma of Sabah's earliest hairstyling efforts, the family was gathered around the black and white portable television set which was, along with the phone, a gift from the oldest son, George. By now there was no apprehension or anxiety related to Sabah's haircuts. On the contrary, he had become so accomplished that his sisters had spread the word. Sabah's services were now being sought after by a growing number of neighborhood girls. Though he hadn't yet been allowed to cut hair at the salon, he had become far less hesitant in describing himself as a hairdresser. Sabah casually styled his sister's hair as the family sat watching the flickering, hypnotic glow of the television.

Mrs. Toma said shook her head and muttered softly, crossing herself. "There he is again."

It was the Baghdad evening news program, complete with a newscaster in a suit, white shirt, and tie reading the latest stories from behind a reputable-looking wooden desk. A single headline glared out at them from the screen:

"ABU TOBAR INVADES AL AMEEN NEIGHBORHOOD"

The newscaster's voice was a bored drone: "Another infamous attack occurred today, in the Al Ameen neighborhood, marking the sixth time this month that The Father of the Machete has struck in the Baghdad area."

Suddenly, the image changed. The small television screen displayed interior shots of a modest family home.

"Girls, don't look," Mrs. Toma said. "Father, turn it. Turn the channel. *Please.*"

But no one moved. The family stared in horror and morbid curiosity at television images which, in recent months, had become routine throughout most of Iraq. A series of extremely graphic photos paraded across the TV. These were not simply crime scene photos; they were worse than that. It was as though the film and photos had been taken with one goal in mind: to present the most horrific scene of human carnage imaginable in the least amount of time.

The newscaster continued. "The family, both Shiite and known Communist sympathizers, reportedly had an extensive cache of weapons, including several handguns, rifles, and ammunition, in direct violation of state policy criminalizing the private possessions of weapons by any civilian."

Mrs. Toma shook her head in silence.

Sabah asked the question everyone in the country had been asking. "Who is this Abu Tobar? Why can't they catch him?"

"Because," Mr. Toma said grimly, "he's everywhere."

By now, the Baathists had control of the entire country and everything in it, including the media. Newspapers, radio, and television were under their control, each manipulated and exploited to produce the maximum amount of fear in the general population. But nothing was more effective than the character of Abu Tobar. On every television across Iraq, several times a week, the nightmarish exploits of this monster would be reported by state television in the grisliest, most graphic detail.

At the time, the character was both intentionally presented and viewed by most Iraqis as half reality, half myth, but all horror. The only families ever murdered or attacked were either apolitical, anti-Baathists, communists, or were secretly concealing weapons, and this fact soon became more than coincidental to even the least discerning citizens.

Only later, many years later, did Sabah realize just how evil the entire campaign had been. The murder of these innocent families was horrible enough. But this regime not only brutally murdered hundreds of families under the guise of a fictitious person or persons named Abu Tobar, they took sadistic pleasure in creating a story about this character, promoting his exploits as though human slaughter were a game.

Whatever the motive behind the creation and promotion of The Father of the Machete, the message was clear: conceal a weapon in your home and your entire family would die. As propaganda it may not have been successful in turning public sympathy toward the Baathists, but these were not people who were interested in sympathy or even had the vaguest idea what it meant. They were only interested in fear, and they were world class experts at delivering that product.

Within a year of Abu Tobar's introduction, the country was in a state of spellbound horror and submission. Any last traces of rebellion or resistance were gone, blown away like a shamal sending desert dust and sand flying, settling finally into a dark and windless night. There was nothing for anyone to do but go about their lives, performing the everyday chores and tasks that might allow a person or family to stay alive for one more day.

CHAPTER TEN

★ ★ ★

A Second Home

★ ★ ★

I t seemed that the darker his country grew under the control of this new and monstrous regime, the more comfort Sabah took, not in the safety of his own home, but in his new family at the Tokalon Salon. Unlike his one-room home, the school, or even the houses of wealthy friends within the neighborhood, the salon was a refuge and haven. At that time, many of the wealthier families in Baghdad were Baathists and regular clients of the salon. Though a staunch anti-Baathist, Mr. Moghadam welcomed their business for two reasons. First, if he didn't, there was always a chance they would shut the salon down. But a far less dramatic reason was Mr. Moghadam's emphatic subscription to the old adage, "Keep your friends close, and your enemies closer."

There was no tension or stress in the salon related to restricted topics of conversation. Tokalon employees were not oppressed by the first and most important rule of any large corporation, the requirement for constant self-editing and monitoring to avoid offending one's co-workers. In every company in Iraq, this fundamental law was intensified by the proliferation of the Baathists. The practice of speaking in banal generalities and keeping workplace conversations safe—and, by extension, keeping one's job safe— radically accelerated as the Baathists increased in power.

It would be difficult to say why the Tokalon was a preferred salon of many Baathists. Perhaps the Baathists were responding to what most people respond to—a warm, positive environment filled with bright people and spontaneous expression. The salon had never been a hotbed of political discussion, either before or after the regime took power. The topic was never self-consciously or awkwardly avoided. It simply wasn't of interest. Perhaps, oddly, this was what the Baathists found so refreshing. Was the salon a small vacation from the relentless obligations of their party, no matter how heartfelt their commitment might be to it?

Or perhaps this was a place where political ideologies were, at least temporarily, put aside and replaced with a more compelling and binding human attribute: wealth. For whatever reason, the salon was a happy place. It became brighter and happier because the world surrounding it was growing darker and more unhappy with each passing day.

One evening, as Sabah was finishing up the day's sweeping, he glanced up from his work to find Mr. Moghadam standing in front of him. Before he could say a word, Mr. Moghadam reached out and pressed something cool, hard, and metallic into Sabah's palm.

"Take care of this," Mr. Moghadam said, his eyes fixed unwaveringly on Sabah's. "Don't lose it."

Confused, Sabah looked down at the object in his hand—and saw that it was a new, shiny brass key, recently copied. He stared at it uncomprehendingly for a moment, and then realization trickled into him like cool, clear water.

The key to the salon. Mr. Moghadam had given him the key to the salon.

He gaped at Mr. Moghadam for a moment, then looked back down at the key. It felt magical somehow, heavier than it should be in proportion to its size. If he had been knighted at that moment, he could not have been more honored. That this man should place this much trust and confidence in him, allowing him unlimited access and entry to the place that had become his second home, nearly brought tears to his eyes.

"Sir, I will guard it with my life," he said, with such intense sincerity that Mr. Moghadam had to smile.

He knew Sabah well enough to understand that the words were not a meaningless cliché; Sabah really meant what he said. This boy was one of the few people who could say something like that and be credible.

Mr. Moghadam patted Sabah on the shoulder. "I know you will. You've earned it. Just be sure and treat this place like you do your own home."

"Oh, much better than that, " Sabah said.

Mr. Moghadam laughed. "Oh, yes?"

"You've never seen my home."

"Well, it doesn't matter where you live, what matters is how you live there."

★ ★ ★

It was almost eight P.M. The last employees were leaving for the day, and as Sabah headed toward the front door of the salon, he saw Baligh, MaMhar, and Faraj gathered just outside the open door. Sabah took a moment just to look at them, marveling at how worldly and adult they seemed despite only being a handful of years older than he was. What would he himself be like, he wondered, when he was twenty-two, twenty-five, thirty? Would he have Mazhar's playful friendliness with women, Faraj's brash honesty, Baligh's easy confidence and grace? Would he wear cream-colored silk jackets and ascots like Mazhar, or roll his own cigarettes like tough, bearded Faraj, or be the star of the Tokalon like Baligh?

He was caught up in his imaginings, trying to envision his own bright future, when the sound of Baligh's voice brought him back to reality.

"Mazhar, why don't you lock up? I left my key at home."

"I don't have my key today. I came in late, remember? Faraj, you take care of it."

Faraj's voice, always louder and gruffer than the others', was edged in panic. "I never bring my key, you know that! We better catch Jamil before he drives away!"

Sabah found himself stepping forward, out of the shadows and into view of the three men. "Wait!" he said, and they all turned to look at him.

Sabah pulled the freshly-made key out of his pocket. Without another word, he pulled the heavy glass door shut, placed his key in the lock, and twisted it. He tugged on the door twice, making sure it was secured, then turned around.

The three men hadn't moved. They were still staring at him with blank, unchanged expressions. Finally, Mazhar spoke.

"This man deserves a drink."

"Absolutely," Faraj said.

"Couldn't agree more," Baligh said. "Tonight it's on me. You have time, don't you, Sabah?"

Sabah had time like Cinderella had time for the royal ball. He had never been invited out by these men and, for a moment, he was speechless.

"Sure, I-I'd like that very much," he managed.

"You do drink, don't you?" Faraj asked.

Sabah gave an uncaring shrug. "Of course, all the time."

He'd never had a drink in his life. But fifteen minutes later, he was sitting at one of the many riverfront casinos of the city, surrounded by his mentors. Baligh ordered a large fish, just caught that day from the river, along with a tall bottle of clear liquid that looked like water to Sabah. Baligh carefully poured the liquid into tiny glasses. They were cute but didn't seem practical to Sabah. He'd need to refill those a lot of times to make one normal glass of water.

"To the key holders of the Tokalon," Baligh said, holding up his glass. Mazhar and Faraj followed suit.

"No beer for you today," Mazhar said. "Now you're a man and you'll drink like one. Today, we drink arak. To Sabah."

Sabah watched the three men down the clear liquid in single gulps. He drew in a deep breath and did the same thing.

What he drank tasted something like black licorice laced with fire. It didn't taste nearly as bad as it felt. He immediately gasped then coughed. The three others laughed.

"All the time, Sabah? Really?" Baligh said.

Faraj grinned, his swarthy face and neatly trimmed beard making him look more like a desert prince than a hairdresser. "Sabah when you go to confession this week, don't mention us by name." The men laughed and Rashid added, "Sabah, what happens when you get thrown off a horse?"

The drink had rendered Sabah temporarily mute. He looked at the men with wide, watery eyes, wondering what had just hit him, which caused his companions to laugh even more. After a few seconds, he managed to shake his head.

"You get right back on, my friend," Faraj said, and filled the four glasses again.

The three lifted their glasses but didn't drink, their eyes on Sabah, waiting for him to drink first.

Sabah hesitated. He was reminded, somehow, of seeing a doctor as a little boy. He vividly remembered the first time a needle had punctured his skin. There was a completely unexpected sharpness to that experience. This drink, whatever it was, may not have been quite so painful but it was just as surprising and nearly as unpleasant. He wasn't at all sure he wanted to do it again. But there was no way he could avoid it. He was being honored tonight by the men he most admired. They continued smiling, holding their glasses and waiting. After a moment, Mazhar notched his glass up another inch and nodded to Sabah as if to say, *Come on, let's go.*

To the key holders of the Tokalon, Sabah thought, and downed his glass.

The second time wasn't quite as bad as the first and by the sixth time, Sabah not only didn't know if he liked it or not, he didn't care. The talk flowed as freely as the drink, full of laughter and affection, and time passed for Sabah in a warm haze of friendship and inebriation.

A beautiful eight pound barbel, caught that day and served whole, had been placed on the table when they were on their third round. It had been covered in lemon slices, sage, and dill weed. Rarely had Sabah seen such a magnificent display of food. Now, all that remained of it was a head, tail, and cleanly picked skeleton.

Baligh was leaning forward, his forearms resting firmly on the white linen of the table, his hands folded and fingers interlocked. In the candlelight, his face looked particularly pensive. Sabah would soon learn that drinking and reflection went very well together.

"Do you know how many people working at the salon have keys?" Baligh said. "Do you?"

Sabah wasn't sure if the question was being posed to him or to the group in general. Nobody else seemed to be sure, either, and so eventually Baligh answered his own question by raising his right hand. Four fingers were extended.

"You know what?" Mazhar said. "I love this salon. I love it. I've been here five years. Best years of my life. I love you guys. I mean it. But you remember how long I waited to get a key? A *year*." No one said anything and Mazhar continued as though someone had. "That's right," he said, agreeing with the silence.

"I remember," Faraj said.

"That's right," Mazhar said again. "And look at this guy. He's here, what? Six months? And he gets a key? I mean … what's goin' on here?"

"Hey, lemme tell you something," Faraj said. "You take a look at that kid."

"I'm lookin'!"

"Are you?"

Mazhar lifted his head and gazed blearily at Sabah. "Yes!"

"This kid," Faraj said, slowly and deliberately. "This kid … I'm telling you, this kid is going somewhere."

"Where's he goin'?" Baligh said.

Faraj seemed to consider this for a moment, then answered firmly, "Places."

"Places?" Mazhar said. "Where is that?"

"You know," Baligh said, snickering as he poured more arak into his glass, "it's that little town south of Najaf, where they herd goats."

Baligh and MaMhar laughed, but Faraj shook his head, his intense dark eyes fixed on Sabah's.

"Don't listen to them, Sabah," he said. "They're just jealous."

It was becoming difficult for Sabah to listen to anyone. Nothing appeared to be staying still. His friends' overly earnest faces, oddly hovering and disconnected from their bodies, seemed to be on a crazy, tilted merry-go-round.

"No, really, I'm just messing with you," Mazhar said to Sabah. "Actually, you're smarter than me. Seriously. But I'm sexier." He shrugged and gazed heavenward. "Sorry, but those are the facts. What can I do about it?"

One jab was countered by another and the arak kept coming. Suddenly, Sabah felt as though he'd been slapped or as if a chiropractor had twisted his head. A burst of sobriety shot up and through him like a single firework, accompanied by a flash of panic. What day was it? As the laughter continued around him, he tried to think carefully, something which was nearly impossible through the fog of alcohol. It was … Friday? Yes, of course. It was Friday. There was no school tomorrow. Speaking of tomorrow, was it tomorrow already or was it still today? And where was he, anyway? With these final questions, Sabah plunged into oblivion.

★ ★ ★

It was dark when he woke up on a large, comfortable sofa. His shoes were off, a pillow was under his head, and someone had covered him with a blanket. He had never felt so disoriented in his life. On the other side of the room, he could see the outline of someone sleeping on a bed. He sat up on the edge of the sofa and noticed that his shoes were on the floor, right at his feet. So far so good. He wasn't dead, blind, or physically maimed in any recognizable way. Then came another of those awful panic rushes. The key, where was the key? He reached into his pocket and immediately exhaled. He felt the metal contours and pulled it out, letting the sight of the key complete his full sense of relief.

Sabah was thirsty, maybe thirstier than he'd ever been in his life, and he wondered why. He also wondered why his head hurt so much. Had he been in a fight? He lightly touched his face. Everything seemed to be okay. Still, he was a little worried about looking in a mirror. What time was it? He looked around the room and saw an alarm clock on a small table near the bed.

Moonlight shone through several open windows, giving the room an astral, phantom quality. The white and gray color tones, combined with the relative quiet of whatever neighborhood he was in, magnified Sabah's anxiousness. He stepped quietly toward the alarm clock. It was one of those traveling clocks that could be folded into its small leather case but, when opened, looked like a little triangle. The hour and minute hands were luminous. From several feet away, Sabah could see that it was almost five A.M. He was in trouble and he knew it. But maybe, possibly, if he got home in time, his parents would still be asleep. Sometimes he came home late from friends' houses after they'd gone to bed. If he moved fast enough, he might make it back in time, but where was he? And who was lying curled up on the bed? Sabah tiptoed closer and saw that it was Mazhar, sound asleep and snoring.

Very quietly, Sabah walked across the room to a door and opened it. He'd stepped halfway through it before he realized it was a closet. Gently closing the door, he glanced around the room for other options. The only other door led down one flight of stairs. Now he was getting somewhere. Walking down the stairs, he entered a room that was immediately both strange and familiar. Strange because he had never seen it empty and in darkness before. Familiar because it was the salon. He had known there was an apartment with several rooms above the salon. He also knew that Baligh lived there. Now, he had actually slept there.

Under other circumstances, this realization would have carried a considerable sense of accomplishment but right now, all Sabah could think about was getting home as quickly as possible. He unlocked the salon door. The pride he'd felt in receiving the key was replaced, at this moment, by a strong and very practical sense of gratitude. In moments he was running for home.

There was no traffic and the sidewalks were relatively empty. This was good. If he ran fast enough, he could be home in twenty minutes, about fifteen minutes before his mother would be up starting breakfast for the family. As he ran, he tried to remember what had happened the night before. He remembered a big, delicious fish, raised voices, and laughing, but beyond that he wasn't sure of anything.

Not so much arak next time! he promised himself.

If there was a next time, anyway; if he hadn't done anything too stupid!

Worried he might have done something that had embarrassed his friends, he tried harder to remember. Before he could make much headway, though, he saw a man up ahead, in the middle of the long city block, trying to lift his push cart over a high curb and onto the sidewalk.

As Sabah approached, he could see that the man was heaving with all his might, his thick arm muscles straining, but the cart wouldn't budge. He thought about stopping to help, but knew he didn't have enough time—he would barely make it home in time as it was.

Just as he'd decided this, he drew close enough to make out the features of the man's face. His steps slowed and he halted in the middle of the street.

It was Gabir.

CHAPTER ELEVEN

★ ★ ★

The Beginning Of The End

★ ★ ★

"Sabah!" Gabir exclaimed, lowering the handle and letting the cart rest on its stand. He wiped a forearm across his brow. "What are you doing here?"

Sabah gave an embarrassed grimace. "Do I have to tell you?"

"What happened? You look horrible." Gabir offered a wry, knowing smile. "Don't tell me. Arak."

Sabah forgot his embarrassment and stared at his friend. "How did you know?"

Gabir laughed his hard, wheezing laugh. It was the kind that shook his whole body and always made Sabah smile. It was kind, real, and full of life, and never at another person's expense.

"The word's out. The whole town's talking about it!"

"*What?* No! Are you kidding? Who's talking?"

Gabir just laughed again.

"Tell me!"

"I just saw your mom and a priest looking for you," Gabir said, deadpan now.

Sabah looked at his friend for a moment, then sighed. "Really? No! You're joking, right?"

"Maybe." Gabir said, playfully.

"Really, how did you know I was drinking arak?"

"I don't know Sabah, it's hard to explain. The day after … It's just a certain kind of scrambled eggs face. I don't know. Takes one to know one I guess. So, you gonna help me with this cart or what?"

"Maybe …"

"You better, you little snot, or I'll tell your big brother."

Sabah grinned and went to stand beside his friend, and soon they were both gripping the handles of the cart, tugging and heaving to try to pull the cart's wheels over the high curb.

After at least a full minute of this, the cart hadn't budged more than an inch, and the two let go of the handles with matching gasps of exhaustion.

Gabir leaned his back against the cart and spent a moment catching his breath. Sabah wondered how many times Gabir had already tried to lift the cart, and suddenly felt grateful he was here to help his friend.

"I was here yesterday," Gabir said between breaths. "Great day … great. Sold everything. So I put twice as much on today. Only problem is the stupid thing's too heavy."

Sabah looked around for anyone else who might be able to help, but the streets were nearly empty at this hour. One man was walking on the other side of the street and Sabah thought about calling him but decided not to, fearing the call for help might embarrass Gabir, a man who took such pride in his own strength and self-sufficiency. Then the man crossed the street without being asked and Sabah watched him approach. It was dark. The street lights were sparse and dimly lit. The man was no more than a shadow. Only when he was nearly halfway across the street, moving closer to Sabah and Gabir, did they both realize he was a policeman. There was a time, not long before, when that wouldn't have been particularly noteworthy. If anything it would have been welcomed. But not now. Gabir and Sabah both knew better. Now, the police were *them*.

They both kept their eyes on the approaching policeman. Gabir spoke quietly, without turning his head. "Don't say anything. Let me talk to him."

If Sabah's hangover had partially dissipated during his run, now it vanished completely in a rush of adrenaline and dread.

The policeman was in his early thirties, stocky and sturdy but not particularly large. He wore black boots and a wide black leather belt. His shirt and pants were heavy green canvas. He approached with a slow, quiet confidence. He'd not only caught a criminal red handed, he'd caught someone who had nowhere to run. This policeman had seen enough of street peddlers to know that the man would never abandon the cart that was his livelihood.

"Hey, buddy, what's goin' on?" the policeman asked, in what seemed to Sabah a grotesque impersonation of casual conversation.

"Just trying to get my cart on the curb, officer."

"I can see that," the policeman said.

"New curbs, what can you do? They're all over the place. This one's just a few weeks old."

Gabir's efforts to ingratiate himself with the poker-faced officer made Sabah cringe with discomfort.

The officer said nothing; Gabir went on, a bit nervously, "They make them so high now. I don't know why anybody would—"

"What were you doing in the street in the first place?"

The question was so abrupt it jarred Gabir into silence.

"Don't you know," the policeman continued, "that peddlers can't push carts in the streets anymore? You have to cross at the signal lights."

"I know that, officer," Gabir said, more quietly now.

"So, you're breaking he law."

Gabir swallowed. "Well, sir, you see, the nearest signal light is about six blocks from here, and well, the cart is heavy, and I'm coming from the other direction, and—"

"You intentionally broke the law," the officer said in a hard voice. "Are you stupid or something?"

"No sir, I'm not stupid." The words were soft and strained. It was a sound that reminded Sabah of something but he couldn't place it. What was it? It was like alley cats in the middle of the night. The low, quavering moans, unnaturally long and ominous, that would explode into a fury of hissing and shrieks. He felt sick.

"You intentionally broke the law," the officer said again.

"I was just trying to get—"

"And you say you're not stupid?"

"Officer, please ..."

"Do me a favor. Shut up. Just shut your big mouth."

The policeman reached to the side of his belt and unclasped one of the square leather satchels attached to it. He pulled out a citation pad.

"What's your full name?"

"You're giving me a ticket?"

"I'm not asking again. What's your name?"

"Sir, I'm just trying to make a living. That's all. I'm just doing what I've been doing all my—"

Before Gabir could finish, the policeman grabbed up his baton and, in one sweeping motion, slammed it into Gabir's left tricep. Gabir didn't move, not even a flinch. It was as though, at that moment, Gabir had become a marble statue. Sabah had always respected this man's strength and quiet dignity. That respect would have bordered on awe had Sabah not been so terrified by the current circumstances.

Something was at work in Gabir. It had been building slowly over many years, so slowly that no one, not even Sabah, had noticed it.

It wasn't just the bureaucracy, the new laws, restrictions, and ordinances that had been making his life so much more difficult over the past few years. It was the hidden power behind the laws. It was the constant, growing pressure of that power, manifesting itself in some new way every day. It was the sense that nothing was his anymore. The people of Baghdad were becoming prisoners of the city they lived in. The city, one day at a time, was being slowly suffocated.

Like anyone else's life, Gabir's was defined in a large part by a sense of space. He had grown accustomed to the little world he lived in and his little life within his native city. He wasn't wealthy and never would be. He would not travel throughout the world or even, very often, to other regions of his own country. That was fine. He had made his peace with that. But even that little bit of comfort, the last remnants of dreams that would never come true, were being stripped away from him. His sense of space was decreasing, growing smaller and smaller, until he now, when he had been cornered in a state of constant claustrophobia. In the most real way, at this moment, Gabir was every non-Baathist man, woman and child in Baghdad and Sabah knew it.

As Gabir's world contracted around him, the seeds of injustice and wrong, wrong in the largest, noblest sense of the word, had been silently growing within him. Something was eroding, and had been for a long, long time. But now, with his arm stinging and the officer's cruel, condescending face only inches away, the last precarious boulders of order had been upended. The avalanche was imminent. Gabir's time was at hand.

For Sabah, time seemed to slow. The policeman was staring at him, eyes wide, perhaps trying to understand why his baton strike had failed to produce any kind of reaction. Then the officer's brows contracted in angry determination and he swung back the baton, and even though Gabir knew it was moving with the speed of a snake's strike, it seemed to take hours for the baton to lurch forward toward the side of his head.

He watched the moment unfold in detached fascination and, as if he'd practiced his response a thousand times before, his massive hand intercepted, enveloped, and halted the policeman's hand. They froze there, the baton hovering a few inches away from Gabir's head, the policeman's face a comic mask of shock and fury

Sabah could not move or think. Gabir continued to hold the policeman's arm, unmoving, in a bizarre mockery of a dance.

"Sabah, go," Gabir said, in a strong voice that was strangely calm. "Now."

Sabah didn't move. He was paralyzed with indecision, not knowing, under these surreal circumstances, whether staying or going would be the most dangerous thing to do.

Gabir's head jerked around to look at him, his eyes wild. "Now!" he yelled, and his voice was like a gunshot. "Go!"

It was the last time he would see his friend's face, and the last expression he would ever see on it. Why this? Why did it have to be this? It had always been a kind face, a gentle face, patient and non-judgmental. A face Sabah was always happy to see and a face that made him happy. But that face was gone. Like the face of fire as it consumes that which it destroys, this was the face of pain, alive and fully exposed, leaping out in a final act of self-determination, even if that meant self-destruction. This was a face that left Sabah empty, completely without hope. But he had no choice. He turned and ran. In another moment, he heard a man's agonized scream.

Sabah stopped just once to look back. Gabir had forced the officer's hand back over itself in a one hundred and eighty degree angle, so the top of the policeman's hand was now almost touching the top of his forearm. The man collapsed to his knees in agony, Gabir looming over him.

"Who's stupid now? Huh? *Who's stupid now?*"

Sabah stood watching from the end of the block. The man's screams were echoing off the buildings lining the empty boulevard. He was in pain and would be slow to act—maybe there was still a chance. Gabir could run, get away, go into hiding. But even as he thought it, Sabah knew it wouldn't happen. Gabir would not run. He would stand and face whatever came. To do otherwise, he would not be Gabir.

A police patrol truck appeared, then, turning the corner of the intersection where Sabah was standing, just as Gabir took the front of the policeman's shirt and belt into his massive fists. In perfect weightlifting form, Gabir lifted the officer over his head and, letting out a primal, agonized scream, he threw the man halfway across the wide boulevard, perhaps twenty feet. The man's body landed with a horrible thud and rolled several more feet, where it lay motionless in the middle of the road.

The patrol truck, with three policeman inside, had turned just in time to see the body in mid-flight.

The truck skidded to a stop and all three men jumped out. Two of them raced toward Gabir and a third went to the man lying in the street. Though he was nearly fifty yards away from the scene, safe in his anonymity, Sabah could not make himself leave or stop watching. Was there anything he could do for his friend? Nothing but hopelessly watch a life being destroyed, either by itself or others. It hardly mattered which. As this life was reaching its end, Sabah felt something in him break apart. Something in him was drifting away. Was it hope? Was it his family? Was it his country? Was it his God?

Within seconds, two more officers were unconscious at Gabir's feet. The third policeman, seeing this, ran to the truck. Sabah could hear, even from this distance, the distinct clicks and static of the patrol truck's radio. The policeman was calling for backup. Sabah found his eyes turning to Gabir, who was standing quietly by his date cart. He seemed calm. He was arranging the contents of his cart as though this were just another day, making sure everything was well-organized before his first customer arrived.

Another police truck came, then another, and another. Sabah didn't count them, but within ten minutes there must have been twenty policemen surrounding Gabir. It took no less than all of them, all at once, to subdue him. Sabah had always believed he was friends with the strongest man in Baghdad. Today, he knew it beyond all doubt. Yet there was no joy in this confirmation. In fact, there was only a bottomless, endless sorrow.

Why didn't they shoot and kill him at this instant, right where he stood? Sabah couldn't understand. He knew they were completely capable of it. What they did do was perhaps worse. Gabir was handcuffed, his arms outstretched, held aloft by chains connected to both sides of the patrol truck's frame. He sat with his shirt off on the back gate of the truck. His head hung down so low that his chin rested on his neck. Sabah couldn't tell if he was conscious or not. All he could feel, for sure, was the pain on his face.

It was dawn. The morning had started with his own flight, and fear of retribution in a world that no longer seemed to matter. At this moment of the day, so often associated with hope, Sabah felt an emotion he so rarely experienced he barely recognized it. At this moment, Sabah felt lonely and utterly alone.

Even then, with a final tearful glance at his friend, Sabah wanted to scream to him, "Break the chains friend. Break them. You can break them. Run! Run, Gabir!" There was still a chance, there was always a chance. The words kept repeating themselves over and over again, in a kind of mantra that seemed to transcend the horrible event he had witnessed. The words would continue, at various times from this moment forward, until they would finally resolve themselves into a crystalline vision of his own destiny: *Run ... run ... run ...*

CHAPTER TWELVE
★ ★ ★
The Al Rafiden Social Club
★ ★ ★

G abir's beating fractured and splintered Sabah in ways no one could
have understood or predicted, least of all Sabah himself. For nearly
five years Sabah and his entire country had been slowly suffocating
within a Baathist choke hold. Sabah had more than his own share of
personal encounters with them. But this was different. Seeing what they
had done to this man, in the way they did it. It was more painful and
terrifying to Sabah than anything the Baathists had done to Sabah himself.

Constriction, constraint, suppression, surveillance; they'd all been
growing, like a disease, into every aspect of Iraqi life. Like most of his
country people, Sabah had dealt with this new regime with a combination
of compliance and avoidance. If Sabah and the Iraqi people were anything;
they were tolerant and long-suffering. For most Iraqi's the Baathists
were just another yoke to be carried. This newly acquired fear had, in a
terrible way, become a companion to their own poverty and depravation,
conditions most Iraqi's could not even label because, for their entire lives,
they had known nothing else.

For Sabah, though, the episode with Gabir had triggered something.
Like everyone else, Sabah's world was shaped and controlled by the
claustrophobic climate created by the Baathist's. But at this moment, Sabah
couldn't help also feeling a kind of expansiveness. He was, unknown to
himself, making a decision below the level of thought and reason. Even the
inchoate inception of an unformed idea was enough to slightly energize
Sabah.

Even so, for the next month the changes in Sabah were obvious to his friends, family, and especially his co-workers in the salon. Though his beard was young and thin, it was noticeable enough when he stopped shaving it. His usual scrupulous attention to hygiene, grooming, and wardrobe seemed to be on a leave of absence. His increasingly disheveled appearance was as mysterious as his mood, which had grown far more somber and distracted. More than all this, Sabah consistently demonstrated something so foreign to his nature he almost seemed like another person. Sabah had become pensive.

He was so unlike himself that Mr. Moghadam thought he might be seriously ill.

But Mr. Moghadam clearly understood the limitations of his relationship with Sabah. He was not Sabah's peer or confidant. Though he knew he was respected by Sabah, even admired as a role model, Mr. Moghadam would not invade Sabah, pressing for explanations or answers. That was a job best left to Sabah's co-workers. Mr. Moghadam took Rashid aside and spoke with him. Rashid was aware of the change in Sabah as clearly as Mr. Moghadam and was more than willing to help. It was quickly agreed that Rashid would spend some time with Sabah in a non-work setting, a place where personal problems might be more readily discussed.

Rashid approached Sabah indirectly. It wasn't a practice of the salon or his personal style, but the circumstances called for the smallest trace of guile. They stood together at the back door of the salon during a smoke break.

"What are you doing after work?" Rashid said.

"I'm supposed to see some friends," Sabah answered listlessly.

"Really? You mind if I join you?"

Sabah glanced at Rashid. None of his salon friends had ever expressed an interest in being a part of his school or neighborhood social circles. Nor had Sabah ever invited them. He had always considered the men of the salon to be older, more sophisticated. He'd assumed that a group of younger boys, barely out of high school, would be of little interest to men of such experience and worldliness. Had Sabah not been in his current state of mind, he would have been excited by the suggestion. He respected and admired Rashid. Introducing him to other friends would have been an honor. Now the suggestion only provoked a mild curiosity.

"I'm not sure I'm going," Sabah said.

"Why not?"

Sabah shrugged but said nothing and continued smoking his cigarette. Rashid didn't force the issue, sensing that any effort to pry wouldn't be helpful.

"I don't know," Sabah said, after several long moments. "I guess I haven't been feeling very social lately."

Rashid glanced at Sabah but didn't let his gaze linger. It wasn't a moment for direct eye contact. Instead Rashid said, as casually as he could, "Well, maybe you should. Might be good for you. I know I could use a drink."

Sabah looked at Rashid now. Sure, why not? Though Sabah had been drinking more than usual lately, it had been alone. He hadn't had a drink with a friend in weeks. Maybe if they drank enough he might even find a way to laugh again.

Sabah and Rashid went straight to the social club after work. Sabah's other neighborhood friends, including Hattam, Wallid, and Milad, wouldn't be there for an hour or so. There would be others, too, perhaps. It was Hattam's birthday and any event in the neighborhood was a good excuse to gather and have a good time.

The Al Rafiden Social Club was a popular gathering place for many of the young men in Sabah's neighborhood. The interior featured unpainted cinderblock walls, concrete floors, and a dozen folding card tables. On mild summer evenings like this one, however, the patrons preferred the equally luxurious outdoor gardens with their assorted picnic benches and plain white light bulbs, the latter suspended on long electrical cords between tree limbs and metal posts. Though the club could have made a bomb shelter look inviting, it was the perfect place for young men, who knew little of the world, to relax, drink, and laugh.

Sabah and everyone else who went there felt like they were in their own living rooms, even if many didn't have a living room or even knew what one was. The place was completely without pretense. It was conducive to behavior consistent with itself: plain, direct, and unaffected. In fact, if the gathering had been anywhere else, Sabah probably wouldn't have gone. It was about the last public place he could go in his current emotional state. Anywhere else would have been too tedious.

"I'm confused Sabah. Is this a restaurant or a barnyard?" Rashid asked sitting down at an outside table.

"You don't like it?"

"I love it," Rashid said, smiling and slapping Sabah on the shoulder.

Sabah could tell that he meant it and he smiled. "It's great isn't it?"

"Remind me to wear my gas mask next time," Rashid said, and lifted his glass to toast Sabah.

Sabah laughed and it made Rashid smile. He hadn't seen Sabah laugh for weeks.

Rashid had ordered a carafe of arak. He was optimistic that he would get the whole story out of Sabah with or without alcoholic assistance, but he wasn't taking any chances. If he couldn't get it out of him, the arak was sure to. By the time the rest of the group arrived, Sabah was feeling no pain, which was a considerable accomplishment considering the amount of pain he was in.

"You know what?" Sabah said after awhile. "I've been thinking about something for a long time."

Okay, here we go, Rashid thought. "Well be careful, don't hurt yourself," he said dryly, but Sabah didn't seem to hear.

"I think … what I wanna do … is leave this country."

As he finished the words, for the first time, Sabah turned his head and looked directly in Rashid's eyes. Rashid stared at Sabah. This was the last thing he expected to hear. Before Rashid could even decide what question to ask, the rest of the group arrived.

Sabah hadn't seen his friends for some time and he realized, only at this moment, just how much he'd missed them. Hattam, Wallid, Milad, Hashim, and several others from the neighborhood arrived and the table instantly erupted into hugs, back slaps, and laughter.

Two hours later, it was dark and the seven friends were still at the table, which was now covered with carafes, bottles, and glasses. A slight breeze felt refreshing in the warm evening air. The light bulbs overhead slowly swayed. As the group continued drinking and talking and laughing, they were completely unaware of being observed by someone at the next table.

Ahmid was from the neighborhood. He was slightly older. They'd grown up with him. They all knew who he was and what he'd become. The other five young men with Ahmid were busy with their own stories and jokes, but Ahmid remained quiet, preoccupied by the only group in the social club more exuberant and boisterous than his own. For Ahmid, happiness was, itself a state owned commidity, the distribution of which was under his sole control and authority.

Rashid was sitting next to Sabah on the wooden bench of their large picnic table. Though he liked the group and was enjoying himself, he hadn't forgotten his purpose.

"Hey, Sabah," he said, putting an arm over Sabah's shoulder. "It's good to see you having fun."

Sabah, suddenly grown serious, studied his friend for a moment. "I'm sorry Rashid."

"Sorry for what?"

Sabah shrugged and took a drink. "I don't know. For not being me."

Rashid felt a small pang somewhere in the center of his chest. He paused before he spoke again.

"You're serious? You really want to go?" Rashid asked, even as their group erupted in laughter.

Sabah eyes met Rashids, and what Rashid saw in those eyes was someone who was truly and completely unhappy. For a few moments Sabah had been silent, thinking, right next to Rashid, but completely alone. Then Sabah opened his mouth to speak.

"Hey! You wanna stop being so loud?" someone screamed.

The group, including Sabah and Rashid, went silent, turning in unison toward the sound of the voice. It had come from Ahmid, who was now standing rigidly at his own table, his face twisted with anger and hatred.

Milad instantly recognized him and was disgusted. "Why don't you start with yourself Ahmid?" Milad retorted. "Have a drink and relax."

Hattam's hand gently touched Milad's arm and Milad slapped it away. Hattam's eyes were fixed on something. His head jerked, almost imperceptibly, as a cue, and Milad's eyes followed Hattams. Both young men were looking at Ahmid's gun and holster. Very few people carried guns and everyone knew who those people were.

But Milad didn't need Hattam's reminder. He knew Ahmid was a Baathist and he certainly knew who *they* were. But even knowing this, it just wasn't conceivable to him that this mean, unhappy little boy, this sad person he'd grown up with and known nearly his entire life, could really be a threat. Not him, and not in this place. The Al Rafiden Social Club was the one place everyone in the neighborhood came because they knew there were no differences here. This was where everyone was free to be whoever they were. It had always been that way. It was beyond Milad's imagination that anyone could be so primitive and uncivilized that they would not understand and respect that.

Milad stood up. He would not be looked down to at this moment. "What's the problem, Ahmid? We're here having a good time, just like you. Look at us! You're just like us. Laughing, drinking, having a good time. Ahmid we grew up together! So what is this? You're the noise police?"

By now, the tables immediately surrounding the two groups had quietly emptied.

Ahmid didn't answer Milad directly. Instead, he glanced at the group he was with. He took one step back away from his table. As if this were a signal, everyone else at his table stood up. All of them were carrying guns. Nearly at the same moment, everyone at Sabah's table stood up. Something in Sabah, in his whole group in fact, was beyond fight or flight. Neither was an option, so they simply stood where they were, frozen and helpless.

Ahmid had been waiting for this moment for a long time. He'd become a district leader in the party and the group he was with was under his supervision. He could have killed Milad on the spot, but it wasn't necessary and might create complications. The truth was, Ahmid found fulfillment in creating new ways to inflict pain and fear. He took the gun out of his holster as he came closer to Milad.

"Ahmid, we'll be quiet! Milad sit down. OK?" Hattam said urgently. "All right? We'll be quiet!"

"Shut up," Ahmid said.

By now, Ahmid had raised the gun and was holding it under Milad's chin. Sabah didn't want to look but found he couldn't look away, even as Rashid got a grip on his shirt and tugged him to the back of the group.

"You want to be friends, Milad?" Ahmid said softly. "You want to be my friend?"

Milad swallowed visibly, his eyes locked on the barrel of the gun. "Is that what you want?"

Ahmid gave a faint smile. "You know what I want?"

Milad shook his head.

In a single moment, the buried fury of an entire lifetime was released. With a brutal backhand swing, Ahmid slammed the butt of his gun as hard as he could into the left side of Milad's jaw. Milad's entire head twisted at a forty-five degree angle as Sabah heard an unfamiliar sound, something like glass or china hitting a concrete floor.

The circle of social club patrons surrounding the scene immediately scattered in all directions. Milad had hardly hit the ground when Sabah saw Ahmid on top of him, slamming his gun handle again and again into Milad's jaw. At the same moment, apparently seeing that the party had started and not wanting to be left out, Ahmid's gun-carrying colleagues randomly started beating anyone they could get a hold of.

Sabah felt a violent jerk on the back of his shirt. He turned, instinctively raising his arms in self-defense, only to see Rashid gesturing wildly for Sabah to follow him. Sabah hesitated, looking back at where Milad lay on the ground, still being beaten by Ahmid. By now, Wallid was also on the ground being beaten by two other members of Ahmid's group.

The social club was in complete chaos. People scattered in every direction, knowing gunfire could erupt any moment. A minute passed.

Breathless and panting, Ahmid looked at the handle of his gun. He wiped it clean on Milad's shirt. Kneeling and straddling Milad, Ahmid paused to catch his breath.

He spoke quietly in a voice only Milad could have heard, if Milad had been conscious and able to hear it. "Well, look at you now, Mr. Popular."

Then Ahmid stood up and studied the crowd. Except for his own friends, the patrons in the social club had either gone or were hovering in the perimeter shadows of the courtyard. Ahmid put his gun back in his holster.

"The man doesn't love his country," he announced to anyone still able to hear. "I don't hate him because he's popular. I hate him because he's not a patriot."

Without another word, Ahmid walked out of the courtyard. His subordinates followed him. Rashid and Sabah had remained untouched. Milad had been at the epicenter of the mayhem and had received, by far, the most damage. He was alive, but he had lost seven of his upper and lower front teeth and would be hospitalized for several days.

Sabah and Rashid left the club and walked along dark streets of

Baghdad on a moonless night. Though Rashid was walking next to Sabah, speaking with him, trying to piece together the events of the evening and make sense of them, Sabah was no longer listening. The streets were very dark but Sabah was in a darker place, a place deep within himself.

CHAPTER THIRTEEN

★ ★ ★

Mrs. Al-Ghamdi's
Gentle Touch

★ ★ ★

The events of the past month, Gabir and now Milad, were creating a seismic shift in Sabah's attitude, outlook and values. There were his parents and home. There was his church and his faith. There was the Tokalon and the beautiful, more complete perspective of the world his work place offered. Each of these strands created a single, indestructible rope of identity which was Sabah. But now, indivudally, and as a whole, the strands were beginning to fray.

He felt himself adrift, but not lost, floating away on an irresistable tide. Yet, other than one comment he made to Rashid on the night Milad was beaten, Sabah had not spoken to one human soul about his deepest feelings. It was unlike him, and he knew it. But his secrecy was something that overpowered him. Sabah understood the vague fantasy of departure from Iraq was a childish dream, a naive ambition that needed to be controlled. But he could not control it.

But the reality of his situation would not allow his dream to be anything more than that. With Saddam Hussein now firmly in control of the country, it would be easier to win the lottery than to get a passport or visa. Every day on his way to work, Sabah walked by the passport office. It was an older building and one that was very familiar to him. He'd seen it his entire life, and for most of those years, it had been just another anonymous governmental institution, a building as nondescript and uninteresting as a post office.

Now, there was a line of people three days long waiting to get in. People of all ages and from all walks of life were sleeping on the sidewalk, camping there twenty-four hours a day for a chance to have an interview that might last ten minutes. And that was only the first step. Getting the passport stamped to leave the country was nearly as difficult as getting the passport itself. Sabah had made repeated commitments to himself to get in that line. And he had broken just as many of those commitments.

On this day he passed the line again. Sabah's natural joy, enthusiasm and love for life had been slowly bleeding out of him for two months now. Nothing seemed to have any meaning or purpose any more. Even that wonderful, delightful, thrilling adventure most people called work, had grown tiresome for Sabah. In fact, the last thing he wanted to do at this moment was go to the Tokalon Salon.

Mrs. Al-Ghamdi was Sabah's first scheduled appointment of the day. Mrs. Al-Ghamdi was the forty-three-year-old wife of an Iraqi ambassador and high ranking official of the Baath Party. Like many of the other ladies in the salon, it was difficult to gauge which aspects of her appearance were natural beauty and which had been carefully constructed. Most of the salon clients, particularly the older women like Mrs. Al-Ghamdi, were refined in their tastes, skilled in their fashion coordination, and perfectly groomed but never florid or overdone. Sabah simply couldn't tell where her style ended and innate beauty began.

She also was, perhaps, the only exception to the golden rule Sabah had been taught when he first arrived at the salon. The rule that said to never burden customers with personal information, but only to be available to listen to theirs. Sabah, learned, very early on, that Mrs. Al-Ghamdi was as a big a soccer fan as he was. But it was much more than this mutual interest which reversed the roles so strictly enforced by the salon. For whatever reason, there was something about Mrs. Al-Ghamdi that put Sabah completely at ease.

She was funny without being mean, smart without being condescending, beautiful without being arrogant, curious without being nosey, opinionated without being didactic. In short she was the physical embodiment of grace itself and Sabah adored her. He had attended to her dozens of times and Sabah could not remember one occasion, when she did not surprise him with some new fact or story or smallest piece of information he found fascinating and useful. She was of a world Sabah had never seen. The world itself was her home and whenever Sabah was with her, he was warmly invited into it.

As Sabah was carefully trimming her hair she began to describe a championship soccer match she had seen, many years, in the Royal Box at Wembley Stadium. Suddenly Sabah stopped and took a step to the side so he could look at her.

"I saw that match!" Sabah exclaimed.

"You did?"

"Yes! Live! Here, in Baghdad, on color TV!"

As the words left his mouth, he felt foolish and slightly embarrassed. In his enthusiasm he'd forgotten who he was talking to. He realized how pathetically prosaic he must have sounded. He had no reason to be concerned. Mrs. Al-Ghamdi was as fond of Sabah as he was of her, precisely because he was unpretentious. She smiled at him even as he blushed, then thought for a moment as he resumed cutting.

"Sabah, have you ever been out of Baghdad?"

"Once, when I was little, we went to Mosul. For my grandfather's funeral."

Sabah stopped trimming for just a moment and looked into the mirror. He saw Mrs. Al-Ghamdi gazing back at him. He couldn't interpret the expression precisely. It wasn't pity, exactly; it something closer to tenderness, perhaps even love.

"Would you like to visit London?"

"More than anything in the world."

"You'd need a passport."

"Mrs. Al-Ghamdi, I don't know if you have been there lately, but there is a line in front of the passport office for miles and miles. So many people want a passport now. And they say even if you wait, you probably won't get it."

No one was more aware of this than Mrs. Al-Ghamdi but she said nothing, offering only her deepest attention as Sabah continued trimming her hair. Suddenly she lifted her arm and with the gentlest touch, placed her outstretched fingers on Sabah's arm. She had never done this before and it startled Sabah, so much so that he completely stopped his work and stared at her.

"Sabah, you are not happy are you?", she asked.

Sabah said nothing. The question both surprised and disturbed him. He didn't want to answer but he didn't need to. His face was his answer. He felt as though he might start crying, and physically, consciously prevented himself from doing so. He had not moved. He had not even not even shaken his head.

"It's OK. I know. I understand," Mrs. Al-Ghamdi said, very softly now. "Now listen to me Sabah. There are things you and I can never talk about. Do you understand?"

Sabah wasn't sure if he did or not but nodded and said nothing.

"I know you Sabah. Believe it or not, I may know you better than you know yourself." She paused and looked again, straight into Sabah's eyes.

"Do you see my handbag? Could you hand it to me please?"

Sabah handed her a small Louis Vuitton purse. She opened it and pulled out a business card. She handed it to Sabah.

"Tomorrow is Thursday. I know you get off at 4 on Thursdays. Tomorrow, when you leave work, go directly to the passport office. Do not get in the line. Go to the reception desk inside and hand the person this card. Tell them you have an appointment at 4:30. The man who's name is on this card will be expecting you. We will say nothing more about this. Not to anyone. Do you understand Sabah?"

Sabah had never seen this side of Mrs. Al-Ghamdi. Her intensity and deadly serious expression chilled him. He felt weak and unable to move. She squeezed his arm and smiled then nodded officially closing the subject. She looked at the mirror, tilting her head in various angles.

"As always, beautiful work Sabah," she said simply completely back to herself again. In another moment, she said good-bye and walked away.

Sabah didn't fully understand but he did know this much, there was the world he lived in and right next to it there was another world. Often Sabah saw the people in that world, but he could never see the world itself. It was a place where people knew things he didn't know, did things he couldn't do, and lived in a way he could never live.

Like many of the customers in the salon, Mrs. Al-Ghamdi was a member of that world. Beyond that, he didn't know much else. He had never viewed Mrs. Al-Ghamdi, or anyone else in his life, in terms of what he could gain from them. In, fact it had never even occurred to Sabah to do so. It was this simple, uncomplicated truth that, so often, brought to Sabah what he had never sought.

Somehow, this great, gracious lady, his friend from the salon, knew someone else and this was how life was in Baghdad. In a perfect world, work and dedication might be rewarded. But the only way to be blessed by fortune's smile, at this time, in this place, was to know someone.

The next day, at exactly 4:15, Sabah walked into the lobby of the passport building, up two flights of stairs, and through several long corridors, leaving the din of the lines and crowd farther behind with each step. Finally, he reached a door with a number that matched the one on the business card given to him by Mrs. Al-Ghamdi

Within minutes, he was seated in front of a desk. A young woman appeared and placed a tray with hot tea on the table in front of him. She poured the tea into a small glass and handed it to him, smiling. Sabah smiled back. The room was quiet and eerily calm, as though he had somehow passed into the very eye of the storm. Within thirty minutes, photos had been taken, forms had been filed, and Sabah left the building, passport clutched tightly in hand.

Elated, enveloped in a surreality rendering him nearly numb and senseless, Sabah walked past the endless line, all of them, desperately hoping for what he now belonged to him. As he walked images of faces flashed through his mind. He saw them so clearly, as though they were right beside him. Mr. Naifeh, his high school vice principal, holding Ali's head against the chalkboard. Mr. Moghadam, the first day he'd met him in the little café where he and his father had worked. Then he saw the eyes of Mrs. Al-Ghamdi, holding his arm in the salon, just the day before.

Why had they done these things for him? He'd done nothing for them. He hadn't given them anything, sacrificed anything for them. They weren't his family. They owed him nothing. And yet here he was, one simple step away from being able to leave his country, if and when he decided to.

Walking by these thousands and thousands of people waiting to get into the passport office, Sabah was gripped by a gratitude so deep, so pure and overwhelming he thought he might burst at any moment. As all consuming as it was, he wasn't sure where that gratitude should be directed. Who or what had brought this about? Was it God? He knew it wasn't luck. It was bigger than that, deeper and far more mysterious. Somehow he knew he was in the realm of the sacred, though it was a realm without face, name, or form. *Why?* he kept asking himself. *Why me?*

One after another, after another, Sabah looked into the faces of people waiting in that line. With each face the question became a silent chant, matching the pace of his footsteps, even as he began to weep.

CHAPTER FOURTEEN

★ ★ ★

The Deputies For Moral Enforcement

★ ★ ★

As the holder of a passport, Sabah felt like he was in a poker game and had been dealt a third ace. He held an almost guaranteed winning hand, but he wasn't ready to play it just yet. Despite all he had seen, all the ugliness and fear, the growing shadow of repression creeping into every aspect of daily life, Sabah was not yet fully ready to leave his country.

He considered what was holding him back. Was it his family? It would be the first and most obvious answer, but he knew immediately this wasn't the case. He loved his family and was close to them, but he knew that he was ready to leave them. Was it his friends or the salon? In fact, it wasn't one thing at all but a fabric of people and circumstances which, when woven together, not only created a life filled with a sense of meaning and purpose, it was the only life Sabah had ever known. Even if Abu Tobar continued his killing spree, if Gabir was in prison, if Milad was in the hospital, all that horror and darkness had not yet entirely extinguished the simple joys of his life.

He had been at the salon nearly seven years now and was in his second year of college. His circle of friends had continued to grow. There wasn't a day in his life that someone wasn't calling him, asking him out, or driving by the salon unannounced to pick him up and deliver him to this social gathering, party or event.

Still, there were constant reminders that the larger world was changing, like the day he'd gotten off the bus near campus and was walking to class.

It was early morning and the sidewalk was crowded. Sabah saw a man riding a bicycle on the sidewalk, coming toward him. Before he could move, the man brushed against him, lost his balance, and nearly fell over. He caught himself just in time and glared at Sabah.

"Why don't you watch where you're going,?" the man said.

He was about Sabah's age, perhaps a year or two older. He was wearing a uniform of some type. There were so many new uniforms on the streets these days that Sabah couldn't keep up with them. Half the time he didn't know if they were local or federal police, military, or some new branch of law enforcement he wasn't even aware of. Whoever or whatever they were, a uniform signaled trouble, because they all led to the same place.

"I'm sorry, I didn't see you," Sabah said, and for some reason, perhaps related to impatience, pride, the people of influence in his own world, or simply having a passport, he added, "I think the sidewalk is for pedestrians, isn't it?"

"You telling me the law?" the man said.

"I'm not telling you. It *is* the law."

"What's your name?"

"Sabah. Sabah Toma. What's yours?"

The uniformed man studied Sabah for a moment. "You're kind of a smart mouth, aren't you?"

"Not at all. I'm just a student, going to school."

"I don't think so. I think you're going somewhere else. I think you're going over there."

The young man shifted his head slightly to the right and Sabah's eyes followed the movement, to a police station directly across the street.

"Really? What have I done?"

"What have you done? I don't like you. That's what you've done. I think we need to ask you some questions. So, let's go."

"Okay. No problem." But Sabah didn't move. He stood perfectly still and looked the man in the eye. "But I think you should know that if you bring me in there, you may not like what you find out. In fact, it may be a big problem for you."

The young man in uniform was standing as still as Sabah. For several long moments, the two men stared at each other, not blinking, playing a very serious kind of poker game as people swarmed by and around them on the busy sidewalk. Part of Sabah was confident, based on his vast network of friends and acquaintences. He felt a small degree of protection from the Baathists, at least the lower ranking members like this person seemed to be.

Another part of him didn't have any idea who this person was or how dangerous he might be. But that part was worn down, so exhausted by this man and countless others like him that he no longer cared what they could to him. Either way, at that moment, there wasn't a trace of fear in Sabah's face.

The silent stand-off stretched on for another few moments, then the man gave him a disgusted look and shook his head.

"Get out of my sight, " he said..

"Have a good day," Sabah said, and walked away.

This was what the larger world had come to. This was the world of Iraq outside one's own home and immediate circle of trusted friends. The moment any Iraqi citizen crossed the border of his or her own home or neighborhood, they entered a world of masks. It was a world where someone who looked and acted just like you might have the power to kill you and not be punished for it.

It was a world where poker games, exactly like the one Sabah had just played, took place every day. Sabah knew this. Despite the deep, strong ties within his own world, the growing sense of claustrophobia was becoming more suffocating than ever. Even as he was adding friends, a fence was going up around all of them, compelling Sabah to stay within that fence at all times. Going outside that secured area was becoming too dangerous.

His friends had become ever closer and Khalid was one of the closest. Of course, there were his salon friends who, over the years, had transitioned from mentors to peers. Khalid, on the other hand, was Sabah's age. They'd moved through life together for the past eight years, and not just any eight years. These were the pliant, unformed years of puberty and adolescence when so many experiences are first time experiences and emotions are never more varied or vivid. They had passed through the refining fires of youth together and forged a friendship that was closer, in some ways, than Sabah's relationships with his own brothers. As they both sensed this strange constriction of the world, the dark mist of distrust constantly hovering everywhere and nowhere, their reliance on each other grew ever stronger.

They went to visit Milad at his home the morning he returned from the hospital. He'd already undergone one operation but would need at least one more if his mouth was going to be restored to its original condition. They made every effort to keep the tone of the visit light and cheerful. They even got Milad to laugh a couple of times, though it hurt him because the laughter pulled at his stitches. They didn't stay long but promised they'd be back soon and left their friend alone to rest.

Though Khalid and Sabah put on happy faces for Milad, they left the hospital angrier than they'd ever been. Sabah was seldom filled with hate. He was often deeply confused and curious when bad things were done to other people or even to himself. But now there was no other way to describe what he was feeling. He hated Ahmid for what he had done. It was so wrong, for so many reasons. To do that to anyone was wrong, but to do it to Milad, a person who showed such kindness and generosity to everyone he met? That crime was unforgivable.

Khalid and Sabah got home just before noon and sat down on the front steps of Sabah's family's house. The steps faced a side street which would have been fairly busy on a weekday, but it was a Saturday. The street was quiet except for a few younger kids playing and yelling just down the block. There was a soccer game in about an hour at the park, but Sabah wasn't in the mood.

The visit with Milad had left Sabah visibly upset and Khalid was conflicted on how best to deal with it. After all, Sabah never said no to a soccer game.

"It might be a good idea," Khalid said after awhile.

"You go," Sabah said. When Khalid just stared at him, he gave an uncaring shrug. "Go on! What else are you gonna do?"

"I don't know. Nothin'."

For several seconds they were silent. Sabah and Khalid both stared straight ahead, into the quiet street.

"Whatever," Sabah said. "Why not? If I don't play I'm gonna mope. Right?"

"That's what I say!" Khalid agreed.

Just at that moment, a group of four girls they'd never seen before came into view. They were walking toward Khalid and Sabah, on the same side of the street. They were school girls, maybe a few years younger. The girls definitely weren't from the neighborhood. Neither Sabah or Khalid recognized them, but they were a very nice looking group, carefully dressed and made up. Any one of them would have been a head turner. All four of them together created quite a sight. Even so, Khalid and Sabah said nothing as the group passed by.

As they passed, the group of girls seemed to knot closer together, twittering and murmuring to themselves. Two of them sent shy smiles and furtive glances toward Sabah and his friend.

Sabah and Khalid continued to watch them whisper and giggle as they moved farther down the sidewalk. A few moments passed before they noticed the two uniformed young men standing at the bottom of the steps, just below them. Sabah had never seen them before, but with a single glance, he knew all he needed to. With these two there would be no salutation, no polite chit-chat, and certainly no introductions.

Neither Khalid nor Sabah had ever seen these particular uniforms and neither recognized the patch, either an emblem or logo, sewn onto the long sleeves of their brown shirts. The men were older, both perhaps in their early- to mid-thirties. The variety of law enforcement positions, as much as the power-hungry simpletons who filled them, was becoming almost farcical to Sabah. These two men would have amused him had he seen them in passing. Now, as they confronted him, he knew that whatever their purpose was, it wasn't going to be a laughing matter.

"What are you doing?" one of them asked.

Sabah and Khalid exchanged glances, first because they didn't know whom the man was addressing. More importantly, the question didn't make sense. It was obvious what they were doing. They were sitting on the front steps of their home.

"You were looking at those girls weren't you?" the man went on with what seemed to Sabah a stern, "caught you red-handed" expression. The look on this grown man's face somehow reminded Sabah of a mother finding her little boy's hand in the cookie jar.

Sabah and Khalid looked at each other again, becoming more perplexed with each question.

"We saw you looking at them!" the man persisted.

"Yes!" Sabah finally blurted out, forgetting to filter his irritation. That was the first thing you had to do when speaking with any man in uniform: never appear insolent.

The man speaking took a step closer. As he did so, Sabah and Khalid noticed the unmarked Volga, a Russian-made governmental car. It was double-parked and idling in the street right behind the men. A third man in the passenger seat was sitting casually with one foot in the car and one on the ground. A siren light on the car roof was spinning quickly, alternating in blue and red.

"Yes," Sabah said again, quickly assuming the standard servile tone most citizens had been trained to display in these situations. "We were looking at the girls."

"You were harrassing them, weren't you?"

"No!" Khalid said, softly but firmly. "We weren't harrasing them. We didn't say a word to them."

"Don't lie, punk!" the second officer barked. "We heard what you said!"

"Officers," Sabah intervened as delicately and rationally as he could. "I'm sorry, I don't even know if that's what I should call you. I apologize. Sir, *we* apologize ..."

"We're Section Deputies for the Department of Moral Enforcement."

Sabah had never heard of this and had had no idea such an organization existed. For a moment, but not much longer, his natural curiosity was at odds with his subservient role. He genuinely wanted to know what that meant but he didn't dare ask for more information.

"Both of us witnessed it," the officer said. "We heard you. We saw you. The way you leered at those girls. The way you dishonored them."

"Dishonored?" Sabah echoed. "Sir, please. This is our home ..."

He was relying on a method he often used in volatile and difficult circumstances, when communication had unraveled and he was facing an impasse. He would back away from the immediate issue and try to approach it step-by-step, until it could be completely and mutually grasped by everyone involved.

"All we're doing here is just sitting. That's it. We're just sitting in front of our house, like we've done our whole lives. We're not bothering anybody. We don't want to bother any—"

"You know what?" the first man said. "You've got a big mouth. Anybody ever tell you that?"

Sabah stopped talking instantly, gripped by the familiar paralysis and powerlessness he'd felt so many times before, in so many similar situations.

Actually, yes, they have, he thought to himself. Of course, he said nothing.

"I think we're going to need question you," the man said.

Sabah didn't know what that meant and his last hope vanished when the man spoke again.

"Get in the car. Both of you."

For a long moment, Sabah and Khalid remained seated, both wondering if this could be some kind of prank or cruel joke. Then one of the officers pulled something out of his leather holster. It was a billy club, perhaps made of wood, though it was hard to tell because of its leather handle and heavy black laquer paint.

"I said move! Now!"

Rashid and Sabah stood up and walked down the front steps of the home Sabah had lived in for more than eight years. Both of them knew they might never be back.

CHAPTER FIFTEEN

★ ★ ★

The Breaking Point

★ ★ ★

Two of the officers sat in the front seats of the small two-door sedan. Sabah sat in the middle of the back seat, Rashid on his left and the third officer on his right. The sedan was small enough for their shoulders to touch, and had Sabah not been holding his knees tightly together, their knees would have been touching also.

As the car rattled through the badly paved and bumpy city streets, Sabah turned and glanced at Khalid. Their eyes met and Sabah realized he was seeing a mirror image of himself. Khalid was bordering on shock. This wasn't happening. They weren't really in this car. They weren't really going wherever they were going. And where were they going? Sabah had no idea. He glanced out the car window and couldn't guess, based on the street they were on or the direction they were traveling, what their ultimate destination might be.

"Sir," Sabah began, not turning his head and speaking as meekly as he could. "Perhaps, since my friend doesn't live where I live, perhaps … he could go to his own home."

None of the three officers reacted in any way. It wasn't possible that they hadn't heard him. Knowing he was being deliberately ignored, Sabah desperately struggled to control the fear and rage crippling his capacity for reason. There had to be some way to get through to them, to at least save Khalid.

"Sir, he didn't do anything. It was me. It was only me. It wasn't—"

With the speed, fury, and efficiency of a snake strike, the man seated next to him slammed his elbow into Sabah's face, just above his chin and below his bottom lip. The force of the impact was so great that Sabah's head crashed into the back window of the sedan.

For a few seconds there was nothing but haze. Then his surroundings slowly materialized again. He could taste something warm and tinny. When he looked down, he saw that his shirt and pants changed color.

"That's what happens to people with big mouths. Now keep it shut until we tell you to open it."

An hour later, Khalid and Sabah sat together in a small interrogation room. Though terrified and in pain, Sabah was coherent enough to notice that the building they'd entered wasn't a typical police station. At one time it could have been anything, a home, a store, or a market. But like so many buildings in Baghdad now, it had been confiscated and modified to meet the needs of the current regime.

Some windows had bars over them. Others had been hastily covered in brick or cinderblock. A metal gate surrounded the front door. The building possessed the standard accoutrements that, by now, every Iraqi citizen was familiar with. This was a governmental building, and those who entered it didn't always come out again.

Harsh, uncovered fluorescent light filled the small room, accentuating the perforated pattern of black dots on the asbestos ceiling tiles. The yellowing tiles were, themselves, covered by water marks. The gloss grey, oil-based paint on the walls of the room was chipped and fading. The linoleum floor was filthy and warping.

Sabah and Rashid sat silently in metal folding chairs, facing a small, unvarnished wooden desk. Sabah doubted the room could be less inviting or hospitable, even if someone had tried. But then, perhaps they had. This was their particular genius, after all, the ability to make everyone ill at ease, at all times and in every way.

Suddenly, a door opened. Khalid and Sabah jerked their heads around to see the man who had hit Sabah in the car and another man, someone they hadn't seen before. The new man was in his late forties or early fifties, overweight and with a full beard. He sat down at the desk opposite Khalid and Sabah and placed a single manilla folder on the table. For a moment, he regarded the two young men in silence, letting the tense atmosphere build, and then he slowly opened the folder.

The fat man wheezed slightly as he spoke. He dwarfed the folding chair he was sitting in, seeming to swallow it with his girth. Sabah thought the chair might actually collapse under the man's weight.

He asked questions to both Khalid and Sabah, questions related to their residences, schools, hobbies, friends, and families. One question led to another and another. Each one was more senseless and irrelevant than the one before.

The man seemed to take great pride in the logical progression of his interrogation. He portrayed, with every word and gesture, a competence and precision that would not be confounded, even by the best efforts of riffraff like these two. The man's officiousness, as much as his body odor, was making Sabah sick to his stomach. He'd been asking questions for well over an hour. At every moment, he was letting Khalid and Sabah know he would be getting to the bottom of this incident. This was the most disturbing aspect of the experience because, of course, there was no bottom to get to.

"You're a hairdresser. What kind of work is that for a man? What are you, some kind of pervert?"

The second officer who had brought Sabah into the station was still in the room, standing guard at the door. He chuckled at this, and he and the fat man shared a grin.

Sabah interpreted the question as rhetorical and remained silent. It was best not to speak unless he was absolutely sure he was required to.

"What's that all over you?" the fat man said suddenly. "What happened to your lip?"

They were the most obvious questions he could have asked and it had taken him almost seventy-five minutes to ask them. Sabah's lower lip was a grotesquely inflated, purplish balloon. It made it difficult for him to speak clearly.

"That man hit me," Sabah said, risking a glance at the man by the door.

"Did he?" He turned his gaze to the officer at the door. "Did you hit him?"

The younger man contrived to look both shocked and indignant. "Of course not, Captain. He's lying."

"Then how did it happen?"

"He fell as he was getting into the car. He hit his lip on the curb."

Sabah summoned the final shreds of his patience and self-control. He remained silent. The fat man looked at Khalid.

"You were there?" he asked.

"Yes sir," Khalid answered.

"Well?"

Sabah's gaze went immediately to his friend, but Khalid wasn't looking at him. He was staring down at his hands, a tense, conflicted look on his face.

If he agreed with Sabah, they could both be accused of lying. If he agreed with the officer, he would be condemning Sabah. It was a horrible moment, the kind that would test the full measure of any man's courage and loyalty.

Neither Sabah nor Khalid knew what the outcome of this long afternoon would be. They both knew this much; it was possible that both of them could be killed for nothing more than being in the wrong place at the wrong time. Even if that place was Sabah's own home.

To be loyal or to live, to be truthful or to live, to be brave or to live. In a hundred cities throughout their entire country, at that very moment, thousands of men and women faced the same choice Khalid was facing. It was their way of life now and everyone knew it, though this did nothing to alleviate the excruciating agony when it happened to *you*.

Sabah and Khalid were best friends. There was nothing Khalid didn't know about Sabah, and the same was true of Sabah for Khalid. As their country and world had become, over the years, a more and more dangerous place, they had grown closer to each other. They had started to see themselves like two gunfighters in those American western movies they loved so much, desperately outnumbered and standing back-to-back, courageously fighting off the bad guys.

Finally Khalid glanced at his closest and dearest friend. The interrogating officer had gotten up from his chair and lumbered over to the two young men. He stood looming over them, waiting for Khalid to speak, the full weight of his authority and power falling over them like a dark, threatening shadow. This was a man who could make a person disappear, and none could challenge him.

Khalid's head dropped, and his words were hardly more than a whisper. "He fell."

Sabah's eyes had been on Khalid, and now that the answer had come, he didn't turn away. He waited for his friend to look over at him, to at least spare him a glance that said, *I'm sorry, I had no other choice, please forgive me*, but the glance never came. Sabah was still waiting for it when a massive palm exploded against his cheek, nearly knocking him to the ground. The fat officer stood over him.

"This is a very serious accusation," the man growled, "and a very serious lie."

As Sabah stared up at him, there was no accusation in his gaze, just utter disbelief and a pain that only comes from the very center of a person's heart.

The fat man returned to his desk, lowered himself into his chair, and closed the manilla folder.

"Get him out of here," he said, sounding bored. "Oh, and show him what we do to liars."

The younger officer nodded and opened the door. Immediately outside were two other officers. Only when they were outside the interrogation room did Khalid glance at Sabah with what seemed an infinite amount of guilt, sorrow, and regret. Sabah wanted to smile at him and forgive him, but as the officers led him away from Khalid, all he could do was stare at his friend, his face a mask of pain with eyes made bottomless by the single word, "why".

★ ★ ★

A half hour later, in a holding area in a small, windowless room somewhere toward the center of the building, Khalid heard the screams. For a moment he prayed, *Let it be someone else, please let it be someone else.* But then he heard the cries, "Stop ... please ... stop!" and he lost all hope. He recognized the voice. It was Sabah.

Moments later, Khalid heard a door open and voices echoing in a corridor. There was the sound of footsteps and shuffling, then his own cell door opened. Sabah had been half-carried, half-dragged to where he now stood, propped against the door frame. He was bruised, and out of breath. Before he could regain his balance, he was pushed forward and he fell to his knees, putting his hands out just in time to stop his face from smashing straight into the floor. The cell door slammed behind him.

Khalid rushed over and knelt beside his friend, trying to help him up, but Sabah shoved him away. For several moments, Sabah stayed where he was, on all fours, his head down and his gaze on the floor, his breath coming harshly. Khalid sat down and didn't move.

Both men, buried in their own private worlds of pain, said nothing. There was nothing to say. Finally, after more than a minute, Sabah regained the strength to sit up. He leaned back against a wall of the cell, his head hanging down.

When the silence was broken, it was Sabah who broke it. He looked up and straight at Khalid, his face was not the same as when he came in.

It was a sight Rashid would remember to his dying day.

Sabah's voice was dry and cracked, harsh with finality: "It's over."

Khalid stared at him, and it was a long moment before the meaning of these words finally sank in. When they did, he opened his mouth to protest, to argue, to explain—but he knew there was nothing he could say. Guilt curdled in his stomach, vile and bitter, and all he could do was close his eyes and think, *I'm sorry. Sabah, I'm so sorry.*

★ ★ ★

It was entirely possible that the two could have remained in the building for weeks or months, or been permanently disposed of at the whim of one person or another. But mercy came in the form of the night shift captain, a man named Kazom. Looking over the daily report log, he noticed two new additions in cell number C4. He made it a practice to introduce himself to each new arrival, not to establish his authority, but strictly out of humanitarian interests. Sometimes a new prisoner required obvious medical attention, which was usually both caused and disregarded by the day shift. Some new arrivals were so young, and the environment so terrifying, that they would sob and cry all night, keeping other detainees awake. Captain Kazom did what he could to help with the pain. He was oddly suited to his work, a man of compassion in a heartless place.

On his nightly rounds, he passed by C4 and looked in through the door's small window. He saw two young men, awake and talking. He opened the door.

One of the young men had his back to the door; as Kazom stepped inside, the young man turned—and Kazom saw his shirt changed color. His face was bruised.

Without a word, Kazom left the cell, locking the door behind him.

Sabah and Khalid stared after him, not sure what to make of this brief, wordless encounter. Within moments, however, the door opened again and the captain was back, this time holding a towel. He handed the towel to Sabah. It was white, clean, damp, and warm. Sabah looked at the man, not sure what he was supposed to do.

"For your face," the man said gently. "Go ahead, son."

Sabah hesitated, then gingerly brought the towel to his swollen face. "Thank you," he said quietly.

"I'm Captain Kazom," the man said. "What happened?"

Both Sabah and Khalid froze. They couldn't go through this again. They couldn't answer one more question and risk suffering the consequences of that answer. On the other hand, they couldn't remain silent. It was late at night now, past midnight. They were both exhausted. For the moment they said nothing, desperately trying to decide on the best course of action. Kazom recognized their hesitation. He'd seen it a hundred times before.

"It's okay, really," he said, his voice soft and tentative, as if speaking to a frightened animal. "I'm not here to hurt you."

Khalid didn't trust him. Strangely, though he'd been the torture recipient, Sabah did.

Sabah explained the events of the day, including Khalid's failure to stand up for him at that critical moment.

"I was afraid!" Khalid said, exasperated, tired of saying the words and hearing himself say them.

Kazom had been listening and nodding. He put a hand on Khalid's shoulder.

"He knows that. He understands. You understand don't you?" he asked Sabah.

The answer was yes, though Sabah was so hurt and angry that it was almost impossible for him to admit it. Khalid stared at Sabah, searching for some acknowledgement to the question. Sabah glanced at Khalid and instantly recognized the immeasureable pleading in his eyes.

Sabah eyes found Khalids and then, Sabah slowly nodded.

Only at this moment did Khalid begin to cry.

112

"I'm sorry, I'm sorry, I'm sorry …" Perhaps he wanted to say more, but right now he wasn't capable of it, his sobs choking his words.

Kazom had seen it all before, friends turned against friends, brothers against brothers. It was all part of the plan to create and preserve only one loyalty while destroying all others. Kazom was a sensible man with a sense of purpose in everything he said and did. He had only so much time with these two. So many others would need to be seen on his nightly rounds.

"What do you boys do? You work, go to school?"

"I'm a student," Rashid said. "I do both," said Sabah. Short answers were becoming a reflex for them both. Despite this man's apparently good intentions, Sabah knew that short answers were safe answers.

"Where do you work?" the man asked Sabah.

"I work at a beauty salon, as a hairdresser."

"Really? Which one?"

"Tokalon Salon."

"No kidding?" Kazom smiled. "My sister goes to that salon."

"Really?" Sabah said, and found himself genuinely interested despite the circumstances. "What's her name?"

"Mahra. Mahra Kazom. Dyes her hair red all the time."

Sabah's face lit up. "Yes, I do know her!" In fact he'd seen her go upstairs with Mazhar more than a few times at the salon for some "extracurricular" services. "Very nice lady," he said. "Very nice."

"Thank you! She loves your salon. Raves about it!"

"Thank you," Sabah said, smiling for the first time in nearly twelve hours. It felt more like a lifetime.

Kazom was smiling too, but after a moment, his smile faded. He looked at the two young men and slowly began to shake his head. The conversation had been moving in a promising direction. The mood had been brightening, but now it had quickly shifted again. Khalid and Sabah instinctively recoiled and braced themselves. It was a conditioned reflex, triggered by gestures, movements, or intonations typically indiscernable in a terror-free world.

"Why?" Kazom asked, posing the question to no one in particular. Was he speaking to himself, Rashid and Sabah, or some higher authority beyond all the power of this world?

Kazom looked at the boys. He'd made his decision and he stood up.

"Get up," he said. "You're getting out of here."

Sometime after midnight, Khalid and Sabah were walking, free again, through the quiet streets of Baghdad. They said little on the way home. For Sabah, there was no anger, resentment, or hard feelings. For Rashid, there was no remorse or paralyzing guilt. They were both floating in the brisk night air, high on adrenaline, joy, and relief. They were alive and they were going home. But for Sabah there was something else. There was an absolute stillness and calm, the aftermath of a final resolve.

Being connected to that rare tranquility was a second kind of joy for Sabah. For the first time in his life, he realized he would find light in the darkest places. Even in the most evil people on earth, there could be goodness. This realization resonated in his heart. Sabah glanced at his friend as they walked in the stillness of the moonlit night. Sabah lifted his left arm and put it over the shoulder of his friend even as the words even as the words came to him once again, "It's over."

CHAPTER SIXTEEN

★ ★ ★

Departure

★ ★ ★

For most refugees in 1975, the path out of Iraq, and ultimately to America, was a long, twisted, and disjointed journey. Very few people could get a visa stamped for direct transit to the United States. Getting a visa stamped at all, to go to any country for any reason, was never guaranteed. As was the case with most tyrants, the Baathists' policies and procedures were defined by a generous amount of insecurity and paranoia.

Like all dictatorial regimes, Baathist's fanatically controlled and manipulated their public image. Opinion among Iraqi citizens was of no consequence. The party's image outside of Iraq, on the other hand, was monitored with manic obsessiveness. Saddam Hussein held a plethora of psychological neuroses, but foremost among these was the desperate need to be recognized as a great leader on the global stage. For Saddam Hussein, the person who could do the most damage to whatever sick, demented self-image he'd constructed was the person leaving Iraq.

Obtaining a passport and visa under this regime was hard enough. This process, and the long journey to America, was a little like a single salmon swimming upstream, giving its all to find a way home. It was a perilous journey against all odds, requiring the full focus of one's life force. But for those who made it, unlike the unfortunate salmon who could only live long enough to mate and die, there was the promise of a second life. To arrive anywhere outside Iraq would be a dream come true, but America, this was the realm of the gods. It was also the last country any Iraqi citizen would be allowed to travel.

There were many paths to get to America, but one of the more common was the trip to Greece. From Greece, it would be possible to get to Mexico, and from Mexico, it was possible to get to America. There would be unknown obstacles at every step in the journey and ultimate success was never assured. Who could know, when one's full strength had been summoned to launch out of the stream and over the next waterfall, if a bear would be waiting to instantly and permanently end the journey? Still, like the salmon, these were thoughts that never entered the refugees' minds. They were all driven, Sabah included, by a single message, a message far beyond word or even thought. Like their own heartbeats, simultaneously unnoticed and life giving, it was a silent inner prayer pleading without end, *freedom … freedom … freedom.*

"Why are you going to Greece?"

Sabah had been in line half the day and had finally arrived at a window that looked something like a bank teller's station. A thick plexiglass plate separated Sabah from a dour looking man seated on a high stool.

"I'm going to visit my cousin," Sabah said. "He's at school there."

He knew that the harder he tried to keep his tone casual and conversational, the more he would fail. Here was another moment, like so many before, when his destiny, his very life, was being held in a balance, this time by someone displaying that special indifference so unique to bureaucrats. The expression on the man's face was marked with a blend of complacency with traces of disdain. More than anything else, the man seemed bored. They were separated only by that worn sheet of plexiglas, but emotionally, they could have been in different universes.

With his left hand, the man was holding the passport open, unfolded and pressed against the top of his desk. As Sabah watched, the man opened the lid of a small tin box. There were several boxes by him, and they were all ink pads. One was green, another black, and another red. The man opened the box with the green pad. He lifted a large, heavy rubber stamp, hit the green ink pad, and stamped the passport.

"Have a good trip. Next!"

Sabah knew he should leave. He should simply thank the man and go away to let him continue his job. But for just a moment he couldn't move. After a second, the man realized Sabah was still standing there and looked up at him.

"Yes?"

"Thank you," Sabah said.

Sabah thought he saw a flash of recognition, as though something in this man, only at this moment, knew and understood what this thank you had meant. Then, with the force of a sudden, unexpected slap, Sabah knew he'd revealed too much. He turned and quickly walked away.

As he left the building, he wondered if perhaps the man received this kind of effusive gratitude every day. Perhaps he recognized it for what it was and made no sign of it. Perhaps he saw nothing and didn't want to see anything. Either way, Sabah would soon be doing something else he'd never done before: he'd be purchasing a ticket for a flight to Athens. Before anything else, though, he had to see Mr. Moghadam.

Sabah was scheduled to work the next day at the salon. It would be a bittersweet goodbye, in some ways even more poignant than saying goodbye to his own family. Whoever he was today, whatever Sabah Toma had become during his twenty-two years in this world, it was far more a result of this single place than anything else in his life. How does one say goodbye to a such a place? Sabah was, by nature, a person of propriety and tradition in a land defined by both. Showing the proper respect and gratitude to Mr. Moghadam, as well as to his dear friends Baligh, Milad, Rashid, and Mazhar, was of the highest importance to Sabah.

But how? How could he repay them? It wouldn't be possible, but he hoped that they would at least know that he loved them.

Walking the final block toward the Tokalon, Sabah saw a flower peddler on the street. From the moment his passport had been stamped, his world and everything in it had never looked more beautiful. He'd passed this peddler thousands of times and had never purchased a single flower. Today, he bought bouquet, but only after sorting and smelling each one he picked. It was expensive, an extravagance he couldn't afford, but it was the very least he could offer the men who had given him his life.

As he approached the salon, he saw something that didn't immediately register. A large truck was parked in front of the Tokalon. A temporary ramp had been put in place over the front steps. Large, strong-looking men were wheeling furniture out through the front door and putting it on the truck.

Sabah walked past them and into the salon, which was now almost empty. Mr. Moghadam stood at the far side of the room. He was standing beside one of the moving men, holding a clipboard, writing something.

The moving man walked away, toward the front door and Sabah. At that moment Mr. Moghadam noticed Sabah for the first time. Sabah didn't move as Mr. Moghadam approached him.

"Hello, Sabah," he said softly. "Let's go outside,"

The officers had arrived, unnanounced, one hour earlier, right at opening time. The official explanation was that the current administration did not feel it was appropriate for men to be cutting women's hair. No options had been presented. No opportunity to adjust and comply with the new policy had been given. With swift, unexpected, and shocking brutality, the Tokalon Salon had been forever closed.

Fifteen minutes later, Sabah and Mr. Moghadam sat in a small cafe just across the street from the salon, sipping tea and watching the final remnants of their world being wheeled away. Sabah was surprised, and slightly relieved, by Mr. Moghadam's unexpectedly upbeat mood.

"I thought it might happen. And I've still got the girls. We can open another shop. We'll get by. It won't be the same, but we'll get by."

Mr. Moghadam watched the movers for another few seconds, then turned and fixed a steady gaze on Sabah.

"It's not too late for you. You can still get out."

Sabah thought back to that day, so long ago, when he'd been working at his father's little cafe, no bigger than the one they were now sitting at. To Sabah, this man had become nearly as much a father as his own father. As well as he knew Mr. Moghadam, Sabah couldn't decide if his words and demeanor, sitting at this table right now, were a charade, some stoic facade to save Sabah from worry. It would have been consistent with the man Sabah knew Mr. Moghadam to be. Rather than press him for the truth, Sabah reached into his jacket pocket, pulled something out, and placed it on the small, round table between them.

Mr. Moghadam looked at it for a long moment, then picked up the passport and opened it. He studied it carefully for several seconds.

"Greece?" he asked.

"Yes. Then America."

Mr. Moghadam smiled. In this single smile, like a refracted rainbow through a prism, there was understanding, fulfillment, joy, and love. It was a smile only Mr. Moghadam could have given and only for Sabah. Sabah knew he'd made Mr. Moghadam happy. It was the only gift Sabah could have given him and the one present he'd most dearly wanted to give.

They sat together, completely comfortable and shared a long and perfect silence. Mr. Moghadam had expected nothing less from Sabah and, though he wasn't surprised by the news, nothing could have diminished his delight. Finally, Mr. Moghadam spoke.

"Good for you, Sabah. Good for you."

The two men got to their feet and Mr. Moghadam did something he had never done before. He took Sabah in his arms and held him. His words came to Sabah like a patriarch's blessing.

"Go to America. This country is not for you. Go and never come back."

Mr. Moghadam pulled away and held Sabah by the shoulders now. "You just remember, when you get to be a big shot over there, don't forget your friends."

"I won't." Sabah smiled.

The two men said goodbye doubting they would ever see each other again. In fact, Sabah would not see anyone from the salon, including his closest friends. All of them were smart enough to stay one step ahead of the law. Even at that moment, they were making their own plans for survival.

The day of Sabah's departure was like any other day, except that every mundane and routine ritual was marked by the fact that it would be the last one. Taking a shower, opening the small refrigerator, peeling an orange, making tea; the more ordinary the activity the more peculiar it seemed. Finally, the time had come. A taxi arrived at the Toma home. Sabah was not partial to overly dramatic public displays of emotion and his family was no exception. In fact, quite the opposite; they were the last people he would want to be crying with in a public place, surrounded by strangers.

Though his mother and father didn't know it, Sabah would be seeing them again. They hoped it would be true. They prayed it would be true. But only Sabah knew that it was true. And only his perfect knowledge would make it so. As he held his parents and they cried together, he couldn't have comforted them with his own sense well being, his unshakeable knowledge that they would not only be together again, they would be together in America.

The same prescience that comforted Sabah at his home was with him at the airport. He held his older brother, seeing his future almost as a vision, where he and his brother would be together again.

Sabah had never been on a plane before, yet the incredible adventure of flight was completely overshadowed by the knowledge that, within hours, he would be in a different world. Even so, he wasn't prepared for the awesome physical rush as the four massive jet engines began to whine. The forward thrust hit him somewhere in the center of his body. He felt himself being pressed firmly down and back into his upright seat. He watched the tarmac begin to move by slowly, then quickly becoming a blur, even as the g-forces grew stronger and stronger. He listened to the engines roar and, as the jet separated from the ground, he instinctively clutched his seat's armrests.

As he watched the world fall away Sabah thought to himself, *This must be the feeling the freedom.*

PART II
THE IMMIGRANT

CHAPTER SEVENTEEN

★ ★ ★

Waking Up In a Dream

★ ★ ★

For almost ten years, Sabah had lived in a world where anyone, at any moment, could disappear and never return. He had adapted to these conditions, along with millions of his fellow countrymen. They all knew about Abu Tobar. Everyone knew someone who was missing and would probably never be seen again. It might be a neighbor, the friend of a friend, someone in school, a relative, or even a family member.

For many years, death had been closer, more real, and more imminent. It constantly hovered over every aspect of day-to-day life, not unlike a global epidemic like the plague or Spanish Influenza. From this adversary, there was no safety or defense. Fate alone determined one's life expectancy and each person knew it. In a way, the entire country lived in a kind of schizophrenia.

On the one hand, the horror was relentless. It was as painfully close as it was amorphous and omniscient. It was felt more often than it was seen and it was seen constantly. Most people understood that acknowledging it, or even allowing the shadow to preoccupy one's thoughts for even the shortest time, would lead to intolerable levels of hopelessness and despair. A certain amount of denial was essential if one was to function even at a minimum level. During Sabah's formative youth and early manhood, the mantra of the common man was to go about one's business quietly, while not intruding on anyone else's. During those years, the already minimal dreams and aspirations of the average Iraqi were reduced to ashes. The expectations for one's lot in life were exceeded simply by leaving one's family in the morning, performing a full day of honest work, and then returning home that evening uninjured and alive.

The energy required to avoid thinking about the new regime often exceeded the energy required for work itself. But the capacity for adaptation is so fundamental to what a human being is, it might be seen as both a foundation and cornerstone. Life did go on. Perhaps without the same hope and joy, but like those stubborn weeds and bushes pushing their way up through the cracks of concrete freeways or the many other manufactured monuments of man's presence on the earth, life prevails against all adversaries, even against all odds. The desire to stay alive is simply stronger than our fear of death.

During those years, Sabah had done far more than stay alive. He had, unlike so many of his countrymen, actually thrived. His life had not been defined by placing blinders on and treading the same path, day in and day out, for years and years. If there is a life force in all of us, its intensity must vary and burn at as many different levels as there are people. In Sabah, throughout all the days of his life in Iraq, the flame not only wasn't extinguished, it had actually grown brighter.

He was aware of the shadow and was as terrified by it as anyone else in his country. It had been in the very air he breathed, like a perpetual smog. Even so, his unique circumstances, particularly the constant opportunities for learning and entertainment provided by the salon, had more than offset the oppression crippling most of his countrymen.

Despite all this, and his own massive expectations for what his post-Iraq life would actually be and feel like, Sabah wasn't prepared for what he was now experiencing. He was gazing down from thirty-two thousand feet at a sea of royal blue water. Clouds drifted in and out of view. Miles below, chains of small brown islands dotted the blue backdrop. He was halfway between Turkey and Greece, less than an hour from arrival in Athens. Not until this moment had he known the full extent of the Baathists' influence over his entire being. They were behind him now, in a world literally more than a thousand miles away.

It wasn't real. In less than an hour, he would step off this jet. He would be in a place where Baathists didn't exist and if they did, they were a miniscule minority, without power of any kind. They had terrorized Sabah's country for nearly half of his life. Sabah knew each person was responsible for managing that terror, determining the extent to which it would control their lives. In this regard, he believed he'd done quite well. In fact, he didn't believe he was affected at all. But he had been, profoundly. The full weight of it fell on him only now, as he looked out a jet window at the beautiful world below.

It had been a subliminal fear, operating at a constant low level in the back of his mind. He realized it now, the way we notice something only when it stops, like the hum of a refrigerator suddenly stopping in the still of the night. It simply wasn't there anymore. It wasn't a sound, scent, image, or anything else directly connected to his physical senses. It was something in the realm of the mind and perhaps also of the heart. Something had just turned off and it was gone. Sabah had known excitement, joy and hope. These had never been extinguished. But this was something different. He wasn't sure he'd ever felt it before.

If fact, he wasn't sure he even had a word for it. He wondered for a moment, and tried to remember. Even as a little boy, years before he even knew what a Baathist was, had he experienced it then? He wasn't sure but he didn't think so. He didn't think it was a feeling a little boy was capable of experiencing. Then he realized, with all the surreality of waking up in a dream, what it was. For the first time in his adult life, Sabah knew he was at peace.

He had a similar feeling when the jet's tires hit the runway in Athens. In the overwhelming excitement of leaping into a world of freedom, not to mention the thrill of travel itself, he'd been completely unaware of his instinctive fear of flying. The instant the plane touched down, Sabah sighed and relaxed his grip on his seat. He was safe again. The peace he felt perfectly merged with his fully restored sense of physical safety.

Staring out his window, trying to take in every detail of this new world, the first thing Sabah noticed was the quality of the light itself. It was mid-day and cloudless in Athens. He thought he might be imagining it but the light appeared, somehow, to be brighter, more pure. This world seemed to appear in higher resolution and clarity, the same way, many years later, the HD television would transform standard television.

In the years and decades to come, tens of thousands within the Chaldean sub-culture would find their way out of Iraq. Each person who made the journey paved the way and made the path that much clearer and easier for those who would follow. Similar to the first, ancient European explorers sailing off to discover the New World, the first wave of Chaldean refugees literally traveled into the unknown. And like their European counterparts, they formed tiny colonies or communities where they could band together, relying on each other for security and comfort in a strange new place.

Sabah was not the first to leave but he was among the first. He estimated, based only on rumor and word of mouth, that it would take him about a year to get a visa out of Greece to somewhere in North America, most probably Mexico. Even in Greece, a direct visa to the United States was nearly impossible. In fact, it would take Sabah eight months. During that short time, the Chaldean immigrant population in Athens would grow from three to over a hundred.

Sabah's cousin, Sammy, had been in Athens for almost two years on a student visa, though Sabah was never quite sure where his cousin went to school or what he studied. The most commonly requested and frequently granted visa in Iraq was for students studying outside the country. Though Sabah hadn't been in close contact with his cousin since the days of childhood, they had kept in touch over the years. Most recently, they'd exchanged a series of letters and phone calls detailing Sabah's arrival in Greece.

Whenever Sabah asked Sammy for details on what he was doing in Greece, Sammy would say something like, "Oh you know, the usual thing. Studying, still trying to graduate."

Sammy was the same age as Sabah. He should have been, like Sabah, close to his junior year in college, but he never gave specific information about what level he was at in his studies. Sabah, always the diplomat, never pressed anyone on information they were obviously reticent to provide. This was never more relevant than with a relative like Sammy.

Since Sammy's departure from Iraq two years earlier, Sabah had been following his cousin's new life with great interest. He knew Sammy had left with the long range goal of reaching America. But here his cousin was after nearly two years, standing in the airport terminal in Athens, smiling as Sabah emerged from the boarding gate.

Whatever slight suspicion or consternation Sammy had provoked in all their previous communication instantly disappeared. The young cousins recognized each other immediately. They warmly embraced, kissing each other's cheeks. Sabah was genuinely thrilled and delighted to see Sammy. In minutes they were in a taxi.

"Sammy," Sabah said, staring out the open window of the taxi. "What *is* this place?"

Sammy was slightly heavier and less fashionable than Sabah, but was just as personable. He laughed out loud. "Don't you know? This is Jesusland. This is it! The land of milk and honey."

The city was a blitzkrieg on Sabah's senses. Nearly dizzy from the visual and sensory overload, he desperately tried to process and assimilate every detail flooding past the open taxi window. Then, out of this shifting, fantastic kaleidoscope of new information, one massive component commanded his attention like a hammer slamming into his head.

"Sammy, what is *that*?"

Sammy leaned forward in his seat and looked up. It was a standard-sized billboard on top of a four-story office building. The billboard showed the face of a beautiful woman, her hair seemingly blown back by the wind. Next to her pouting, glossy red lips, well-defined cheek bones, and heavy eye shadow was a bottle of Black Velvet whiskey. Sammy looked back at Sabah and, for a moment, couldn't put it together. What was what? The billboard, the lady in the billboard, the whiskey? Then Sammy laughed, though he wasn't sure who had most provoked his laughter, himself or Sabah.

"I think I've been here too long," he said.

Sabah just stared blankly at him, not knowing what anything meant, least of all his cousin. Sammy just kept laughing. Then, seeing the exasperation on Sabah's face, he blurted out, "It's a billboard!"

"A what?"

"It's an advertisement. Like a magazine advertisement, except bigger."

"Why?" Sabah asked.

"Why what?"

"Why would you want to take a picture of someone's face, make it as big as house, and put it on top a building?"

"Oh, they're not just on top of buildings, look at that one."

Sabah snapped his head around to look and sure enough, there was another one right along the side of the boulevard, held aloft by a massive framework of wood and metal. This one had a photo of a car on it. Then he saw another billboard and another, each one featuring some product or service, usually accompanied by an attractive smiling face, a phone number, or both. These billboards were all over the place.

"That's crazy!" Sabah said.

"No, that's capitalism. Free enterprise system at work, Sabah. You're in Jesusland, but you're also in the Land of Stuff." When Sabah just stared at him, Sammy grinned and gave his cousin a reassuring pat on the shoulder. "You'll get the picture fast enough. But trust me, you're gonna love it."

"I already do, and I don't even know what you're talking about."

The taxi was passing near the center of the city now, close to Sammy's basement apartment, moving more slowly through the narrower streets. Sabah, still reeling from the effects of the billboards, had almost reached his processing limit when he was dealt an even more severe blow. For most of the thirty minute drive from the airport, Sabah had concentrated on larger objects such as buildings and billboards. There were older buildings here, like in Baghdad, but there were also just as many contemporary office buildings sleekly covered in sheets of dark plate glass. Their precise, geometric lines and angles seemed to symbolize a world of predictability and efficiency.

Sharp, Sabah thought. This was a country on the move and he liked it.

Now they were traveling slowly enough for more details to emerge. For Sabah, details generally came in the form of people, and even in these extraordinary circumstances, he was guided by instinctive reflexes. The sidewalks were filled with mid-day shoppers and business people walking around or dining in quaint, cozy outdoor cafes. Sabah found his eyes drawn to as many of them as he could individually evaluate. Everyone was so different! For Sabah, the diversity of people was almost breathtaking.

He was vaguely familiar with some of the nationalities, clothing styles, and skin colors creating this fantastic moving patchwork. At one point in his life, he may have seen one person similar in appearance to a person he was seeing right now. Perhaps years would pass and he might see another person who looked similar to someone else in this Athens crowd. Baghdad had always been insular and homogenized but never more so than after ten years of tyranny. Now, with a single glance out his taxi window, all his memories had been assembled and expanded ten thousand times. He was seeing people from all over the world. In fact, Sabah was convinced he was seeing the world itself.

Even above the beautiful, living mosaic of people, the fascinating buildings, and his first course in capitalism, Sabah could not believe the women. They weren't wearing anything! He had seen mini-skirts in the salon, of course. He knew what the contemporary western fashions for women were only because he had seen them so often at work. But this was something else entirely. Not only were they barely covered, they were so stylish! It was as though this entire city was one big Tokalon Salon. He was tempted to stop the taxi right there and walk the rest of the way to Sammy's no matter how far it was, just to be on the sidewalks or in the cafés where these beautiful women were.

"Careful, Odysseus," Sammy said, noticing the direction of his cousin's attention. "There's lots of sirens in this place. You don't want to end up shipwrecked like me."

Sabah glanced at his cousin. Sammy was smiling but Sabah noticed that the smile didn't reach his eyes.

Something had happened to Sammy. Sabah knew it. Sammy had planned to go to America. His student visa had been, as so many were in Iraq, a sham and a ploy. Was Sammy even in school? He had no idea. One thing was for sure: after two years, Sammy was still in Greece. But why?

He would find out in time but right now, as he got out of the taxi and stepped into a new world and a new life, Sabah couldn't care less.

CHAPTER EIGHTEEN

★ ★ ★

A Rendezvous With Democracy

★ ★ ★

S abah arrived in Athens with the equivalent of five hundred dollars. If he managed the money well, it might last three months. He knew he would need to find work at some point, but that seemed far beyond the horiMon. Sabah seldom felt regret. In fact, the emotion was completely foreign to him.

He'd spent the past eight years of his life making a very good income, with the benefit of constant financial and material support from devoted parents. He'd never worried about saving money, though, and even now, he couldn't bring himself to regret all the many uses he'd found for his paychecks.

"Sabah, you've got a hole in your pocket," his mother had always said to him.

She might say it while cooking, cleaning, or during one of those rare moments when they were alone, sitting quietly together at home. She was never stern with Sabah. He couldn't recall even once receiving anything like a lecture from her. She would toss out her observations casually and offhandedly. She might just as well have said, "I think it's going to rain tomorrow."

Was it her lack of emphasis, her failure as a disciplinarian that had brought Sabah to this point?

No, Sabah thought, *I messed up all by myself.*

He chuckled quietly, then sipped his Turkish coffee.

It was the afternoon of his arrival. Sammy had a few brief errands to run. Sabah had wandered into one of those many sidewalk cafes they'd passed on the way from the airport. Sammy would be joining him in a little while. For now Sabah sat alone, basking in the warm late afternoon sunlight, not having any idea where he was or where he wanted to go first. Thank heavens he would have a tour guide in the form of his cousin.

Mom, Sabah thought, even as he watched the amazing parade of people streaming past the cafe. *What else did you try to tell me that I never listened to?*

Suddenly, Sabah felt the slightest twinge of panic, like the moment someone realizes something's missing—their keys, wallet, or anything of value. A kind jolt went through him. What did she know that she hadn't taught him? What hadn't he *allowed* her to teach him? Now she was more than a thousand miles away, and learning anything from her, whether he wanted to or not, was no longer possible.

He saw her face clearly. Did she know how much he loved her? In the midst of his new paradise, Sabah felt a moment of anxiousness. Had he told her, shown her, given to her in a way that she knew?

He took a sip of coffee and looked into the busy boulevard, dominated not by carts, pedestrians or peddlars but by cars and trucks. The answer was yes. Yes, of course she knew, because he *did* love her and he had shown it, many times. They would both live, now, only with longing for each other until the moment they were together again, never with regret for anything unspoken or unexpressed. The same was true for his father.

Sabah was relieved and knew that he had just survived his first wave of homesickness.

Yes, he had been an independent young man, as independent as any young man could be living in a prison masquerading as a country. But home had always been there. Wherever his home had been, in all its many locations, it had been modest and meager but always well-managed by his parents. They had always proudly taken care of themselves and each one of their children. They had never failed in this sacred duty. It was who they were. It was what their lives had become. Perhaps only now, sitting in this café on his first day in Athens, did Sabah fully realize how much he'd relied on their support, in one form or another, every day of his life.

When he was younger, he had often gone to the market with his mother.

She would carefully consider each purchase, never haggling or negotiating. If what she wanted was offered at a price that was acceptable, she would purchase it. Carefully, methodically, and with unrelieved concentration, she would collect all the things she would need to feed her family.

Even as she did this Sabah would be standing close beside her. Yet he would be in his own world, distracted as little boys are by countless tiny details and diversions.

I should have paid more attention, Sabah thought to himself as he waited for Sammy to arrive.

Now, for the first time in his life, he would be doing that shopping on his own. How many times had he torn his clothing only to find it sewn, cleaned, and neatly folded, waiting for him on his bed? How many times had his mother nursed and cared for him when he was sick? Sabah made a mental note not to his tear his clothes or get sick.

Starting right now, this very moment, Sabah knew he would, in every way, learn to take care of himself.

Sammy reappeared then and Sabah was happy to see him, in part because he'd interrupted a rather sober reverie. There would be plenty of time for that but right now it was time to explore and that's exactly what they did. Over the course of the week, Sabah and Sammy did almost nothing but take city buses to nearly every square block of Athens, as Sammy did the best he could to explain what they were seeing.

Ancient cities filled with deteriorating stone and marble ruins were one thing Sabah was familiar with. He knew where the world's first advanced society had formed. He'd been there. He'd seen Babylon. Even the Baathists couldn't take away the pride he felt in this aspect of his national heritage. Architectural antiquities were, for Sabah, the least impressive aspect of this amazing city. In fact, he was growing slightly impatient with Sammy's overly enthusiastic praise of Greek history. Every location, and every building in that location, had a story, a story Sammy clearly loved to tell.

Then, just like that, Sabah knew.

They were eating sandwiches in a park when Sabah looked at Sammy.

"You're not going to America are you?" Sabah asked, trying not to make his words sound like an accusation.

Sammy was quiet for a moment, then sighed. "Probably not."

"You love it here."

Sammy seemed to consider this for a moment. "It's enough for me," he said.

"Well, it's not for me."

He waited for Sammy to say something, defend himself in some way, but Sammy said nothing. He just ate his sandwich and looked at Sabah.

"It would never be enough for me," Sabah said.

Sammy smiled at him. "Never say never."

Sabah didn't return the smile. "By this time, next year, I'll be living in America."

Sammy simply smiled and nodded, though the doubt was clear in his expression. After a time, he started picking up the assorted plastic bottles and paper plates from their picnic feast.

"Come on," Sammy said, "I saved the best for last."

They boarded a city bus and rode in silence for awhile, Sabah looking dully out the window trying to reassure himself his cousin's fate would not be his own. He would get out of Greece. He *would* reach America.

The bus rounded a corner, then, and Sabah saw it in the distance, high on a single hill. Out of the dozens of ancient buildings he'd seen that week, it was the only one he recognized. How strange, Sabah thought, to see only an image or photograph of something your entire life, and then to see the real thing with your own eyes. Though it was made of ancient, crumbling stone and was not actually alive, the vibrancy and surprise experienced at his first glimpse made it seem so. It was the Acropolis and at its heart, the Parthenon.

He had seen it in school books and had, perhaps, studied its significance at some point in his distant past, but at this moment, Sabah couldn't remember what he'd been taught. As the bus came closer and he saw it more clearly, he had a sense that this place was very important, almost sacred. But not like a church, not holy or even mystical. There was something else about it, something he couldn't identify. It was as though questions, perhaps just one question, needed to be answered. The building was posing both the question and the answer but as he walked around the crumbling columns, Sabah couldn't hear or understand either. His thoughts came to an abrupt end at the sound of a single word.

"Democracy," Sammy said.

They had walked up the hill to the Parthenon in silence. Sammy had let his cousin be. He knew what Sabah was feeling, even if Sabah didn't. It had happened to Sammy the first time he was here. The force of the place, the first time, had been almost overwhelming. To a large extent it still was.

In those first few moments, Sammy left his cousin alone. They had been standing still for a full minute, as close to the building as the cordon rope would allow, before Sammy had spoken.

Sammy was sophisticated enough to know that the concept and practice of democracy had not been invented in the building they were standing next to. But he also recognized the universal human need for physical objects to simultaneously symbolize and commemorate man's most sacred ideals. The entire world had designated this single building as such, and for the highest ideal of all. That had been enough to inspire his reverence and, Sammy was sure, it was much more than enough for Sabah.

"What is it?" Sabah asked, awe permeating every word.

Sammy was so closely attuned to Sabah at this moment there was no ambiguity in the question. He knew what Sabah meant. He realized he didn't have the wisdom to answer Sabah with the grace and eloquence such a question deserved. Several more moments passed before Sammy spoke again.

"It's you," he said at last.

Sabah looked at his cousin, not completely understanding.

"It's me," Sammy continued. "It's every person, in the whole world, who is free. It started where we're standing, twenty five hundred years ago."

Sabah stared at the building again, though his focus had shifted slightly. Was he seeing just a single column of broken marble? Or was he taking in the entire structure, trying to let this image and moment emblazon themselves on his memory for the rest of his life? Sammy wasn't sure which it might be. Then Sabah turned, faced his cousin, and spoke.

"It's America," Sabah said, with the intense earnestness Sammy had seen in his cousin all their lives. But now it was even more exaggerated, as if Sabah were almost performing a self-parody. It seemed funny to Sammy but laughter, now, would have been rude if not hurtful.

Instead, Sammy smiled and said gently, "Well, it's the best of what America is."

★ ★ ★

In fact, Sammy was in school. He was attending a city college in Athens. Sabah's arrival just happened to coincide with a break in the school's schedule. Sammy was also working, being paid under the table as an unskilled laborer. He'd applied for the Greek equivalent of a green card and had become quite proficient in the contemporary Greek language. After a week of playing tour guide, Sammy returned to his regular schedule of school, study, and work, though he still allowed himself ample free time to enjoy the city with Sabah.

For the next two weeks, Sabah was mainly left to his own devices. He would walk for miles, all over the city, taking in every museum, store, shop, art gallery, or theater he came across. As he explored the city, he passed by a men's clothing store and saw a suit in the window. It immediately reminded him of Mazhar or Mr. Moghadam. It was the kind they wore, of the finest Italian fabric and design. To Sabah, the suit said "success." Sabah told Sammy, the same day he saw it, that he would own that suit.

Sabah loved American movies. There were so many more of them here and he went to see all of them, enthralled, even if they were both spoken and subtitled in languages he couldn't fully understand. And the record stores, completely unreal. They must have had every record ever made. He wished he had a million dollars to buy a whole store. But in a city of nearly incomparable history, filled to overflowing with compelling products to purchase, Sabah's most profoundly felt first impressions were for the spacious, neatly organized, wax-floored and fluorescent-lit supermarkets.

His family's experience in acquiring food, at least over the last ten years, had been to wait in line for hours so they could receive whatever the government made available. They were accustomed to stale loaves of bread, a little rice or potatoes. There was never enough of anything. The concept of variety was as foreign as that of freedom. So walking on squeaky clean floors in a warehouse-sized building, passing perfectly ordered shelves with row after row of products, was staggering to Sabah.

His first encounter with a supermarket had been inadvertent and incidental. The store was next to a movie theater. Sabah had already purchased his ticket for the next showing. With some time to spare he'd wandered in, curious. Three hours later he was still there while an unused movie ticket remained wasted and forgotten at the bottom of his pocket. To waste money was one thing. To forget to go to a movie, that was unheard of! To do *both*, the only possible excuse was death or a supermarket.

He listed, in the first hour, at least one hundred types of canned or boxed food items he couldn't name or identify. He picked up the cans or boxes, carefully studying them one by one. The images on their labels were as mysterious and confusing as the words printed in an unreadable language. Sabah had no idea what he was looking at. But more than that, much more, there were at least four or five different *varieties* of each kind of food or product. It was just too much. He was getting a headache. How in the world was he going to buy and prepare his own food in this city? He thought it would be best to just give his money to Sammy and let him take care of it, which was what he did.

Sabah was never bored, not because he found ways to constantly entertain himself, but because truly inquisitive people seldom are. Still, they can grow restless. Toward the end of his first month in Athens, Sabah had already used a good portion of his savings. His older brother, George, had promised to send more money, but Sabah hadn't relied on his family for money since he was fourteen and he wasn't about to start now.

Being able to find a good job was rare in Iraq. Within the unskilled lower classes, which included most of Iraq, including the Toma family, any job was rare. Only now, facing his prospects in Athens as a non-citizen unable to speak Greek, did Sabah realize he'd started to take the salon for granted. For years he'd received a generous income, unjustified by scholastic achievement or even that very long road known as the "dues paying process." More than that, he'd worked in a place where he was constantly connected to the most important people in his city. Sabah knew people and he'd been known by them. In his own small way, he had become someone in Baghdad.

All of that was gone now, but Sabah didn't regret it for a second. He'd traded it all away and would've gladly given everything else, if he'd had it to give, for this new world of freedom. For the past few weeks he'd been able go where he wanted, when he wanted, how he wanted. He could do and be whatever he wanted. He could drink ouzo in a small café and dance like Zorba the Greek, which he often did. Before his departure from Iraq, he'd actually practiced dancing like Anthony Quinn so he could hit the dance floor at full speed on arrival.

He could do all this without anonymous uniformed police officers, moral standards officials, or any of those other governmental thugs forever monitoring and spying on him. Every day in Greece was a celebration, a holiday. But even the happiest man, made delirious by his first taste of unadulterated freedom, eventually understands he must earn his daily bread in order to survive and make his way through this world.

Sammy was a good, reliable worker. A recommendation from him was not without weight to his employer, the owner of a small construction company. By the end of his first month in Athens, Sabah found himself with a hammer and chisel in his hands, often standing on a ladder at ceiling level, retrofitting the older concrete buildings of the city.

His job was a simple one and didn't require sophisticated instructions or explanations. The boss, a balding Greek man with gnarled hands and a dark, weather-worn face which made him appear older than his forty years, would simply point to a section of wall or draw a blue chalk line across a concrete ceiling. With his hammer and chisel Sabah would, blow by blow, piece by shattered piece, follow that line and create a channel into which electrical wiring would eventually be placed.

It wasn't the easiest transition for a man who'd made his living holding scissors. At the end of his work day, he would stand over his small kitchen sink soaking his deeply blistered and bleeding hands in warm water. A small price to pay, Sabah thought, for a chance to support himself. In fact, he'd expected nothing less. If he needed to do this work every day for a year, if it took him one step closer to America, he would do it gratefully. But Sabah would find Greece no different than Iraq in one very important way. No matter where he went, opportunity would be his friend.

CHAPTER NINETEEN

★ ★ ★

New Friends

★ ★ ★

Man is a habitual creature. We quickly form new routines and patterns, regardless of how dramatic the changes in our world may be. We organize and impose order on our lives without recognizing the illusion fundamentally connected to these efforts: the illusion that we alone can shape and control our own destinies. No one is more devoted to this illusion—some would even call it a myth—than the man who works the hardest. Though Sabah played harder than most other young men in Iraq, he also worked harder. He was the perfect candidate for conversion.

He would soon be twenty-three. For the first time in his life he was fully embracing the principles that would define him as a man. Far above all others was the belief that all good things in life, anything worth having or achieving, began with work. Even now, at the genesis of manhood and self-creation, he was already repelled by the notion of "luck." Eventually, many years later in America, he would reject the idea of luck with the ferocity of an atheist denouncing the idea of God.

He was here, in Greece, alive and on his way to America. This was so because every day for the past nine years, he'd had a dream. The dream had been like a young seedling which he alone had watered, nurtured, protected, and fulfilled. Yes, he had been given help along the way in unexpected ways, sometimes even from strangers. He would never forget these people. He would be grateful to them until his dying day, but had it been luck? There were only two realities for Sabah. There was himself and there was God. Precisely how, why and when God intervened in Sabah's destiny was God's business. For Sabah, everything else was up to him.

Sabah knew his path to America would require even more assistance, from how many people he couldn't begin to guess. These people were unknown to him now, but they would appear without his seeking them, as they always had before. Perhaps they would help him, perhaps they wouldn't. But if they did help, would it be luck?

Never, Sabah told himself.

With a most delicate interplay, the relationship between Sabah's notion of luck and his faith in God would gently rotate and sway within him, like those beautiful mobiles in the Tokalon salon. Though his Chaldean faith was alive Sabah's lifelong friendship with, and devotion to God, had been tempered and cooled by the painful memories of half a life time. Only after several more years, and many more strange twists of fate, would the embers of Sabah's faith fully re-ignite again in a sublime reconcilition with his God, a God who had patiently waited for Sabah. But now, in Greece, Sabah's faith wasn't in the cool, dark, stain-glassed church where his mother would kneel and light candles three times a week. For now, Sabah's faith was in himself.

Ramsey arrived in Athens nine weeks after Sabah. Though he and Sabah had never met before, Sammy's parents had grown up in the same village as Sabah's parents. That this simple fact connected the two so closely speaks to the power of family ties within the Chaldean community, both in Iraq and throughout the world. Sabah's general philosophy when it came to friends, or any other combination of people under any circumstances, had always been "the more the merrier." He'd looked forward to Ramsey's arrival for this reason and, though three men would be sharing a room that was already crowded for two, the rent would be less, and that was fine with Sabah.

What Sabah *wasn't* ready for were Ramsey's jeans. Sabah knew about Levi's, real Levi's, the kind they made in America, the kind Marlon Brando and James Dean wore. He'd even seen them in Athens. They were far too expensive to buy new and, as of yet, he hadn't found a used pair in any of the thrift or re-sale stores he'd searched in. In terms of building his wardrobe, Levi's were Sabah's highest priority.

Ramsey was in the little flat with Sammy when Sabah arrived from work. With Sammy's help, Ramsey was unpacking his single suitcase, fitting his things wherever he could in the cramped one-room apartment. Their backs were to Sabah. Sabah immediately noticed Ramsey's worn and faded jeans with their tiny red tag. Ramsey's white polo shirt was tucked in and Sabah also noticed the leather patch in the belt seam. Finally, he saw the unique stitching across the seat of the jeans. The pattern of the thread always looked like the top of a heart to Sabah. He knew instantly: these were Levis.

It didn't make sense. Sabah knew that, like himself, Ramsey had never been out of Iraq before. Not only that, he had rarely been out of Baghdad. How could he have gotten a pair of Levi's? Though gripped with curiosity, Sabah said nothing about the jeans as Sammy and Ramsey turned to face him. Ramsey was taller than Sammy and slender, though not skinny. He was gracefully proportioned. To Sabah he looked like an athlete but not a soccer player. What was it? A swimmer, a gymnast? No, Sabah thought. He looked like a tennis player.

Perhaps it was the little green crocodile on the front of his polo shirt, his toned forearms, or simply the aura of gracefulness surrounding him. What surprised Sabah the most, though, was that he was fashionable. He was like Milad, Rashid, or Baligh. He was something Americans called "cool" and he was the last thing Sabah had expected.

Standing next to Ramsey, Sammy appeared to be even more of a fashion catastrophe than he already was.

"Hey, Sabah, say hello to Ramsey," Sammy said, obviously delighted by his friend's arrival.

"A pleasure, Ramsey," Sabah said, with unforced sincerity.

They shook hands and Ramsey offered a huge smile to Sabah. "I don't believe it. I can't believe I'm here."

As he spoke, Ramsey glanced out the pavement-level window of their apartment, watching people walk by even as he continued unpacking.

"Sound familiar Sabah?," Sammy asked giving Sabah a knowing grin. "Sabah's been here two months and his eyes are still glazed."

Ramsey smiled, then turned and faced Sammy and Sabah, who were sitting at the only piece of furniture in the room, a small wooden table with two stools.

Ramsey gave Sammy an amused look. "So this is the closet, right? Where's the the rest of the place?"

Sabah and Ramsey shared a serious glance and Ramsey saw it. He smiled. "Just messing with ya", he added.

"What are you talking about?" Sabah asked. "This is a palace! You should see where I grew up!"

"Are you kidding?" Sammy said. "How about *Ramsey*? We all grew up like sardines."

The truth of the words showed in Ramsey's knowing smile.

"Anyway," Ramsey said, "I'm grateful, really. I brought you a little something from home."

He turned his back and dug through what was left in his suitcase.

"Ramsey, you didn't need to bring ..." Sammy was saying.

"Yes, I did. I know we're all in this together, but I really appreciate what you've done, Sammy. So, here you go."

Ramsey turned and beamed a slightly bashful but beautiful smile, the kind that only happens when it comes with a gift. He was holding the neck of a large bottle in one hand. The label was facing Sammy. "Here's to Athens and here's to *not* being in Iraq."

Sammy offered a slightly perplexed smile and said nothing. It wasn't the right reaction. In a heartbeat Sabah realized Sammy didn't know what the bottle was. Why should he know? Sammy had always been more conservative in his personal life, more orthodox in their shared Chaldean faith. Sabah was genuinely surprised Sammy didn't know what it was but Sabah was even more surprised at himself for feeling slightly irritated.

"It's arak, Sammy," Sabah explained in a perfunctory tone.

"I know you're not much of a drinker," Ramsey said. "But sometimes you just have to celebrate, right?"

"Unless you celebrate *all* the time," Sabah said.

Ramsey had arrived from the airport with Sammy late on a Friday afternoon. Of course Sabah knew what school days were. He'd gone to school his whole life and those days fell on Saturday through Thursday in his Muslim country. The salon had been closed on Monday. Even so, that day wasn't used for recreation as much as taking care of the chores and duties he didn't have time for during the rest of his week.

This new Greek lifestyle and it's unique rhythm of five days on, two days off, five days on, two days off, was suiting Sabah very nicely. The truth was, despite work that left him with calloused hands, an exhausted body, and barely enough to pay his food and rent, he'd never had it easier. And he knew it.

What he didn't know was that his western metamorphosis had already begun. Nothing could tarnish or diminish his constant exhilaration at simply not being in Iraq. But for young men, worlds and memories fade, even the worst kind of memories, and with surprising speed. The horrors of one world are replaced by the repeated daily tasks and rhythms of another. Now Sabah had discovered that very western concept of the weekend.

Gratitude was the foundation of Sabah's life, a prelude to any activity related to work or play, but he couldn't help the slow ground swell of anticipation rising in him, beginning on a Monday morning. It would build in size and intensity throughout each weekday until, on Friday, he would find his typically optimistic mood, even brighter and more expansive. It was the weekend! It was time for fun, and having fun was something Sabah was very good at.

His time with Sammy had been enjoyable, but almost as though he'd been with a chaperone or tour guide, even a teacher. He had seen things, been places, learned things. All of this had been wonderful and Sabah would be forever grateful to his cousin for offering his home and knowledge. But it hadn't been like the old days with his friends from the neighborhood. Sammy could never be like Baligh, Rashid, or Milad.

With the arrival of Ramsey, perhaps at the very moment Ramsey pulled the bottle of arak out of his suitcase, Sabah realized he'd been missing something in his new world. There was an entire aspect of Sabah's personality which had been dormant in Greece. The Sabah that had been nurtured by Baligh, MaMhar, Faraj and his world at the Tokalon was missing in Greece. With the appearance of Ramsey, this side of Sabah would quickly re-emerge.

There was never a conscious choice for Sabah. It was never a question of discarding one and selecting the other. His affinity for Ramsey was present from the moment they met, as was Ramsey's for Sabah. They quickly fit together as neatly and easily as the interlocking teeth of a closing zipper.

"So, where'd you get the jeans?" Sabah asked Ramsey on that first

Friday night. Along with Sammy, they were sitting in a neighborhood café close to the flat. Sabah had been in it before but had never seen it like this. Now there was a trio of traditionally dressed Greek musicians standing in the corner of the room, singing and playing bouzoukis on a slightly elevated platform. Sabah and Ramsey had finished half a bottle of ouzo by themselves while Sammy's glass remained half full.

The room had filled since their arrival. The laughter of the crowd, along with the constant music, made it necessary for Sabah and Ramsey to nearly yell. This was making Sammy wince slightly. To Sabah and Ramsey, however, the overall volume of the room, including their voices, seemed exactly as it should be.

"A year ago there was this English archeology student traveling through my parents' village. He traded them to me."

Sabah considered this for a moment, in that slow, deliberate way drunken people do. "What'd you give *him*?"

For several long moments, Ramsey studied Sabah with an intense seriousness.

"My sister," he finally said and downed another shot of ouzo.

Sabah, surprised into silence, simply stared at Ramsey. Suddenly both men laughed at the same time.

"That's bad," Sabah said.

"What? My sister's not worth these pants?"

"I'd have to see your sister," Sabah said.

Ramsey looked at Sabah, shrugged then casually added, "My sister's uglier than a warthog," he said, pouring their glassed full once again.

This put Sabah over the edge and he started laughing in a way he hadn't laughed for months, wildly and uncontrollably. The familiar numb disorientation was beginning to feel just right but it got better because, at that very moment, the musicians started playing the only Greek song Sabah knew. It was the theme music to the movie "Zorba The Greek."

A pretty Greek girl was dancing by herself, alone in front of the musicians. The three young men admired her for a moment.

Sabah jumped out of his chair. "I'm dancing."

"Go for it! Do it!" Ramsey shouted after him.

"What's he doing?" Sammy said, looking dumbfounded.

"Being an idiot!" Ramsey said and cheered Sabah on.

In moments, the café's attention was focused on the dance floor couple. They were moving together with such perfect synchronization they could have been Ginger Rogers and Fred Astaire. Side by side, their arms alternately interlocked between shoulders and waists, they moved forward, sideways, around chairs, and between tables, bending, jumping, sliding, and gliding to the ever faster tempo of the music. Sabah raised both arms and tilted his head so far back he was staring straight at the ceiling.

"WOH – PAH!" he howled, and the cafe went crazy, cheering on this exotic dervish who knew nothing about Greek dancing but looked like epic poetry doing whatever he *was* doing.

His partner was enjoying the moment as much as Sabah. With her own movements and vocal exclamations, she was constantly inspiring Sabah to ever greater theatrics. By now Ramsey was simultaneously awe-struck, horrified, and laughing so hard he couldn't breathe. Sammy, perhaps the only sober person in the room, not only didn't find it funny, he was disappointed in Sabah.

With the inscrutable, impeccable and mysterious timing often found in drinking, Sabah ended his performance, exactly at the moment the music ended, with a magnificent flourish. He dipped his partner and held her so low to the floor her long hair brushed against the tiles. He pulled her up again and gave her a long, deep kiss. Whistles and cheers filled the cafe. It was the best kind of night. It was a night to be remembered and a night completely lost to memory.

The next morning the three went out for coffee. They walked along a route Sammy and Sabah had taken dozens of times before. As they walked, Sammy did something that was completely, thoroughly impulsive. How often do actions occur independent of conscious intent? All the time, and in countless ways. Infinite variations of circumstances, events, and chains of events are permanently strung together like a circle of prayer beads, moving within and through us from birth to death. Who knows why we do the things we do, exactly when we do them? How much of our behavior is planned and how much is unplanned? In the end, probably very little of the former and much of the latter.

So it was that on this morning, Sammy changed the course of Sabah's destiny, not because he wanted to but because he wanted to do something else, something of far less grandeur. Sammy wanted Sabah's attention, loyalty, and devotion—in short, his friendship, which seemed to be rapidly slipping away. He wanted Sabah to know that friends were for fun but family was forever. He would show his cousin that relatives were interested in more than just his entertainment; they were interested in his life.

"Sabah, why haven't you looked for a job there? We pass it all the time." Sammy posed the question casually. They were walking by a beauty salon.

"You know why. I don't speak Greek. What am I gonna do there? That's a place where people need to talk to you. You need to talk to them. That's how it works."

"Come here," Sammy said, and he took Sabah's arm.

"Are we gonna eat or get haircuts?" Ramsey said. "I'm hungry!"

"Give us a minute," Sammy said. "Or come in, whatever you like."

With that, Sammy opened the front door of the salon and pulled Sabah in. It was a small and simple place, with three chairs and sinks. Compared to the Tokalon, it was completely unimpressive, but it had a certain charm and coziness that appealed to Sabah.

A woman wearing glasses glanced up from where she stood behind a small reception desk. She spoke in Greek.

"May I help you?" she asked, looking slightly startled at the sight of a man dragging another man into the salon.

Sammy answered her in Greek and they continued speaking for a few moments. Sabah had no idea what either of them were saying. The, woman, perhaps twenty-five or twenty-six, removed her glasses and stepped around from behind her desk. For the first time, Sabah noticed her long, slender legs and her light complexion. With her glasses off, he saw her light brown eyes, almost the color of parchment paper, set above a triangular, gently sloping jaw and chin. Neatly trimmed short blonde hair framed her face. Her eyebrows were carefully cropped but not rigidly so, nor did she wear her makeup in such a way that any part of her face drew more attention than any other part. Mascara, lipstick, and blush—it was all there, but where was it? Sabah could only see the whole of this face, all at once. Her name was Jaqueline, and she was a Greek woman of classic beauty.

"You speak English?" she said to Sabah.

"I do, yes. A little."

"And you worked in a salon in Baghdad for eight years?"

Sabah hesitated. She had spoken a little too fast. He thought he'd understood her but he was thinking a little too long. Seeing this, Ramsey quickly interrupted and then, just as quickly, Sabah recovered.

"Yes, that's true," Sabah said. "Eight years."

The woman studied Sabah carefully for another moment.

"Can you start this Monday?"

"Sure, he can!" Sammy said. "He—"

But Sabah interrupted Sammy, speaking quickly in Aramaic.

"What is it?" Jaqueline asked.

"He says he must give his current boss notice he's leaving."

"I see. Of course. What's good, then? Shall we say … a week from Monday?"

This time Sabah understood Jaqueline without his cousin's help.

"For sure," Sabah said, smiling. "I'll be here."

"Good." Then, almost as an afterthought, Jaqueline smiled and said, " I guess it would be a good idea if I knew your name."

"Sabah. Sabah Toma, Miss. Thank you. I grateful to you. Thank you."

"Nice meeting you, Sabah. I'm Jaqueline." She extended her hand.

A handshake seemed insufficient. Sabah wanted to kiss her hand but knew that would be out of the question. Instead, he held her delicate hand perhaps a moment longer than he should and said again, "Thank you, Miss."

Sammy was delighted. Whatever instinct had prompted him to drag Sabah into this salon only minutes earlier had obviously been a good one. Sabah was ecstatic and couldn't stop praising his cousin for his help. It would be a new and better job, for sure, one much better suited to his talents and disposition. It would also be the last thing he expected: a siren's song.

CHAPTER TWENTY

★ ★ ★

Plans Interrupted

★ ★ ★

I t was Monday, December fifth, the day before the official start of the
Greek Christmas season. That season begins on December sixth, Saint
Nicolas Day, and ends January sixth, the day of Epiphany. Neither
Sabah nor Sammy had realized how fortunate their timing had been when
they'd walked into Jaqueline's shop a week earlier. The next month was
going to be the busiest period of the year by far, and Jaqueline had been
looking for extra staff.

Sabah was due to arrive at the shop when it opened, at exactly nine
A.M. He was standing at the front door at eight forty-five, excited for
so many reasons. First, and most obviously, he didn't have to pick up a
hammer and chisel today. That alone was enough for him to dance his
way to his new job. Next, he knew that whatever he was going to earn
today, it would be more than he'd been making at his construction job,
probably a lot more. But most importantly, towering above the other
factors contributing to his hope and optimism, he would be working with
Jaqueline.

From the moment they'd met, he could tell, just by way she looked
and smiled at him, that she was attracted to him. And he felt exactly the
same way toward her. He stood at the front door knowing that he'd not
only be spending all day with her, he'd be getting *paid* for it! What could
be better than that?

It was a typically beautiful winter day in Athens. Clean, crisp air in the
morning would quickly give way to comfortably warm sunshine. At eight
fifty-five, a taxi pulled up in front of the salon and Jaqueline stepped out

wearing a fashionable jacket with matching wool scarf, a short skirt, and brown leather boots. She looked like something out of a fashion magazine and Sabah smiled. She returned the smile.

"How did I know you'd be here, waiting?" she asked as she unlocked the salon door.

"I don't know," Sabah said. "You're smart?"

"Maybe." She headed inside before he could reply. "Give me a second to do a couple of things and I'll get you set up."

Sabah watched as she went to her reception desk. She turned on her Ansophone and Sabah heard a beep, followed by a woman's recorded voice in Greek. He realized it was a telephone answering machine. He'd heard of them but had never seen one. As fascinated as he was by new technology of any kind, he resisted the impulse to go to the reception desk and look at it. Instead, he saw a broom, picked it up, and began sweeping.

Jaqueline, busy listening to messages and writing notes, didn't immediately notice what Sabah was doing. When she looked up, she was surprised. She'd hired him as a hair stylist. She had another girl, still training, who did the cleaning and sweeping. She was about to tell him this but stopped herself. Some instinct told her not to interrupt him. She sensed that if she said anything to him, if she told him he didn't need to do what he was doing, it wouldn't have been well received. Their relationship wouldn't have improved, working or otherwise. Instead she just watched him for a moment, moved by this handsome young man's unassuming manner and humility.

"Sabah," she said finally, and he stopped sweeping. He looked up at her. She continued slowly and clearly, "If someone doesn't speak English or you have trouble understanding someone, be sure and tell me."

"Okay," Sabah said.

"Even if I'm busy, it's okay."

"You got it." Sabah smiled and Jaqueline smiled back.

Saint Nicolas Day started the holiday season with a bang. It was a day of widespread parties and celebration filled with eating, drinking, and singing. The day before a holiday was always busy in a salon, when ladies made their final beauty preparations for special events. Today was no exception. From the moment the door opened, customers streamed into the shop. Jaqueline and Sabah immediately started working as a team, Sabah washing and shampooing hair and Jaqueline cutting it.

The truth was, she was a little nervous about Sabah's styling ability. She liked him but how did she know, for sure, what he was able to do? After all, this was her shop and these were her loyal customers. She couldn't lose sight of fact that no matter how attractive he was. Even so, she *had* hired him to cut hair.

The moment for his first test came sooner than she expected or preferred.

It was only ten A.M. and there were already two customers waiting, both of them preferring Jaqueline to cut their hair, each saying they'd be happy to wait. Sabah had said nothing at each request but only shared a glance with Jaqueline. When a third lady arrived, Jaqueline couldn't wait any longer. The woman was a new customer and Jaqueline hadn't done her hair before. This was it.

"Sabah, perhaps you could take care of that lady?" Jaqueline said, without the slightest pause in her own work.

"Of course. Ma'am?" Sabah gestured to a chair near where he was standing.

When the woman had seated herself, Sabah asked in English, "What can I do for you today?"

The woman answered in a mixture of Greek and English, speaking so quickly that Sabah understood neither. He glanced up at Jaqueline. Despite her kind promise, he could see that at this moment, she was in no position to be a translator. Fortunately, Jaqueline had dozens of fashion magazines neatly arranged on a coffee table. Sabah had noticed them earlier. He lifted his palm to the woman now sitting in his chair, smiled, and stepped away. In another second, he was holding a magazine open for her, pointing to picture after picture of models in advertisements.

"Which one?" Sabah said.

The woman glanced up at him, not sure if he was joking. His calm demeanor and confident smile assured her he wasn't. She took the magazine in her own hands and flipped through several pages. She stopped, looked up at him again, and pointed to a picture of Catherine Deneuve. In the photo, her hair was long, straight, and perfectly smooth, gracefully curling in over her bosom.

"No problem," Sabah said, and he began to work.

Sabah may not have been the world's greatest stylist, certainly not as good as Rashid or his other friends at the Tokalon, but he was far better than he gave himself credit for. After all, what did he know about other hair stylists outside of the Tokalon, let alone the rest of the world? Sabah was able to do what all highly skilled professionals do, regardless of their craft. He created excellent results in the least amount of time. He worked quickly, efficiently, and flawlessly.

The woman was shampooed, cut, and blow dried before Jaqueline had finished her own customer. Jaqueline had glanced at Sabah several times as he was working, not convinced that his speed indicated competence rather than ignorance.

The woman stepped out of her chair and studied herself in a mirror. Her entire body seemed to relax. Then she turned to Sabah and looked at him closely. Though physically she was far from Catherine Deneuve, her hair could have been an exact match.

"Are you the owner?" she asked.

"No, ma'am, that lady is," Sabah said.

The woman turned to Jaqueline, who had paused in her own work. Jaqueline was not only amazed that Sabah was finished already, but that he'd transformed a plain middle-aged woman into someone who was attractive, if not glamorous. The woman spoke to Jaqueline.

"My friend said you did good work here, but I had no idea. Wonderful, really."

"Well, thank you," Jaqueline said, smiling at both the customer and Sabah.

Before the woman took her leave, she left Sabah a tip in the form of a handful of drachmas, which he gratefully accepted. The other two women waiting for Jaqueline had looked up from their magazines. They'd been watching and listening to the exchange. When Sabah's customer left, the women looked at each other then back to Sabah. One of them spoke.

"Do you have time for one more?" she asked.

"Certainly," Sabah said. His second era of haircutting was off and running.

The day only got busier. By two o'clock, when the afternoon break started and the whole country stopped working for two hours, Sabah had already placed a small pile of tips on the counter. He hadn't even had time to stack and organize it, so the bills simply accumulated there, much like the hair gathering in piles at his feet.

Jaqueline usually saw her sister for lunch. Today they'd be meeting in the salon, as Jaqueline had ordered out for delivery. She asked Sabah if he'd like to join them.

"Actually, I'm meeting my cousin. You know, the one you met last week."

"I remember. The one who told me where you live," Jaqueline said.

The truth was, Sabah had no plans to meet his cousin. The game that had started between Jaqueline and himself had been building throughout the day, usually in the form of glances and smiles. Sometimes they'd been direct, undisguised in their intent. But Sabah preferred the mirrors. Between his clip here or his comb stroke there, he would catch a reflected glance from Jaqueline. Better still he liked that unexpected instant when, together, they found each other's reflections in a mirror. It had been a kind of ongoing dance between them, supporting all the other activities of the day.

At one point, Jaqueline had needed help cutting the hair of a particular customer. Her hair was so long Jaqueline had asked Sabah to hold up the outer layers with both hands while she cut the inner layers. As Sabah held her hair and Jaqueline brushed and trimmed, Jaqueline stepped closer to Sabah, her hand occasionally glancing against his as she worked. Each time it did, his heart would skip a beat and he sensed that hers did the same. Now, some instinct in Sabah told him, *Don't be a pushover. Play a little hard to get.* He already knew she wanted him. Let her want him a little more.

When the shop closed at eight P.M., Jaqueline still had a customer in her chair.

"Sabah, why don't you lock up?" she said.

"If it's okay, I think I'll just go now."

Jaqueline stopped what she was doing. It was an odd, slightly awkward moment for both of them.

"Okay," she said slowly, "but you know tomorrow's Saint Nicolas Day. We're closed tomorrow."

"I know. There's a party at my cousin's right now. I'm supposed to be there."

"Oh. I didn't know. That's nice. Okay, well, we'll see you Wednesday then, right?"

"Of course," Sabah said, and he opened the door to go.

Jaqueline suddenly called to him. "Sabah, your tips!" She was looking over at his shelf where the equivalent of over a hundred dollars in small bills had been hastily discarded. It looked like a small haystack and it was as much as Sabah would've made in a week at his construction job.

"It's okay, leave it," Sabah said.

"What?"

"It's fine, leave it. I'll get it later."

"But Sabah …"

"Really. See you later. And thank you again."

He left with this simple message: I'm not greedy and I trust you. Ironically, though it may have been game, the message had been neither disingenuous or untrue. Even in flirtation and courtship, perhaps especially these matters, it was impossible for Sabah to be anything other than himself.

The last thing Sabah saw as he stepped out the door was Jaqueline's expression of surprise and curiosity. If what they'd been playing all day had been a card game, Sabah was confident he'd just shown the winning hand. With that, he left the shop and walked the few blocks to his flat.

Sammy and Ramsey were there, along with seven other young men Sabah had never met. Most were Chaldean. All were from Iraq. They were mostly Sammy's school friends, members of a rapidly growing community of Iraqi expatriates in Athens. They were young, all in their early twenties, full of life, hope, and dreams. All of them had one more thing in common; they were about to spend their first Christmas season away from home, family, and friends.

Sabah heard them from the end the hallway before he reached the apartment. He walked in and saw them huddled together around two folding card tables taking up nearly the entire floor space of Sammy's basement apartment. They were eating, laughing, and drinking, doing their very best to be their own family at Christmas.

There was one person in the group who attracted Sabah's curiosity more than the others. Perhaps because, like Sabah, he was the only other man in the room who had hair to his shoulders. He didn't have Sabah's beard and moustache, but he was an edgy sort of person, just the kind Sabah was most interested in. His name was Ahmad Murphy and Sabah would soon discover that he was as unusual as his name was. He didn't know it yet, but of the many men in Sabah's life he would call business partners, Ahmad would be his first. Together they would be making some money in Greece. In fact, they would be making a lot of it and making it easily.

Sabah was happy to be with such a festive group. He didn't even know what Saint Nicolas Day was. There was no such celebration in Iraq. But if there was a reason to celebrate anything, anytime, anywhere in the world, Sabah was not only ready, he was first in line. Within a half hour, everyone in the room was his friend. An hour and four shots of arak later, he felt like he'd known them his whole life. Then the apartment buzzer rang. Ramsey wandered to the intercom.

"Yes?" he said.

"Uh, hello, good evening," came a smooth female voice. "Is Sabah there, please?"

The group barely noticed the separate conversation. They continued their animated reminiscing about all things Iraq and, in particular, their adventures in getting out of there.

"Sabah?" Ramsey said into the intercom.

"Yes, is there a Sabah there?"

Ramsey glanced over at Sabah, who was the only one in the group watching him.

"Who is this?"

"It's Jaqueline."

As Ramsey pressed the entry buzzer, Sabah jumped up too quickly, knocking over his plastic folding chair in the process.

"Whoa, easy there cowboy," Ahmad said.

"Right," Sabah said. "Keep going. I'll be right back."

Though Sabah had been impressed, even charmed by Ahmad's proclivity for American colloquialisms, this one hadn't fully registered and Ahmad realized it. He watched Sabah hurry toward to door and leave the apartment.

Sabah didn't want her to come inside. She really didn't need to be in a room full of drunk guys speaking a language she didn't understand, and all of them in desperate need of a woman on top of that. When he stepped out the front door, she was already halfway down the hallway walking toward him. She smiled but said nothing for a moment. Then she lifted up a fat, letter-sized envelope.

"Here," she said.

Sabah took the envelope but didn't open it. Instead he simply held Jaqueline's steady gaze in his own.

"What are you doing tomorrow?" Jaqueline asked.

Sabah smiled. "Oh, wow, my calendar is loaded, just busy, busy."

"Oh," Jaqueline said.

Sabah took a moment to privately enjoy her disappointment, then he added, "Nothing."

She laughed. "You little ..." Her voice trailed off and she gave Sabah a light punch on the shoulder. "I want to take you to lunch. For Saint Nicolas Day."

"Sounds good to me," Sabah said.

Sabah saw the effort this request required in her and he was moved by it. Though he'd known her less than a day, he liked her very much. As he studied her face in the dim light of the hallway, he was moved by a fondness that was placed somewhere near the border of love. Perhaps he had seen her insecurity. Perhaps she had seen his compassion. Who knows what comes before a first kiss? Only the two people who share it and very often, not even them.

Jaqueline took a step toward Sabah and lifted her face to his. As her eyes closed she kissed his lips lightly, with infinite tenderness, and Sabah returned that kiss. It wasn't a kiss of friendship. It wasn't a kiss good night. It was a kiss of promise. She pulled away after what might have been a moment, but how is an event measured when it occurs outside of time? She looked up at Sabah, told him her taxi was waiting, and said good night. Then she turned and left.

Sabah watched her go, standing alone in the empty hallway. Now the whole building, including his apartment, was strangely quiet. Sabah turned toward his apartment and caught a glimpse of six faces, stacked in a row one on top of another, peering out from the slightly open door. The door flew open and Sabah heard several cries in unison. He shook his head and re-entered the room to the collective, back-slapping approval of his fraternity.

But he didn't have time to enjoy their praise and adulation. He let them sit down again as he stood in the corner of the room to read the note Jaqueline had included with his tips. He didn't notice Ramsey looking over his shoulder as he read it. It was just a couple of sentences. But it was the three words at the bottom that leapt out at him as though they were one of those new billboards he saw all over the city. "I love you" were the words he saw and they were exactly what he wanted to see. Ramsey saw them at the same time.

"I love you? I love you, Sabah?" Ramsey asked with unmasked suspicion.

"First of all, it's none of your business, but second, what's wrong with that?"

Sabah emptied the envelope. He and the group saw the wad of bills for the first time. If they'd been impressed with the kiss, they were now an official fan club. They gawked at the dozens of bills in Sabah's hand.

"You like this?" Sabah said, taking a moment to savor the awe in their faces. "Here, take it!"

He threw the bundle into the air and bills filled the room, floating and spinning down like autumn leaves. Hollering and laughing, his friends picked up the scattered bills and handed them back to Sabah.

Sabah took the money again and looked around at the group. "I mean it," he said. "Keep it if you want. I got what I wanted."

CHAPTER TWENTY-ONE

★ ★ ★

Seduction With A Twist

★ ★ ★

The next morning was Saint Nicolas Day. It was a Tuesday but the busy boulevard outside Sabah's basement window was unusually quiet. To Sabah, it seemed more like a Sunday morning. After a time, he heard the sound of single car stopping at the curb outside. Looking out his narrow basement window, he was eye level with the taxi's tires, and just in time to see the car door open and a woman's high-heeled shoe step out. Just as she had promised, Jaqueline arrived exactly at 1 PM. Sabah, always punctual himself, appreciated this behavior in others.

Sabah assumed they'd be going to lunch somewhere in the neighborhood. Sharing the intimacy of this back seat with Jaqueline created an overwhelming anticipation in him, so much so that he entirely forgot to take advantage of this rare opportunity for sightseeing by car. If anyone else had been in the car with him, they would have had half of his attention at best. The other half would have been staring out the window at every new detail in his passing view.

At this moment, however, all Sabah could see were Jaqueline's shining eyes.

They'd been in the taxi about twenty minutes before Sabah even looked out the taxi window. Only then did he realize that this wasn't just a trip around the corner.

"Not that it matters," he said, "but where are we going?"

"One of my favorite places," Jaqueline said. "I think you'll like it."

"I like it already."

Jaqueline said nothing. They were holding hands. She simply smiled and pressed his hand tighter.

In about thirty-five minutes, they had reached a seaside neighborhood. It appeared, to Sabah, as a separate world within a world. He saw a tranquil harbor. It was a light turquoise color he'd never seen before, in water or otherwise. It was also crystal clear. Fishing boats tied to small docks seemed to hover in mid-air. A long stretch of golden sand was perfectly groomed, dotted with striped umbrellas and white wooden beach chairs. In summer, the beach would have been jammed, but now, in December, it was almost empty. At the far north end, a shear granite cliff rose sharply, towering over the beach, giving the entire landscape and community an anchor of stability and safety. It was one of the most beautiful places Sabah had ever seen. Since they'd left his apartment, this was the first time Sabah wasn't aware of Jaqueline. She, on the other hand, was very aware of Sabah, closely studying his reaction to everything he was seeing.

"Nice, isn't it?" she asked in a gentle, quiet voice.

"Yes, very," Sabah said.

"I like it." She paused, then added, "It's my home."

Was it the words or the way she spoke them? Sabah wasn't sure which made him quickly turn and look at Jaqueline.

"You *live* here?"

"Yes. Born here, actually." Her focus shifted past Sabah and out his window. "We're here."

The taxi had stopped in front of restaurant that was literally on the beach. This was no seaside shanty. It was precisely the kind of fine dining restaurant Sabah had almost no experience with. He knew of such places, of course, but had rarely been to a restaurant in Iraq that even had menus, let alone pressed linen, fine crystal, and elaborate sets of silverware.

Jaqueline greeted the maitre d' by name, a detail Sabah found both revealing and impressive. She was, after all, only four or five years older than he was. This touch of worldly sophistication seemed a natural extension of her personality. Her familiarity with the man was befitting of those additional years and did not in any way seem pretentious or insincere.

They were immediately escorted to an outside patio and their waiting table. As Sabah sat down and looked out over the sea, the tranquility of the harbor seemed even greater and more sublime. Mid-afternoon sunlight was shimmering on the dappled water, delicately shifting in a gentle breeze. He heard a seagull crying somewhere in the distance, a common sound to Jaqueline but not to Sabah. He was curious but was too busy taking in the perfection of the moment to ask what it was.

Jaqueline was already looking at her menu. Sabah knew, from movies mostly, this was something that listed what the restaurant served. You could read it and choose something; a very novel concept, Sabah thought. He knew the words would be in Greek so he also knew he would have no idea what he was looking at.

"I'm starving," Jaqueline said. "What would you like?"

She looked up and noticed Sabah's slight hesitation and bewilderment. She put her hand on his knee and said slowly, "Sabah, you get whatever you like, okay?"

Her voice was all kindness and softness, and something inside of him relaxed. "Thank you," he said. "For now, I think a Turkish coffee is good."

"Whatever you like," she said again.

The lunch was long and leisurely. They basked in the tender sunlight as much as they did the savory food. They finished two carafes of Robola, Jaqueline's favorite white wine, which was quickly becoming Sabah's favorite also. They ate perfectly prepared fish and lamb. Now Sabah sat, sipping a final espresso. Jaqueline watched him from across the table, reclining, one leg folded over the other with the ease and grace of a velvet drape. She thought she had never seen a more handsome man in her life.

"Would you like to see where I live?" she asked.

The question was perfect in its inevitability. He'd heard the exact words in his mind a dozen times throughout the afternoon. When she actually spoke them, there was almost a sense of déjà vu. Sabah smiled in perfect comfort and said, "I'd love to."

Sabah offered to contribute toward the payment of the bill, but Jaqueline would have none of it. As he reached for his wallet, she placed her hand on his forearm and pressed gently, shaking her head. She told him softly, but firmly, to put his money away.

Jaqueline lived close enough to the restaurant that they were able to walk to her home rather than call a taxi. Their arms tightly around each other, they strolled along the wooden boardwalk bordering the beach. By now it was close to four in the afternoon. At this time of year twilight came early in Greece, and they watched the orange glow of the sun moving closer to a razor-edged horizon.

Jaqueline owned a two-bedroom, two-bath townhouse. It was only a few blocks from the restaurant and on the same stretch of sand. She opened the front door for Sabah and the sun followed them inside. A bank of windows covered an entire wall of her home, revealing the full panorama of the beach, hillside, and sunset. Sabah drew a sharp breath and let it out slowly. Jaqueline had closed the door behind them and they stood, finally, alone in the stillness and privacy of this beautiful home. They were perfectly satiated and fully intoxicated, more so by the intimate proximity in a private setting than by the wine.

Hours later, seated in lounge chairs outside on Jaqueline's porch, a fire blazing in her outdoor fireplace, they watched the long line of reflected moonlight delicately waiver on the Aegean Sea. They listened to the wave surges softly ebb and flow, shifting the small pebbles forming the shoreline. It was the kind of night that myths were made of.

Though they held hands both had been looking out at the sky and the sea. Sabah picked up his Brandy snifter and raised it just an inch as he looked at Jaqueline and waited for him to turn. She did and two hearts, completely at ease, experienced each other.

"Here's looking at you, kid," Sabah smiled and took a sip of his Courvoisier.

Jaqueline laughed.

"OK Bogey," she answered. "Whatever you say."

Suddenly Sabah's eyes focused just a bit more on her face.

"You know that one?" he asked, delighted that Jaqueline should be familiar with one of his favorite movies.

"Sabah, please," Jackie said.

"What?" Sabah said, still tickled and happy to be the source of a such wonderful chastisement.

"It's only the most romantic movie ever made," Jaqueline said.

"It is! It is! And you're the only girl I ever knew who's seen it!"

Jaqueline was astute enough, even after a few hours of drinking, to take in all that this revelation suggested about Sabah. How provincial, restricted and limited the world of Iraq must be. She didn't doubt it was the truth and knowing, immediately, that it was, made Sabah all the more adorable

159

to her. She said nothing but simply continued to look at him. She squeezed his hand tighter for a moment and released the pressure.

Resisting the impulse to invite Sabah to her bedroom, right at that instant, required all her concentration and will power. That could happen, it would happen, but this was perfect, too, in its own way. For a minute the two had not spoken, absolutely comftorable in their complete silence.

"You like American movies, then?"

"Love them. They're the best. Best movies, best country. It figures."

Jaqueline said nothing for a few moments. For Jaqueline, a bridge had been approached. It had come unexpectedly. Now she was weighing whether she wanted to cross it, though Sabah was completely unaware of both her concentration and indecision. She suspected something and if she was right, it was going to have to be crossed eventually. There would be no choice. Like Sabah, she didn't shy away from things that were difficult. She had made her choice.

"You like America?"

"Well, I've never been there, but I know it's great."

"If you haven't been there, how do you know it's great?"

Sabah looked at Jaqueline again with renewed focus and saw something in her face that immediately sobered him. He raised the back of his lounger up, picked up his legs and swiveled so that he completely faced her. His one hand had not disconnected from hers and with his free hand, he took her other hand in his. Holding both her hands now, staring down at her as she reclined in her chair only inches away, he studied her carefully though not at all critically.

"I just know," he said. "For lots of reasons." Jaqueline's lack of enthusiasm was beginning to make him uncomfortable and he added quickly, "It's the greatest, Jaqueline. It really is. I'm gonna live there."

Jaqueline pulled her hands away. "Are you?"

Sabah didn't like coyness or a lack of directness in any form and Jaqueline, for the first time, was beginning to irritate him.

"Why the questions?" he asked, suddenly sounding so loud and shrill he surprised himself.

Jaqueline said nothing, just shrugged.

"Have *you* been there?" Sabah went on, beginning to sound like a cross examiner.

Jaqueline had looked away for a moment, taking in the radiance of the moon, now much lower and closer to the sea's horizon. She looked back at Sabah.

"I'm an American citizen," she said. "I have dual citizenship."

Sabah had never met an American citizen before. And he had never heard of dual citizenship. Meeting such a person, under any circumstances, would have been of the highest interest to Sabah. But at this moment, in the closest place to heaven he had ever been, with, perhaps, the most attractive women he had ever seen, these were absolutely the last words he expected to hear. Surprise and curiosity canceled out his excitement. He felt like he'd either had too much to drink or not enough and stared at her, unblinking, for several seconds.

"What?" he finally managed to say.

"I lived in Chicago for twelve years," Jaqueline said.

So that was why her English was so good. He'd assumed before that she was just bright and gifted at speaking other languages.

"No! Tell me! You have to tell me about it!"

Jaqueline offered a tired smile. And she *was* tired. It was late now. "Later, Sabah. I promise. For now, can we rest?"

Now Jaqueline sat up, reclined Sabah's lounge chair and gestured for him for slide over. She layed down beside him and covered them both with a small blanket that had been covering her. Now on his side, propping himself up on a elbow, Sabah looked at Jaqueline's beautiful, kind face. He felt a twinge of regret and embarrassment at being so harsh. He didn't know why he'd acted the way he did and that, more than anything else, bothered him.

"Sure, of course," he said, and lightly stroked Jaqueline's hair. "But can I ask just one question?"

Jaqueline opened her eyes. Her expression was taut and tired.

"Only one," Sabah said. "I promise."

"What is it?"

"Why did you leave?"

Their faces were very close to each other now. Sabah could feel her chest rise and fall hear her breathing. The night had become silent.

Finally, Jaqueline let out a soft breath. "I don't like America."

CHAPTER TWENTY-TWO

★ ★ ★

Better Than Paradise

★ ★ ★

Sabah had created an unintentional pattern of hurt feelings and disappointment. Though Sammy, Ramsey, and Sabah all got along very well together, Sammy's basement flat had quickly proved too small. Only a month after Ramsey's arrival, Sabah and Ramsey moved out and into another place a few blocks away. It wasn't a surprise to Sammy. He'd seen it coming but that expectation did nothing to minimize his hurt feelings.

Sammy's cousin and lifelong friend had moved in with someone he'd only known a month. For Sammy, it was an upsetting rejection, though the last person he would reveal this to was Sabah. For his own part, Sabah had mixed feelings about the move. He didn't want to be disloyal to Sammy, or in any way display a lack of gratitude. But all three knew there just wasn't enough space. Sabah had to make a choice between his new friend and his cousin.

His choice, to Sabah's credit, wasn't based solely on the fact that Ramsey was much more of a nightlife companion. It had far more to do with Ramsey's sense of mission about America. Who knew if Sammy would ever get there? In Sabah's mind, Greece had become a kind of sedative to Sammy. After two years here, Sammy's desire to reach America had almost completely dissolved into complacency. If America was heaven, Sammy was in limbo.

Just the opposite was true of Ramsey. Ramsey was the first person Sabah had ever met whose determination to reach America was greater than his own. Unlike Sabah, Ramsey had planned his departure from

Iraq more carefully. He'd actually saved his money and had enough to live comfortably for at least a year in Athens. With all his free time, Ramsey would visit consulates and embassies. He did research in libraries and constantly visited the bars and cafés where fellow ex-Iraqis could be found. Sabah's full time job was styling hair. Ramsey's was getting a visa to America.

This was why Sabah wanted to live with Ramsey. They would help and encourage each other. In the worst case scenario, Ramsey would be a kind of insurance policy. If, for whatever crazy reason, Sabah did lose sight of his mission to reach America, he knew Ramsey would keep him on the straight and narrow, with whip in hand if necessary. In this regard, as in so many other countless instances both past and yet to come, Sabah's instincts did not fail him.

For the time being, Sabah did the same thing to Ramsey he'd done to his cousin, though perhaps not to the same extent. If Sammy had been hurt, Ramsey was merely apprehensive, and troubled with ongoing consternation. By the time of the actual move, Sabah was spending several nights a week at Jaqueline's idyllic seaside home. Despite this, their moving plans unfolded as scheduled during the first month of Ramsey's arrival and Sabah's first month at the salon. Jaqueline was an unknown variable neither had expected. But Sabah firmly reassured Ramsey that their living arrangement wouldn't be affected by any extracurricular activities. Ramsey wasn't entirely convinced.

If Ramsey was concerned, he had good reason to be. Perhaps for the first time in his life, Sabah was experiencing a new kind of adventure, entering deeper and deeper into an actual relationship with a woman. At twenty-three, Sabah was certainly no virgin, but physical intimacy with a woman, formerly such a complete experience unto itself, so self-fulfilling, had now become a gateway to something far greater. For the first time in his life, a woman had become his friend. In fact, a woman had become his best friend.

They would sit together on a beach chair in the early hours of morning, wrapped together as tightly by their single blanket as they were by the silence of the night. They would sip brandy, staring up at a black sky glistening with a million stars. They would basque in a bon fire right there on the sand, just beyond the paved tiles of her porch. The wood from the dancing flames would pop and spark, interrupting the silence with its odd, harmonious rhythm. In this place, they were completely safe from the chill of night and from all other fears.

During these moments, Sabah would ask himself, *What's the matter with this?*

His answer would always be the same: nothing. A beautiful home, a beautiful woman, a beautiful country and world; what more could there be than this? America was there. It would always be there. In time, perhaps, he could persuade her to go there with him. If not to live, then at the very least to visit. They could both be dual citizens. They could come and go as they pleased, anywhere they liked and any time. The whole world belonged to them! What was wrong with that? Again, Sabah would search within his mind and heart for the truth, but still the answer remained the same: nothing.

It was February 1975 and, for the first time in his life, Sabah was considering the idea of getting married. He had said nothing to Jaqueline, nor would he until he was absolutely, one hundred percent sure this was what he wanted. There was do doubt in his mind as to what her answer would be. He knew she loved him. She had told him so many times, as he had her. But offering her an actual proposal of marriage, with all its weight and importance, was held in constant balance by that other massive guiding force in his life: his dream of America. Had this dream, and her refusal to go there, not been part of this equation, he probably would have been married to her already.

It was a dilemma he could not resolve. But slowly, inexorably, his growing attachment to Jaqueline and the life they had together was tilting that balance toward Greece, at least for now. How he wished his father or mother were with him now, or even Mr. Moghadam, Milad, or any of his other friends back home. He knew a man must make his own choices, but even the best men rely on wise words from others.

Over two months had passed since Sabah and Ramsey had moved in together. The previous day, Sabah had called Ramsey from the salon. He'd told Ramsey he had something important to talk about and was a little surprised when Ramsey said the same thing. Jaqueline was going to a movie with her sister and some friends after work and Sabah met Ramsey at a local cafe.

The two friends shared a bottle of ouzo and played some of their favorite songs on a jukebox. Sabah still couldn't believe Ramsey liked American rock music as much as he did. Sabah stood by the machine as Foghat's "Slow Ride" came on. Sabah gyrated his hips, doing an Elvis impersonation, then slowly slid across the floor while Ramsey shook his head.

Sabah sat down and smiled at his friend. He liked to do little things to embarrass friends. But now, Sabah had misinterpreted Ramsey's reaction to his goofy dance moves.

"It's Jaqueline's favorite song," Sabah said.

"That's appropriate."

"What is?" Sabah said, catching the first flush of ouzo.

"'Slow ride, take it easy.' Pretty much sums you up doesn't it?"

There was a coolness and detachment in Ramsey that Sabah hadn't seen before. It was slightly unsettling, though Sabah didn't immediately give in to the feeling. Instead, he just listened to the music and took a moment to compose himself.

"You know what?" he said. "I think so. I think you're right."

"How's Jaqueline doing?" Ramsey asked.

"Great. In fact, that was my news." He took a letter-sized envelope out of his coat pocket and set it on the table. Ramsey looked at it and said nothing.

"It's not what I was planning," Sabah said, and took another drink of ouzo so he wouldn't have to meet his friend's eyes. "But that's life, right? The thing that happens when you're making other plans."

Ramsey's gaze went back to the envelope. "What is it?"

"A letter, to Jaqueline's parents in Chicago. We wrote it together. She wanted their permission."

"To do what?"

"To marry me. I'm mailing it tonight."

Ramsey's face remained tense and unchanged. "Married? Then what? You stay in Greece?"

"For a while, yes. Then go to America. We could live both places."

Ramsey said nothing for a long, uncomfortable moment, leaning forward with his forearms on the small round table and his hands clasped together. Suddenly, he sat back and took something out of his own jacket pocket.

"I have something to show you, too."

"Yeah, you said. What is it?"

Ramsey tossed his passport onto the cafe table. It landed on top of Sabah's letter. Sabah lifted it up and opened it. He stared at it for a moment, at first not sure what he was looking at. Then he realized: it was a stamped visa to Mexico.

"Mexico?" Sabah said. "What's Mexico?"

"It's connected to America, on the southern border."

"It's not part of America?"

"No, Sabah, it's not. And if you weren't in bed, or thinking about being in bed, twenty-four hours a day, you might know these things." Ramsey stopped himself, allowing his disappointment and anger to subside before he spoke again. "I'm leaving next week. My flight's already booked, but that's not the big news."

If there was something bigger than this, Sabah couldn't imagine what it would be.

"My uncle in Detroit gave me a guy's number," Ramsey continued. "I don't know who he is and I'm not sure how my uncle found him, but he's a ... I don't know, a kind of guide. The guy's spent the last ten years doing nothing but getting Chaldeans out of Iraq. He takes them anywhere they want to go in the world, including America! Sabah, I *talked* to him today. He's picking me up at the airport in Mexico City. He told me he can get me to Detroit within two weeks of today!"

Sabah heard and understood every word. They were reverberating in his mind, as though his head had become a tower bell. Ramsey saw his words' impact and said nothing more, letting Sabah fully digest the enormity of this revelation.

"Who's the guy?" Sabah said finally.

"I don't know. George somebody. Tanger something. I don't know, and I don't care, as long as he gets me to America. Sabah ..." He waited until Sabah was fully focused on him, paying complete attention to his words, before he went on. "Listen to me. You can't stay here. You can't stay in Greece. Think! Why did you want to go to America? Who was it for? Was it for you, or was it for your family?"

In an instant, Sabah was there again. Had it been six months or a lifetime, that last moment he'd said goodbye? He saw now, as clearly as he saw every detail of the room around him, his father's face, his mother's, his sisters', his brothers'.

"My mother," Sabah said softly, speaking more to himself than to Ramsey. "She didn't believe me. She didn't believe she'd see me again. She didn't believe I could help them. She didn't ..."

The words trailed off. The song had ended by now and several people at a nearby table were laughing.

Ramsey leaned forward. "Was she right?" His voice was quiet but also hard, unforgiving. "Was she right, Sabah?"

He thought about all the times he'd been lying with his arms wrapped around Jaqueline, comfortable in his new life and asking himself, *What's the matter with this?*

And now, finally, he knew the answer.

If I stay here with her, my family will never get to America.

He knew the truth of it with the clarity of a lightning strike, and a new resolve began to build inside of him.

"Sabah," Ramsey said again. "Was she right? Was your mother right?"

He took a deep breath and let it out slowly. "No," he said. "No, she wasn't."

Ramsey nodded, a grim sort of relief on his face. "Good. I don't know who your parents are to you, Sabah, but I know who mine are to me. They gave me my *life*. If I don't go to America, I can't return theirs. Do you understand?"

He did. The next question came without hesitation: "Where did you get the visa stamped?"

For the next hour, the two friends discussed, in the most minute detail, where to get visas stamped, how Ramsey would refer his tour guide to Sabah, miscellaneous travel costs, and a thousand other details related to leaving Greece. They drank more ouzo and were soon laughing, but not once that night was Jaqueline's name mentioned again.

CHAPTER TWENTY-THREE

★ ★ ★

Plans Restored

★ ★ ★

For Sabah, the conversation with Ramsey was like an alarm clock going off during REM sleep. He awoke severely dazed, disoriented, and unsure of his surroundings. The past few months had been like a dream, but there was no doubt now that he was back. The old mantra had stirred to life. Ramsey's words had been the alarm bell and the clock had started again in Sabah. With each tick of the second hand, the chant had been reborn: *America, America, America.*

The letter he'd written with Jaqueline was thrown away, though Sabah never told her. The question of what to do with Jaqueline was unresolved. It also became a lower priority as his focus instantly shifted to plans of departure. Jaqueline sensed Sabah's growing distance even as he tried, unsuccessfully, to assure her that there was nothing wrong.

If Ramsey had been attempting a moon landing, Sabah could not have waited with more interest or anxiousness. Both of them knew this much: there was no direct route to America. They'd been to the U.S. Consulate in Athens at least half a dozen times in search of visas. Each time, they'd arrived with some new half-baked ploy or stratagem.

On one occasion, Sabah had been there and had believed his conversation with the consul was going well. The man appeared friendly and receptive. Sabah was optimistic.

"You're going to school in the United States?" the man asked, reviewing Sabah's application.

"Yes sir," Sabah answered.

"What will you study?"

Sabah smiled. "Well, everything I hope."

"Sounds like a pretty full schedule," the man said, smiling back. Then, after a slight pause, the man leaned back in his chair and spoke again. "Let me ask you something. If I gave you another kind of visa, one that would let you stay in America as long as you like, would you still want to study there?"

The truth slipped out before he could stop it: "Probably not, no."

The consul's demeanor shifted dramatically. Up to that moment, he'd been warm and cordial. At that, his lips pursed and his eyes narrowed.

"Get out of my office. Now!" he barked.

Sabah left the office without another word.

No, there was no direct route to America. The fact that Mexico had not occurred to Sabah or any of his Chaldean friends, as a logical point of entry, was a monument to both their innocence and ignorance. Each step of their journey to America carried its own horizon. There was no second, third, or fourth step. There was only this step: *Get out of Iraq and this never ending nightmare. Go anywhere you can, however you can.*

Once you escaped from Iraq, there would be no road map, no street signs conveniently saying, "This way to America." Every rumor had to be followed, every avenue explored until, eventually, a door would open.

That door did open for Sabah, in the form of Fernando, a manager in the Mexican consulate. But not before Sabah had received word from Ramsey. Exactly as his friend had predicted, the call came two weeks after that fateful conversation in the café. It was late in the afternoon and Sabah was working with Jaqueline in the salon. She was busy taking care of a customer and Sabah answered the phone.

Jaqueline's intuition had already placed her in alert mode and she instantly picked up on Sabah's tone of voice. This was no customer calling to make an appointment. Sabah's body language and the animation in his voice suggested he was not only speaking with a friend, he was occupied in some extremely urgent business.

Sabah and Ramsey spoke only briefly, limiting themselves to essential facts only. Ramsey had made it. He was on the other side. He was in America and in Detroit. There was no time for long descriptions of first impressions, but Ramsey said this much, "It's bigger than we thought, in every way."

Sabah pressed for more but Ramsey was calling on his uncle's phone. He'd write later but at this moment, time and money were never more closely connected.

Ramsey had already given Sabah the guide's name and phone number before he'd left Greece. Now, he told Sabah he'd spoken with the guide. The guide, George, was expecting to hear from Sabah at any time.

"And Sabah," Ramsey said, "he told me to tell you that there's no guarantee. But he can get most people over and you don't pay until you get across. If you get across, it's six hundred dollars for the trip."

The possibility of not being able to get into America wasn't entirely surprising to Sabah. It was consistent with the other information he occasionally got wind of. His best guess was that there was a one in four chance he wouldn't make it into America, no matter what country he was trying to get in from. Solely based on rumor, hearsay, and word of mouth descriptions, this seemed to be the consistent failure rate. He hung up the phone realizing, only at that moment, what he would say to Jaqueline.

She'd finished with her client and wasted no time approaching Sabah.

"Who was it?" she asked, her tone casual, professional rather than personal.

Sabah rewound his entire conversation and his response to it. Was there anything he'd said or done, anything witnessed by Jaqueline, that would make the information he was about to give less than credible? Though he hadn't looked at her while he was speaking with Ramsey, he was certain she'd been looking at him.

After the micro-second review, Sabah met Jaqueline's questioning gaze and said quietly, "My father's sick."

"Oh, no," Jaqueline said, and he couldn't tell if she believed him or not. "Is it serious?"

"They're not sure but I need to go home for about a week."

What else could he have done? Should he have told her the truth? Is it possible that, sometimes, a lie can be an expression of love? Of course he didn't want to hurt her, but her pain was inevitable. He knew that. Was he simply sparing himself the unpleasant experience of witnessing that pain? Was it a self-serving lie, spoken by a young man who couldn't bear the suffering he was about to inflict on another human being?

Or was it a simple calculation? The possibility remained, even with

Ramsey's miracle guide, that Sabah may not make it to America. And then what? Return to Greece, having abandoned a woman who loved him for a country and dream he loved more than her? And a country, by the way, that she wasn't even particularly fond of? What kind of reception would Jaqueline give him then? Certainly not as cordial as a return from a sick father's bedside.

He did love her. But love wasn't enough. In that most treacherous maelstrom where love, duty, and honor converge, who can say which will ultimately prevail and which will not only be discarded, but thrown out by a violent, centrifugal force? At this moment duty was triumphant, but Sabah was no fool. His journey could still fail. So many things would have to go right and if only one thing went wrong, if the golden door to America did slam shut in his face, he could at least return to Greece and to a woman who still loved him.

What was wrong with that? Sabah thought of Rashid and their night in the police station. Rashid had lied because he was afraid. Sabah wondered, after all his rationalizing and effort not to burn bridges, if he was doing the same thing Rashid had done and for the same reason. Had he lied, finally, because he was afraid? Afraid of losing Jaqueline? He thought it over carefully.

No, Sabah decided. It wasn't fear. He hadn't lied because he was afraid of anything. He'd lied to protect as many people as he could, for as long as he could.

"When do you need to go?" Jaqueline asked, and her voice drew him out of his thoughts.

"Soon," Sabah said. "Within a few weeks."

He saw the concern on Jaqueline's face. She was as sensitive and intuitive as any woman is toward the man she loves. Did she suspect something else? Did she imagine what the truth might be? The front door of the shop opened and two more customers walked in. Sabah was grateful for the interruption.

"We'll talk later," Jaqueline said.

"Sure," Sabah said, and they walked away from each other, returning to the one thing both of them had built their lives on. They got back to work.

What Sabah hadn't expected to hear, in his conversation with Ramsey,

171

was the amount of the tour guide's fee. That, along with the plane ticket to Mexico City and all the additional expenses related to travel, was far more money than Sabah had saved in Greece.

The path had been clearly laid out now. He knew where he had to go and what he had to do. The dream was very close. It was probable that he could be in America within only a week or two from this exact moment. But now he didn't have the money.

Sabah pictured himself as one of those thoroughbred race horses, locked in the tight confinement of a starting gate. Ramsey had started the alarm bell that night in the café, when he'd shown Sabah his stamped passport. But a different bell had begun to ring now. It was the starting bell of a race. The gate had flown open and Sabah could see nothing but a wide open stretch straight ahead. All he had to do now was run. Instead, he was frozen in place, unable to move.

It would take at least a month or two, working at the salon, to save the minimum amount needed for the trip. Sabah lived without regret, but his mother's words came back to him at this moment: *"Sabah, you have a hole in your pocket."* Even now, Sabah had no concept of how to manage his money.

Just this week, hadn't he bought that suit he'd seen his first day in Greece? Hadn't he worn it when he'd met Sammy and Ahmad Murphy for dinner? Hole in his pocket or not, he knew why he'd bought that suit, along with the new black shoes and briefcase that matched it so well. Now, after his phone call with Ramsey, Sabah still didn't regret his purchase but he was struck by this coincidence. The cost of the suit, alone, was exactly the same as the guide's travel fee.

That night, he sat alone in the apartment he'd shared with Ramsey. It was true; since they'd moved there only a few months earlier, Sabah had been at Jaqueline's much more often than he'd been in this place. Even so, Sabah was struck by the emptiness of the room now that Ramsey was gone. He sat on one of the twin beds, looking at Ramsey's neatly made bed and wondering what he could do to earn the most amount of money in the least amount of time. If he needed to do it in the salon he would, but every day mattered right now. Also, he knew that the more time he spent with Jaqueline, the more uncomfortable things would get between them.

He thought about the dinner conversation with Sammy and Ahmad earlier that week. Like Ramsey and so many other Iraqis now living in Athens, Ahmad had been closely and constantly networking with this growing community while Sabah had been with Jaqueline, cloistered in his own little world of contentment. Ahmad was discouraged. At dinner, he'd shown his Iraqi passport to Sabah. It was expired. The Iraqi consulate in Athens had stopped renewing them. Saddam's icy grip extended wherever and however it could, even in Athens.

Ahmad said there were probably a hundred others just like him, in the same situation, living in Athens right now. Unable to renew their passports, they'd all become stranded on their journeys. They couldn't go forward. They couldn't go back.

"Well, I can think of worse deserted islands," Sabah had said flippantly.

"We're not like you, Sabah," Ahmad had answered tersely. " We only have one destination and it's not Greece."

Now, sitting in this neat, empty, and quiet room, Sabah thought about Ahmad's passport. That renewal stamp had looked so familiar.

Frowning, he stood up and went to a small cupboard in the space that served as a kitchen. He opened the cabinet door and moved a heavy pile of plates which had probably accumulated over a period of years, abandoned and added to by each successive tenant.

He pulled out a plastic bag and opened it. His passport was still there, along with a few other important items. He pulled out his passport and looked at it closely. It was still valid, and it held the same stamp as the one on Ahmad's. Where had he seen this emblem before? He turned over the contents of the plastic bag. A handful of memories spilled onto a small table. They were the only things he'd been able to bring through customs at the airport in Baghdad. He held up a few small photos of individual family members, his key from the Tokalon Salon, and some Iraqi currency, assorted dinar notes and change.

Sorting through the coins, Sabah picked one up and looked at it closely.

He froze, looked again, and then put the coin carefully down on the table. His mind filled with a dizzying rush of possibility. He knew that there were two things he would have to do the next day, and seeing Ahmad Murphy would be one of them.

First though, he would have to visit his new best friend, Fernando.

CHAPTER TWENTY-FOUR

★ ★ ★

The Birth Of A Businessman

★ ★ ★

One day, in the not so distant future, the office of the Mexican Consulate in Athens would be a very popular place. But that day had not yet arrived. Within Athens' entire Iraqi community, Ramsey had been the first to find Fernando. Sabah, armed with Ramsey's knowledge, was the second.

Always appropriately dressed for any occasion, Sabah walked into the consulate office wearing jeans and a T-shirt, standard student attire. In most consulates, the unique style, flavor, or character of any country tends to be obscured by that more international convention of bureaucracy. This was certainly true of the Mexican consulate.

It was a small, stark office, located on an unimportant and easily missed side street near the center of Athens. As he entered, Sabah noticed two upright flags placed on either side of a large old wooden desk. One was Greek, the other was the red, green, and white flag of Mexico. A black and white photo of a man, showing only his chest and face, was on the wall over the desk. The man in the photo had black hair and a moustache. He wore a suit and tie and was smiling.

At the sound of the office door, a man looked up from the desk. He wore reading glasses and had the first wisps of gray in his black hair. Sabah guessed he was Fernando. He didn't know for sure and it didn't matter. For most young men in the same circumstances, some nervousness might have been expected. The first thing the man saw when he looked at Sabah, however, was a full, perfectly natural smile.

"Amigo!" Sabah exclaimed as he walked to the desk and extended his hand. It was the only Spanish word Sabah knew, but he said it with gusto.

"Buenos dias," the consulate answered, feeling the firm grasp of Sabah's handshake. The consulate paused and looked at Sabah more closely. He wasn't Greek and he wasn't Mexican. What was he?

"You speak Spanish?" the consulate asked in English.

"No," Sabah said.

"English?"

"Yes, more English. You're Fernando, right?"

"Yes, and you are?"

"Sabah. Sabah Toma. My friend Ramsey told me to talk to you,"

"Ramsey, Ramsey … Oh, the Chaldean guy!"

"You got it!" Sabah said, his smile even brighter now.

"I remember. He was going to Mexico City, to study."

"Exactly."

"And you? You're a student too?"

"Absolutely, I'm gonna join him. With your help, of course."

Fernando looked at Sabah a little more closely before he spoke again. "How come you guys are going to Mexico? Seems pretty far from home doesn't it?"

Sabah didn't discern a lack of trust in Fernando's voice. This was innocent curiosity, not a cross examination. Even so, Sabah felt an instinctive need to supplement his story.

"Oh yeah, but Mexico! I mean, cowboys, Indians, horses, Pancho Villa! 'We don't need no stinking badges.' I mean, we gotta see all *that*, right?"

Fernando smiled and looked at Sabah quizzically, disarmed by the young man's enthusiasm as much as his unique aptitude for blending fact and fiction. He suddenly had an image of this crazy middle eastern kid riding full gallop on a white horse through the middle of the Sonoran Desert, wearing a ten-gallon hat, full leather chaps, and silver spurs, probably firing off two hands guns at the same time.

"Sounds good to me." Fernando smiled. "You need to fill out this form."

"No problem, I love forms."

Sabah was leaning over to fill out the form when Fernando asked, "How many passports you need stamped?"

Sabah looked up, completely unprepared for the question. How *many* passports? Was this man actually saying that Sabah could get more than one passport stamped? Sabah thought carefully but knew he couldn't take too long to answer.

For the second time in less than twenty-four hours, Sabah was seized by the vision of an insanely profitable venture. Never in his life had he seen so clearly, easily, and quickly how to make so much money. And it had happened not once, but twice within a single day.

"How many can you do?" he asked at last.

"Well, not *too* many," Fernando said.

"Is six too much?"

Fernando thought about it for a minute. "No, I don't think so. I think six is okay. But, you know, for six I may need a little something extra."

Just like that, they were in the middle of a negotiation, and Sabah was completely ready for it. "You mean, with mine included, as part of the six?"

"No, yours is done. I mean six more, extra."

"What did you have in mind?"

"Well, I probably know less about Iraq than you do Mexico," Fernando began, smiling. "I hear you got nice carpets there. Anyway, my wife says so. She loves them. Persian carpets?"

"Right," Sabah said, knowing full well that Fernando was talking about a product of Iran, not Iraq. Still, Iraq was no slouch in this department. It didn't matter, anyway. Sabah was already thinking three steps ahead.

"Anyway, she's got a few of them but we have this hallway in our house, about three feet by ten feet, perfect for a long carpet but we can't get one anywhere. Maybe if you asked your family for one, you know, had it sent here, maybe that would be a fair exchange?"

"Fernando, I don't believe this. I swear to you, I have one. Just like that. I brought it from home."

Fernando gave him a disbelieving look. "Are you serious?"

"Yes, for sure! It belonged to the father of my father, but looks perfect. Doesn't look a week old."

"Sabah Toma, you bring that carpet and you've got six passports. They'll be stamped, no problem."

Sabah left the consulate's office and immediately went to one of his favorite bazaars, a place he and Jaqueline would sometimes go on weekends. They both liked to rummage through secondhand and antique stores, searching for odd little treasures. He knew exactly where he was going but it had been several weeks. He wasn't sure it would still be there. When he saw it, he let out a deep sigh of relief. There, completely unfurled, the carpet was hanging by its full length outside the shop window.

He inspected it closely. The carpet looked Persian to Sabah but what did he know? Satisfied that it would do the job, he purchased it with nearly everything he had left, almost a hundred dollars. Before it was rolled up and placed in a bag, Sabah asked a small favor. With a pair of scissors provided by the shopkeeper, he removed a small tag on the back of the carpet, a tag that read, "Made In China."

Later that night Sabah and Ahmad Murphy sat at the small table in Sabah's apartment.

"Of course I know who they are and where they are," Ahmad said, rather impatiently. "I see them every day."

Sabah had invited him over to discuss "a business idea," but so far he'd only been asking questions without offering any information.

"So, what's up?" Ahmad demanded.

Sabah silently took a coin out of his pocket. He slapped it on the table and continued gazing at Ahmad with his frozen grin. Ahmad looked at the coin, then back at Sabah.

"What? You wanna flip for something?"

"Look at it," Sabah said.

Ahmad picked up the coin, thinking it might be some rare collector's item. In seconds he realized that it was just a common coin from Iraq, probably one of those made by the Hussein family.

"Okay, a worthless coin made by a worthless idiot. So what?"

Sabah said nothing. He put his passport on the table and held it open with one hand. With his other hand, he took the coin and placed it next to the green, official Iraqi validation stamp. Ahmad leaned in closer, then closer still. His eyes widened.

"I don't believe this," he said, his voice barely above a whisper.

"Believe it, my friend," Sabah said.

Ahmad looked up, his mouth wide open. The images on the passport stamp and the coin were identical.

"We need a green ink pad," Ahmad said.

"Way ahead of you, buddy." Sabah opened a little metal box which, up to that moment, had been sitting unnoticed on the table. "Did you bring your passport?"

"Right here," Ahmad said and placed it on the table.

As carefully as he could, Sabah pressed the coin on the green ink pad, lifted it, and then slowly pressed it onto Ahmad's open passport. He held it there a moment then carefully lifted the coin. If they'd entered a contest measuring surprise, it would have been a tie. Neither could believe what he saw. It was perfect, a completely identical reproduction of the passport validation stamp.

Ahmad reached for his passport and was about to pick it up when Sabah stopped him.

"Wait," Sabah said. He took two more items from a small paper sack. Ahmad watched as Sabah produced two wooden handled rubber stamps and a second ink pad, this one black. By this time Ahmad was convinced he was watching a magician, some master of prestidigitation.

One rubber stamp featured rotating sequences of numbers and months so it could be adjusted to any date. The other stamp only had a single straight line. Within seconds Sabah had adjusted the date stamp and freshly inked both rubber stamps. One at a time, he pressed them carefully down, right next to the green coin stamp he'd just imprinted. Then he held it up the finished product for Ahmad's inspection.

Ahmad took the passport, his amazement mounting by the moment. It looked exactly like the validation seal and dates stamped at an actual Iraqi passport office.

"Sabah, are you sure nobody's gonna know?"

"Who's gonna know? Some cop at the airport? How's he gonna know who signed this? Even if he could read Arabic, how's he gonna know?"

Ahmad thought about it for a second. It all made perfect sense.

"Here, *I'll* sign it!" Sabah said, taking the passport back. He spoke the words out loud as he wrote them in Arabic. "Colonel Warthog. There you go. Easy."

He handed the passport back to Ahmad with a deadpan expression.

The whole thing was just too absurd and Ahmad let out a loud burst of laughter.

"My friend, we are in the passport business," Sabah said, "And speaking of passports, you wanna go to Mexico? This week?"

This time it was Sabah who burst out laughing, at the expression on Ahmad's face. He looked like he didn't know his top from his bottom.

"Come on, let's go find some Chaldeans," Sabah said. "You know where they'll be right now, right?"

"Sure," Ahmad said.

"Well, let's go! We're gonna be very popular tonight."

Ahmad knew the going rate for all black market documents related to international travel. A reasonable price for an updated passport was a hundred and fifty, but a stamped visa, that was something else entirely. If you could get a visa stamped at all, you were looking at around a thousand dollars.

Sabah knew that as soon as he submitted the six passports to Fernando, the word would get out. Fernando's life, at least as far his obscure little office was concerned, would be changing radically and quickly. If it ended up being for the worse, Sabah would be sorry to hear that. But perhaps it would be for the better. Perhaps there were plenty of other things Fernando's wife wanted.

In any event, by the time Iraqis started lining up around the block to see Fernando, Sabah would be in another hemisphere, perhaps even in America. The experience with Fernando taught Sabah a very important lesson, one that would serve him well in America. Now he understood the role knowledge played in commerce and profit. Knowledge wasn't just power; it was money.

In less than three hours, Ahmad and Sabah had collected four passports. Each one came with five hundred dollars cash. The holders were promised that their passports would be returned the next day, stamped with a visa to Mexico. In the meantime, over the next few days, Sabah and Ahmad collected at least seventy other expired passports which would be renewed at fifty dollars each.

Sabah didn't tell anyone, including Ahmad, how he would get the visas stamped. For his assistance in taking Sabah to those people who could afford five hundred dollars for this service, Sabah didn't charge Ahmad for his own visa. Even for Sabah, it was a generous gesture. Five hundred dollars was, after all, a lot of money. Despite this, there would be one more person Sabah wouldn't charge.

For the next several days, Sabah and Ahmad converted Sabah's apartment into a small factory. It was a rustic place with one of those old fashioned toilets, the kind with the water tank high up on the wall. It had a dangling chain. Each time they "renewed" another passport, Ahmad would pull the chain and the toilet would flush.

"There goes another one," he would say, and Sabah would laugh every time.

Sabah took special pleasure in signing the names of the Iraqi authorities and would speak each one out loud as he wrote it, laughing together with Ahmad.

"General Snotnose."

"Perfect," Ahmad would say.

"Captain Brownshorts," and on it went until Sabah and Ahmad had collected and "processed" over seventy outdated passports. Within a week, Sabah's combined earnings from visa sales and passport updating was well over three thousand dollars. Ahmad didn't do so badly either, earning over two thousand. Everyone was happy, including Fernando, who thought his carpet had once been in the Shah's palace.

Sabah had purchased his ticket to Mexico City and had plenty of extra cash to pay the tour guide. There was nothing left to do now but go. His last evening in Athens, Sabah stopped by Sammy's apartment.

"Well, this is it," Sabah said.

Sammy nodded and for a moment they looked at each other. This had been the first face Sabah had seen in a strange new world. This had been the first home he'd had in that world. This was the only family he'd known for the past eight months. Sabah handed Sammy his passport.

"Why'd you want that, anyway?" Sammy asked.

"Look at it," Sabah said.

Sammy opened it up and saw the visa stamp. He looked back up at Sabah.

"You can go to Mexico any time you want," Sabah said. "You have it, if you want it."

The cousins looked at each other, then embraced and kissed each other's cheeks. It was likely they would never meet again. If they did meet again, in America, their lives would have changed as much as the world around them. Sabah left his cousin and took a taxi to Jaqueline's home by the sea.

It was late February and the winter nights were still cold in Athens, cold enough for the bonfire to feel better than it ever had. Sabah and Jaqueline sat close to each other in their beach chairs, quietly watching the flames. They didn't speak much that final night. Perhaps, Sabah thought, she knew the truth. Either way, he wasn't with her now because of any sense of duty, and certainly not because of guilt. He was with her because she'd been the most important and unexpected part of his journey through Greece. It was a journey he'd very nearly ended, all because of her.

He knew he would miss as much as his own mother and father, though he underestimated his feelings in this regard. He had no idea how much he would miss her, nor the unfortunate circumstances that would make his longing for her all the more poignant. He only knew this much: he was sitting next to a beautiful woman who loved him, and a woman he loved. A woman who would have shared her life with him and with whom he would have shared his own. And only God knew how long it would be before he would find that again.

CHAPTER TWENTY-FIVE

★ ★ ★

The Saint And the Spy

★ ★ ★

George Tajirian was one of only three people on the 1968 Iraqi Olympic Team. He was, perhaps, the greatest cyclist in the history of his country. In 1998 he would be indicted by the U.S. Justice Department for heading a global smuggling network responsible for bringing hundreds, if not thousands, of illegal aliens into the United States.

"This is a big step forward for our crackdown on alien smuggling," then U.S. Attorney General Janet Reno would say.

Was he a mercenary, aiding and abetting terrorists? Was he knowingly bringing enemies of America into a country on the cusp of a frenzied preoccupation with national security? Perhaps many would think so, but Sabah would never be one of them. Neither as the young man who first came to America, or the mature, established citizen he was to become. For Sabah Toma, George Tajirian always was, and always would be, one of the greatest men he'd ever known.

As fate would have it, two of the people who had paid Sabah for the Mexican visas were ready to leave as quickly as Sabah was. Fayez and Sam, also Chaldean and around Sabah's age, were on the same flight to Mexico City. Sabah called George a second time to ask him if two others could be included in the travel plans.

In making this request, Sabah was slightly anxious. He didn't know the repercussions of what might be an important last minute change of plan. But Sabah needn't have been concerned. George's nonchalance was equal to Sabah's nervousness. Sure, George said; no problem. For George, there never seemed to be a problem with anything. In fact, to Sabah, it seemed like he didn't even know what the word meant.

For this reason, more than any other, Sabah was surprised into silence during their dinner on the night of arrival.

As he'd promised, George was at the airport to greet them. He was the same height as Sabah but about ten years older, thirty-two or thirty-three perhaps. The seven years since his appearance at the Olympics had done little to diminish his fitness level. His body was still perfectly lean and his muscles were clearly defined. But it was his bearing that exuded strength, more than his body. There was something about the man that made Sabah feel, instantly, that everything was under control.

He had a friendly face with a strong, square chin. George had a mild case of amblyopia. One of his eyes veered, just slightly, off center. Sabah couldn't tell if the appeal of this man's face was diminished or offset by this peculiar eye. Was it this slight imperfection that made George so approachable and accessible? Or was it George's self-assuredness and confidence, his obliviousness of his imperfection, that generated instant affection? Either way, he was a man in charge and he was exactly who Sabah needed him to be.

Life poured out of the man. He seemed more excited to see Sabah and his traveling companions than they were to see him. How could this be? Sabah was nearly at the doorway of America. The collective anticipation of ten thousand children on Christmas morning might approach Sabah's excitement at this moment. In George's world, his own sense of mission matched Sabah's. Sabah and George were perfectly synchronized by an intensity of purpose.

A pretty young hostess guided the group to one of the restaurant tables. She handed them menus, smiled, and walked away. The group watched her go. George waited a moment then looked at Sabah.

"You wanna be with her?" George asked Sabah as he placed his napkin over his lap.

All three young men stared at George, not quite believing what they'd just heard. Instead of waiting for a reply, George just picked up his menu and glanced at it.

"She likes you," George added. "I think you should be with her. Tonight."

Taking advantage of George's momentary preoccupation with the menu, Sabah, Fayez, and Sam shared a private and bemused glance.

"Try the chalupas," George continued. "Unbelievable."

Both suggestions had been made in the same extemporaneous, offhanded way, as though neither was of greater importance or interest to George than the other.

They were on their third pitcher of margaritas, a completely new drink for Sabah and one, he was finding, that went down as easily as water. The food arrived and Sabah tried his chalupa. In high spirits, the group laughed easily as they ate.

A little later, George's tone became more serious. "I only wanted two things. I wanted to be the best bike rider in Iraq. I did that. Now, I want to get the Christians out of the Muslim countries. That's all. What kind of life did we have back there, huh? Any of us? Even me? Don't answer that. We all know. We know. Millions of them, still back there. Gotta get them out, get them to America. Got to."

George's voice trailed off and a silence fell over the group. For a moment, the dinner had become an impromptu commemoration. Then George spoke again, "But, hey, *we* made it! That's the first step, right?"

"Almost made it, anyway." Fayez said, lifting his margarita glass in a mock toast. "Fayez, if George says you made it, you made it," Sabah said.

"He hasn't even told us what he's charging us yet," Fayez said.

"*I* told you! Six hundred dollars. That's what he charges."

"Seems like a lot of money to me," Fayez grumbled.

"Me, too," Sam chimed in.

"Son, look at me," George said, fully present again and deadly serious. When both Fayez and Sam had given him their attention, he jabbed a finger at them. "You're not goin' to the United States with me. Neither of you. As of right now, you're on your own. I wouldn't care if you each gave me six *thousand* dollars. How are you gonna get into America, huh? You figure it out."

George stood up, wiped his mouth, and dropped his napkin on the table. "Sabah, I'll see you in the morning."

Without another word, he left the restaurant. Sabah, Fayez, and Sam sat in silence, momentarily stunned. After several seconds, Sabah looked at his traveling companions.

"You guys messed up, big time," he said.

Fayez shook his head. "So, now what do we do?"

"He told you. You're on your own! I asked him if I could bring you. He was doing me a *favor*. Don't you get it? Six hundred is nothing, nothing! To get to *America*? Like he said, you figure it out."

Sabah's journey so far had been marked by visits to so many governmental offices he'd become completely desensitized to the importance of one over another. The morning after his arrival in Mexico City, George took Sabah to yet another small, nondescript office. At George's instruction, Sabah kept his mouth shut and sat down in a corner of the room. George took Sabah's passport to a man seated behind a window pane in an even smaller inner office.

The two men greeted each other with a warmth and familiarity that Sabah found encouraging. He expected the meeting to take longer than it did. It was over in minutes. The man in the small office looked at Sabah only once as he was speaking with George, then back at Sabah's passport. He stamped it and handed it back to George. The two men shared a smile and handshake. Then George left the man's office and returned to Sabah.

"It's a transit visa," George said.

"What's that?"

"It means you can only be in the United States for three days, traveling through America to get to another country."

George saw the confusion and concern on Sabah's face.

"Don't worry about it," he added. "They all start this way."

Sabah quickly noticed that George seemed to know a lot of people. Wherever they went, George knew everyone and everyone knew George. From taxi drivers to airport porters, airline ticket agents, and even the attendants at shoeshine or newspaper stands, these people not only knew George, they were delighted to see him, as though his mere appearance was the highlight of their day. Sabah was beginning to feel like he was the personal friend of a celebrity.

Armed with snippets of conversation between George and the people they passed, as well as the few bits of information George directly provided, Sabah began cobbling together a clearer vision of his guide. Sabah realized that he was the traveling companion of an international man of mystery. This was a person who lived in a shadow world of plots, schemes, and intrigue. He was the first person Sabah had ever met who spoke seven languages fluently. For Sabah, George was becoming a real life combination of James Bond and Humphrey Bogart.

Within twenty-four hours, George could and would be anywhere in the world, responding to whatever dire circumstances he alone could remedy. Much of his life was unpredictable and unplanned. At the same time, Sabah had the impression that there were certain well-worn paths in George's world.

How many times had George done precisely what Sabah was doing with him today? How many times had he gone through this particular gate, at this particular airport, past these particular people? Dozens or hundreds perhaps?

Sabah had no idea, but his increasing sense that it was *his* turn, his time for the grand adventure, was somehow humbling. His gratitude was actually growing. Here he was, under the security and protection of a man whose self-appointed mission was to save every Chaldean in the world. And he was doing it in a cloaked network of secrecy that the CIA would be proud of. To Sabah, George was a saint and a spy. More than that, he was the best parts of both.

Even on the jet from Mexico City to Tijuana, Sabah had trouble grasping the idea that, before the end of the day, he would be in America. Looking out his window as they descended into Tijuana International Airport, Sabah's feelings and thoughts could not coalesce into speech. So much was raging inside him, the imminent fulfillment of so much hope, the realization of a dream older than his memories.

George glanced at Sabah. He'd seen it before, many times. George understood what the moment meant to Sabah and so he, too, remained silent.

A while later, they were driving in a taxi toward the border. Sabah was staring out the window, thinking that their surroundings were not completely unlike parts of Baghdad. Half-constructed concrete buildings left unfinished for years, if not decades, were strewn among shacks made of plywood and corrugated metal. A pile of tires here, a street peddler there. If anything, this urban landscape was a bit more industrialized and modern than many areas of his hometown.

"How far are we?" Sabah asked.

"Close," George said. "A mile or two."

"America looks like this?" Sabah asked.

George smiled. "You'll see."

The taxi pulled up to a small shop not far from the border. Sabah saw red letters painted on the window that read "Sastreria - Ropa Para Hombre." And here was another one of those people. The building was a men's clothing shop and an older man, portly but well-groomed, was approaching them. He was probably the owner. He greeted George with the familiarity of a family member. The two men embraced and he patted George on the back.

Sabah had no idea why they were here. In their very brief time together, he had already learned not to ask any questions related to George's choices or decisions. It would be like questioning a hurricane, lightning bolt, or any other unstoppable force of nature. Though he'd never experienced it, Sabah imagined that being with George was something like white water rafting; you just hung on for the ride.

In moments, the shop owner was holding up a red blazer. Sabah turned and placed an arm in each sleeve. The man certainly knew his customers. With nothing more than a glance, the shop owner had selected a jacket that felt like it was custom made for Sabah. Next, the tailor lifted a pair of white slacks off a hanger and handed them to Sabah, along with a white polo shirt. He gestured toward a curtain and small dressing room. The pants and shirt fit as well as the jacket. Sabah looked at himself in the mirror. They weren't his style, exactly. Not at all, actually. In fact, it looked more like a costume than clothing, but whatever, Sabah thought. If this was how they dressed in America, he would wear just about anything.

Sabah emerged from his dressing closet and noticed that George had changed also. He was wearing an outfit exactly the same as Sabah's. The whole thing was peculiar and a little funny. Again, Sabah had no idea what it meant but asked no questions, particularly since George was so involved in his conversation with the shop owner.

Finally, the tailor went to a shelf and pulled down a brown cardboard box. He set the box on a table beside George and Sabah. The box was filled with a hundred or more circular patches. They were all identical, about four inches in diameter. Sabah, who had an unfailing eye for quality in anything, could immediately see how carefully these patches had been made. Each one was intricately woven and accented in vivid shades of gold and blue thread. In the middle of each patch was the silhouette of a man on a racing bike. Encircling this image were the English words "International Racing Team."

Almost in the same amount of time it took Sabah to inspect one of these patches, the tailor had sewn one on Sabah's jacket. From their arrival, George and the tailor had been speaking in Spanish. Sabah couldn't understand a word they were saying, but he could tell now, by their long handshake and second embrace, that he and George were nearing the end of their time in this man's shop. Sabah stepped back toward the dressing room to change into his own clothes and was about to draw the curtain when he heard George's voice.

"Sabah, no. Keep them on. And put the jacket on, too."

Sabah had no idea how close to the border he was. They didn't need a taxi now. As they walked, luggage in hand, George pointed to a large, curved, tan-colored object several blocks away. Perhaps he wanted to reassure Sabah that he wouldn't have to carry his large suitcase too much farther. It hardly mattered. Sabah would have gladly carried the suitcase a hundred miles.

Sabah looked where George was pointing. He couldn't tell if it was a building, bridge, or both.

"You see that?" George said.

"Yes …"

"The other side of that is America."

As they drew nearer to the building, they passed a long line of people, stretching back for several blocks. When they reached the building, Sabah and George passed through an outside gate and turnstile. Sabah could feel its heavy weight as he pushed the spinning gate. The paint on its handles was worn smooth and thin by countless hands and revolutions. Then they were inside, walking through a clean, modern, well-maintained building. Everything about the place seemed orderly, logical, and efficient.

The line of people continued within the building, and it seemed, for the most part, to be comprised of Mexicans. Sabah noticed some lighter skinned people, even some people with blonde hair. They didn't appear to be dressed in the same way, exactly, though he and George were walking by them so quickly that it was difficult for him to identify the differences clearly.

These must be Americans, Sabah thought. They were very close now.

Sabah saw the single line they had been walking past scatter and spread into a dozen separate lines, each filing past a uniformed man or woman seated at a desk. George walked straight toward a desk on the extreme left fringe of the room. Sabah wondered if there was even anyone at this desk as there was no line of people leading to it. As he spoke, George's eyes were fixed on this desk.

"Remember, do not say *anything*."

Sabah took George so literally that he didn't even answer.

George glanced at him, making sure he'd heard him. "Understand?"

"Yes," Sabah said, even as he noticed one of the uniformed men moving toward them.

"Good afternoon, officer," George said. He was absolutely calm.

"Passports," the officer said.

George handed the officer passports for Sabah and himself. The officer opened them, then gave a quick but careful glance at both George and Sabah.

"This is a transit visa," the man said.

"Right. We're going to L.A. We're taking a flight to New York. Then to Paris."

Sabah noticed that the man had been glancing at their jackets and embroidered patches as George was giving him this information.

"We're with a racing team. He's my manager," George said. Sabah understood English just well enough to feel weak in his knees, though he kept his gaze and smile steady.

"Racing team?" the man said.

"Yes. I'm George Tajirian."

"Who?"

"George Tajirian. Professional cyclist."

Sabah could tell that the border agent was having a little difficulty processing this. George immediately came to his assistance.

"Here, look." George pulled a folded newspaper out of his suitcase. The newspaper was dog-eared, worn down by age and travel. George opened the paper and showed the agent a large photograph of two people. One of the people was George. The other person was an older man in a suit and tie. He had a ski nose and dark hair slickly combed back, revealing a receding hairline. The border agent looked back and forth between the photo and George at least two or three times before he directed George to a small office immediately adjacent to his desk.

Sabah didn't go into the office but, through a glass wall, he could see George enter it and show the same newspaper photo to another agent seated at a desk. This was all too familiar to Sabah. The questions, the scrutiny, the passing by one person of authority to another person of higher authority. It was what Sabah had expected. Even if these were Americans, his old fear of the law, however it was dressed, would always be there.

Suddenly, Sabah saw George and the agent in the room laughing together and his heart skipped a beat. George left the room smiling and, at a simple gesture from the second border agent in the small office, the first agent let them pass.

They stepped past the officer—and just like that, Sabah was in America.

"You said the transit visa was enough," Sabah said in an undertone. "Why did you say I was your manager? And what was the newspaper for?"

They were still inside the customs building but quickly approaching the exit.

George stopped and Sabah stopped with him. "Sabah, when it comes to getting into America and, more importantly, *staying* in America, everything helps. You understand? Look." George opened the newspaper again and showed Sabah the photo. "You know who that guy is?"

"No."

"That's Richard Nixon,"

"Who's that?" Sabah asked.

"Well, among other things, he use to be President of the United States. That's me and him! My buddy, right? You got it now? You gotta blow smoke up their behind, Sabah. That's how it works. Everywhere. America included."

With that thought in mind, Sabah stepped out of the customs building and onto the firm soil of the United States.

CHAPTER TWENTY-SIX

★ ★ ★

Phantasmagoria

★ ★ ★

For Sabah, Athens had been a giant step sideways. It was different than Baghdad, but in the ancient roots of its architecture and the convoluted corridors that passed as city streets, a feeling of familiarity reverberated in Sabah. In a relatively short time, he'd assimilated his new surroundings. The moment he walked out of the U.S. Customs building in San Ysidro, however, he was engulfed by an entirely new experience. None of the photographs he'd seen, nothing he'd imagined, had remotely prepared him for his first day in America.

If Sabah's eyes had been a camera, able to freeze frame a single moment, a thousand components within that frame would have been unrecognizable and incomprehensible. His eyes couldn't fix on anything because he was anything but stationary. The simple task of walking meant that one entire world was being replaced by another with almost every step. Every moment, the frame was changing. His head veered and tilted to the left, right, up, down as he desperately tried to categorize every element in this new world.

George guided them directly to a Greyhound bus, which departed almost as soon as they boarded. With a whoosh of the hydraulic brakes being released, the bus began to roll. Within minutes, Sabah was experiencing one of Southern California's chief contributions to Western Civilization, the freeway.

Everything was fast in America. Getting a bus was fast. The bus itself was fast. All the other cars around the bus were even faster than the bus. And those cars—how could there be so many of them and so many *kinds*?

191

There were big ones, small ones, cars in all shapes and colors. Where did they all come from? Sabah didn't know how many people lived in America but he was sure every one of them had a car.

Then there was the road itself; that was the strangest thing of all. It was wide, big, clean, smooth, and went on forever. Sabah tried to count how many lanes there were. Ten or more? He wasn't sure. He wondered how so many buses, cars, and trucks could all be together in the same place, moving so fast, without one massive collision after the next. Throughout their three and half hour ride to Los Angeles, Sabah was sure the bus he was on would be involved in one of those pileups at any second.

He noticed signs constantly appearing overhead or on the sides of this road. They were all the same shade of green. Each sign had words with white letters and numbers. As he studied these signs, Sabah soon deciphered a pattern. The same words would appear multiple times but, with each new sign, a different number would appear next to the word. It was like a countdown because each new number would be less than the one before.

"Why do the numbers get smaller?" Sabah asked. George looked confused by the question, so Sabah clarified. "On the green signs."

"Oh, it means the number of miles left before you reach that particular street."

So *that* was how they did it, Sabah thought to himself. They'd been traveling almost two hours and he hadn't seen an accident yet. Even though Americans drove at speeds that defied common sense, they could plan how they got off this road. Aided by the green signs, they could perform an exit maneuver without killing themselves, or anyone else. It was all so … organized.

"Who thought of that?" Sabah asked.

"I don't know," George said. "Ralph Freeway, who knows?"

"Who's that?"

"It's a joke. Sorry. We're on a freeway."

Sabah looked at George, not grasping the concept.

"The thing we're moving on. The road. It's called a freeway."

A freeway, Sabah thought. So that's what this was called. It was, by far, the best road Sabah had ever been on and there weren't even tolls. Sabah had expected nothing less in America, the home of the free. But wait;

didn't the word "free" mean two things in English? It meant not having to pay, but it also meant freedom. It was a free-way for a free country. The symmetry, the sheer poetry of it, was almost overwhelming. Now it was all making sense. Sabah gazed out his window, his amazement growing each moment.

Finally, Sabah saw a major structure that was vaguely recognizable. It was also completely illogical. They'd traveled over a hundred miles, through an utterly alien landscape, but this was the most bizarre sight of all. There, just to the side of the freeway, jutting above orange trees and roof tops, was a miniature alpine peak covered in snow. *Was* it a structure, or was it an optical illusion? Or had his sense of perspective somehow malfunctioned? Was this mountain less than a mile away or was it a hundred miles?

He stared at it until he was sure. No, it was as tiny as it looked. Sabah's view of America from his bus window had been nothing short of kaleidoscopic mayhem until now, but this totally defied logic. Without turning his eyes away, he quickly nudged George and asked him what it was.

"Disneyland," George said casually.

Disneyland, Sabah thought, allowing the word to reach the center of his consciousness. He was gripped in a sudden stillness, as though standing beneath the Bodhi tree. Covered in goosebumps, he surrendered to the revelation. With his own eyes, he was seeing the highest expression of America, a symbol and microcosm of the dream world he'd entered only hours before. At this moment, he was passing the best of the best. He was *looking* at Disneyland!

Soon, another massive shape began to dominate the constantly shifting landscape. Whatever it was, it was big, like those other, real snow-capped mountains George had pointed out earlier. The mountains had another one of those Spanish names. Sabah wondered, if they were in America why did everything have a Spanish name? He was sure they spoke English here, but the green freeway signs were always El something or San this or Los that.

What was it George called them? The San Bernardino Mountains? He'd pointed them out, saying they were sixty miles away. Sabah had nodded numbly and said nothing. He had rarely seen real, snow-covered mountains. They would have been novel and noteworthy if they weren't one of a thousand other things he'd never seen before in just the last two hours. And now this.

They had to be buildings. What else could they be? In the far distance, perhaps five miles away or more, Sabah was looking at tall, slender blocks of varying heights and widths, all clumped together in one place. This wasn't like the rest of this endless city. Intuitively, Sabah sensed that it must be something like the center of Los Angeles. It looked like that city where the wizard was. What was that city? The Wizard of …?

OZ. That was it. He was looking at OZ. How was it possible? How could there be buildings like these? What kind of people could be in them and what could they be doing?

It wasn't the buildings themselves that continued to pummel Sabah's reason. It was what they suggested. During this entire bus trip, Sabah had been engaged in an unconscious process. He'd not only been looking at America, he'd been looking *for* America. What was that thing he would see that would explain it all to him, the one vision that would unveil this sacred place and unfold its mysteries? The answers to these questions were undiscovered, but now, in a moment something like a sunrise, Sabah sensed that an answer was close.

What had appeared, from a distance, as a gray and black silhouette of enormous block towers had become a vast three-dimensional cluster of shimmering steel and glass. What was this place?

This was knowledge, Sabah thought. This was inconceivable technology and industry. It was efficiency and power on an unimaginable scale. The world, as Sabah had known and understood it, was connected to and built out of the past. The past was constantly present and vice versa. The two were woven together, inextricable components of one world and one reality.

Within minutes, that reality, established and taken for granted over the course of an entire lifetime, had collapsed. It was replaced by a completely new paradigm. There was no history here. There was no past. There was only one eternal present. Sabah saw the present, in America, as a raging river. You couldn't fight it. You could either swim with it or you could drown. As for the future, there was none.

In America, the future was now. These were the final ruminations of an exhausted mind as the bus pulled into downtown Los Angeles.

As it had been in Athens, so it was in Los Angeles. Another horizon had been reached, another threshold crossed. Just like Greece, Sabah's all-consuming goal of reaching America had prevented him from planning what he would do once he got there. Now he was here and he had no idea what his next step would be. These circumstances might have created some anxiousness in most immigrants, or even most tourists. After all, our innate human need for structure, direction, and purpose tends to produce a certain amount of anxiety in the absence of all three.

In spite of not knowing what he would do in the next five minutes, let alone the next five years, Sabah was filled with an inexplicable sense of well-being and peace. His mission was clear: stay in America, work in America, bring his family to America. But how that mission would be accomplished was a complete mystery. He did know this much. He had not come to America to take anything but to earn everything. Only one thing mattered and this one thing was everything.

He was in America and no one was going to make him leave.

In a still and untouchable region of his heart, Sabah knew that everything would be all right. He knew this for two reasons, which were tightly woven together in the fabric of his soul. He knew it because he was Sabah and he knew it because he was in America. Even now, his belief in himself had merged with his belief in America. There could no longer be one without the other. His new reality was this: America was Sabah and Sabah was America.

Sabah did have one contact in Los Angeles, an old friend and co-worker of his father. There was also a vague hope that he might enroll in a beauty school and acquire a student visa. Sabah was preoccupying himself with these practical details when the taxi he and George were in pulled up to a small bungalow in the Silver Lake section of Los Angeles, a neighborhood just a few miles north of downtown.

George had said they were going to a relative's house. That was about as much as George said on any subject and Sabah never asked for additional information. Though Sabah wasn't aware of it, the fact that the home was a mile from the "Little Armenia" section of the city was no coincidence. The Tajirians were of Armenian descent and George's relative was an active member of this tight-knit community. Sabah also couldn't have known that, of the hundreds of immigrants and refugees George had already brought into Los Angeles, Sabah would be the first to be taken to his relative's home.

In taking him here, George was both honoring Sabah and demonstrating trust in him. The truth was that George liked Sabah. George knew that, because of his schedule, his own time would be very limited in Los Angeles. He wanted to give Sabah every benefit he could and this included the hospitality of his own family.

As the taxi pulled up in front of the home, Sabah saw the screen door open. A woman stepped outside and stood with her back to the door, holding it open. She might have been in her late thirties, close to forty. She was dressed conservatively in black slacks and a plain blouse. Her hair was pulled back in a bun. She seemed to be studying her visitors more than looking at them. She stood perfectly still, wiping her hands with a dish towel, as George and Sabah approached.

"He's a young one," were the first words she said.

George didn't respond but kissed the woman on the cheek and said, "Linda, say hello to Sabah. Sabah, this is Linda."

The woman simply took a step back, opening the screen door a bit wider, and said, "Come in."

"Are the girls here?" George asked.

"They're out, but they'll be here for dinner."

Linda had two teenaged daughters. The girls arrived just as Linda was placing the dinner on the table. George and Sabah had already sat down. To Sabah, the girls seemed even younger than their years. They both had a self-conscious silliness about them which Sabah found both surprising and unappealing. He breathed a small sigh of relief. These girls would require no energy on his part. He wouldn't need to pretend he wasn't attracted to them. Sabah ate his dinner quietly.

George and Linda spent most of the dinner speaking in Hayeren, their native Armenian language. Judging from the occasional strained tones of the conversation, there seemed to be a disagreement on something, but Sabah had no idea what it might be.

When it came to matters of his work, George was a person who offered information on a need-to-know basis. Sabah had no way of knowing that

George had brought this woman and her then-toddler daughters into America. Nor could he have known that, over many years, George had helped all of them eventually gain citizenship.

Sabah would never know why he saw what he saw on his first day in America. Was Linda orthodox, conventional, and traditional? Was she worried about reputations, her own and her daughters? Did George find these qualities in any person, even a relative, despicable and repulsive? Sabah would never know.

He slept on a couch in the home's small living room and woke to the sound of raised voices in the kitchen. He lifted his blanket and pulled on his pants and shirt. He walked softly to a doorway next to the kitchen. The door was open slightly, and he could hear the voices within clearly.

"I don't care what you think!" Sabah heard Linda say in English. "It doesn't look good! That boy's not gonna stay here another week."

"Linda, who cares?" George said, sounding exasperated.

"I care! People care!"

"Dumb people!" George was nearly yelling now. "You think I care one bit what people say about your daughters being in the same house with that guy? Do you? You don't know anything about him."

"I don't need to know anything."

"Yes you do! You have any *idea* where he came from? What it took for him to get here, to be here right now? You don't have a clue. It was a lot harder for him than it was for you." George paused, then let out a deep sigh. "I'll tell you what you need to know. That guy out there is better than you. He's better than you and your two daughters put together. That's what you need to know."

George marched out of the kitchen so quickly Sabah didn't have time to move.

"Get packed," George said sharply. "We're going."

Sabah watched George pick up his small travel bag and sling the strap over his shoulder. Before Sabah could say a word, George was already out the front door.

★ ★ ★

CHAPTER TWENTY-SEVEN

The Suit

★ ★ ★

George and Sabah walked in silence for a few blocks until they reached a busy boulevard. Like many cities on many continents, George knew his way around Los Angeles. He was processing his situation with Sabah, even as he was reacting to it. They got on a bus. Sabah had no idea where they were or where they were going.

During a recent trip, George had noticed a prominent beauty school not far from where they were. He'd planned on taking Sabah there, though he didn't think he'd be taking him so quickly. Finding a hotel in the general vicinity of this school seemed like the best plan under the circumstances. The bus passed by the school and George pulled the buzzer. He and Sabah would be getting off at the next stop, which happened to be at the corner of Santa Monica Boulevard and Vermont Avenue in East Hollywood.

They got off the bus and started walking. Farther down the block, George saw a neon sign in the shape of a red arrow. In the middle of the arrow was the word "vacancy." George followed the sign to the front of a four-story brick building. It was a dilapidated residential hotel with occupancy by the day, week, or month.

Perfect, George thought. It wouldn't cost much and the school was across the street.

Sabah was as enthusiastic about his new residence as George. While George waited, Sabah went inside and approached the registration desk.

"How long did you want the room?" the clerk asked. He was a frail elderly man, perhaps in his late sixties. He lifted his cigarette and took a long, deep drag as he waited for an answer.

It was a good question. Sabah had no idea. He knew that, as of this moment, his transit visa would be invalid in three days. At that point he would officially be an illegal immigrant in the United States. This wasn't a particularly daunting prospect. The likelihood of encountering even one of those uniformed customs agents was, at best, remote.

And if, by some wild twist of fate, he was actually confronted by one of these agents, they certainly wouldn't be like the Baathists. They were Americans which meant they weren't thugs, bullies, or killers. He would never be threatened, accosted, or treated in anything less than a dignified way. He couldn't imagine that they would really try and make him leave America. He would just tell them the truth. He was a Christian. America was a Christian nation, wasn't it? Would they send him back to a non-Christian country being held hostage by an insane person who was killing tens of thousands his fellow citizens? Sabah stepped confidentially into America, knowing this simply wasn't possible.

Sabah had been lost in thought for almost half a minute. The clerk was accustomed to these kinds of delays. Guests in this hotel often exercised mental deliberations at check-in. He knew these pauses related to a large variety of personal emergencies, often involving the law. Though the clerk correctly assumed Sabah's slow response was somehow related to illegal activities, they weren't the type most commonly associated with this hotel.

In the end, Sabah decided that three days in this hotel would be fine, for now. He paid cash and carried his luggage through a large, dark lobby. Mismatched furniture was strewn haphazardly across a stained green shag carpet. Two middle-aged black men occupied a set of vinyl Queen Ann chairs. They glanced up from their card game and Sabah smiled at them as he walked by. They didn't return the smile and said nothing. Sabah noticed that the material on their chairs was cracked and brittle.

Yellowing lamp shades dimly illuminated the room, casting a dull gloss on the dark, thinly veneered, wood paneled walls. A sofa's striped, earth-toned fabric was torn in several places. A crack ran the length of a frosted wall mirror, which featured an overlay of a deer standing beside a picturesque mountain stream.

Very nice, Sabah thought as he took in every aspect of the lobby, then entered an elevator to his room.

Later at lunch, George informed Sabah he would need to leave that afternoon. Sabah presumed George was going somewhere else in Los Angeles and wouldn't be sharing the hotel room that night.

"Where are you going?" Sabah asked.

"Ecuador," George said.

It was a surprise, but it also made sense. George was, after all, an international man of mystery. Sabah was sorry to see George go. Though their contact had been brief, Sabah already considered him more than a friend. George had done everything Ramsey had said he would do. George would be remembered by Sabah, for the rest of his life, as the man who had brought him to America.

More immediately, though, he would have been an invaluable resource on the most practical level. Even so, George's imminent departure did not in the smallest way affect Sabah's sense of security and well being. With or without him, Sabah knew he would be perfectly fine. George had recognized this attribute in Sabah the moment they'd met. Perhaps it was this quality, more than anything else, that had endeared Sabah so quickly to George.

Later that afternoon, on the curb in front of his hotel, Sabah watched George step into a taxi. He waved goodbye to his friend. Like so many others in the past year, Sabah had no way of knowing if he would ever see George again. He watched the taxi moving through the traffic until it turned a corner and disappeared.

Sabah knew he was in Hollywood, the birthplace of all those American movies that had taught him so much about his new world. He could see the actual Hollywood sign right outside his hotel room window. If there was any place in America he would have loved to sightsee and explore, it was here. But he'd already been sidetracked once during his mission. It had been a serious mistake, almost a fatal one. It wouldn't happen again. He turned and faced the hotel. Here he was. There was no time, now, for personal interests or indulgences. It was time to get to work.

He went straight to his room and opened his suitcase. It could have been much worse, but the quality and drape of the fabric allowed his suit to hang smoothly, almost without a wrinkle. He placed the jacket and pants on a hanger and hooked them on top of the open bathroom door. He stepped back and studied the suit. It was deep black with sparse, thin white stripes. It looked as good to him now as it had nine months earlier, on his first day in Greece. There was an element of vanity in the purchase. It was a beautiful suit and he had no doubt he'd look beautiful in it.

But that wasn't why he'd bought it. He bought if for this moment. Being in America was the greatest privilege of his life. If a man attended a formal dinner in which he was the guest of honor, wouldn't he wear a suit like this? If a man demonstrated his interest in a woman by purchasing tickets to a symphony or an opera, wouldn't he wear a suit like this? How much more, then, would this suit be needed when he was in America? It was the very least he could do to demonstrate his appreciation and respect for his new home.

Sabah carefully assembled himself. He put on his new white dress shirt, black socks, and black dress shoes. He took the briefcase out of his suitcase and opened it. The briefcase was empty. He organized his possessions and placed them on his bedspread. In a few moments he was reviewing an orderly row of items consisting of a passport, the scissors he'd purchased at the Tokalon Salon, his wallet containing a couple of photographs, and not much else, just a hair brush and a city map he'd picked up in a liquor store earlier that afternoon.

He picked the items up, one by one, then carefully placed them in his briefcase. He closed and locked it. Then, holding the briefcase in his hand, he studied himself in a mirror. He was ready.

It was about four in the afternoon and the lobby was busier than it had been in the morning. The residents of this particular hotel definitely weren't a morning crowd. Now there were a dozen or more people in the lobby as Sabah strolled through it, briefcase in hand. Three men were huddled on the sofa and an adjacent chair. They looked like Mexicans but not exactly like the Mexicans Sabah had seen in Mexico.

One wore a white tank top T-shirt. His black hair, slicked straight back, was covered by a fine hairnet. He had a tear drop tattooed at the corner of an eye. Another man also wore a white T-shirt, but it was covered by an unbuttoned long-sleeved plaid shirt. A third man wore a bandana on top of his head. The group had all been leaning forward, looking at a plastic baggy on an oak coffee table. As Sabah passed, one of them picked up the bag. The men simultaneously straightened then pulled back and away from each other while eyeing Sabah.

"Good afternoon," Sabah said, and smiled.

They said nothing but remained frozen, except for their heads, which slowly swiveled toward him. Their eyes were locked on Sabah.

On the other side the room, closer to the front door, another group was gathered around a small table. There were two ladies, one black, the other white. A black man was with them. The man standing next to the ladies wore a kind of suit Sabah hadn't seen before. It was made of blue polyester and had a wide, flared collar that nearly reached the edges of its padded shoulders. It also had buttoned pockets on the chest. Matching bellbottomed slacks were hemmed high enough to reveal a pair of matching blue, patent leather platform shoes. Several gold chains hung around the man's neck. Though the late afternoon caused the lobby to be even darker now, the man wore a pair of chrome trimmed sunglasses.

Sabah considered his own suit for a moment. He hoped he wasn't too far behind the latest fashion trends in America. As with the group of Mexican men, this group also stopped talking the moment Sabah passed by. They women didn't acknowledge him, even with a glance. Sabah thought the man was watching him, though he couldn't see his eyes. He was stone-faced, looking in Sabah's general direction, but slightly askew. The movement of his head roughly coincided with the pace of Sabah's footsteps.

The women, seated at the table, both wore high heeled shoes and short, tight dresses. It was an impressive display of legs, thighs, and cleavage. Sabah tried not ogle but couldn't help noticing the way one lady's shoe dangled from her foot. Her weight was shifted to one side. She leaned slightly at an angle, one leg hung over the other, moving in a rhythmic sway.

This seemed to be a continuation of fashion trends he'd seen in Greece. He remembered how surprised he'd been then. He'd seen more bare skin on more women during his first week in Athens than he'd seen in his entire life. He remembered how natural and unselfconscious the women had seemed. In fact, Sabah had been impressed by their free expression almost as much as their nearly naked bodies. Perhaps ladies' fashion trends in America were a logical extension of the ladies he'd seen in Greece.

Actually, Sabah thought, it had to be more than a extention. It had to be a conclusion. If the ladies in this lobby wore anything more revealing, they'd have to be naked. That would be fine, too, but Sabah didn't expect fashion trends to cross that line any time in the near future, even in America. Sabah offered another nod and smile to this second group and pushed open the front door.

So far, his reception in his new home hadn't been quite as warm as he would have preferred. He wasn't troubled by this as much as he was curious. Perhaps people in America were just more reserved than people in Greece. Maybe, like himself, they were new to America. They may have been, as he was, unsure of the traditions, customs, and methods of their new world. Who could tell? Sabah didn't give it another thought. He had business to attend to.

Hollywood Stars Beauty School was almost directly across the street from the hotel. It was a busy little factory, with thirty or more students on any given day. A male instructor dressed in a blue smock, not much older than the student he was helping, watched Sabah come in the front door.

Great, the instructor thought, *another vendor, or worse, a salesman.*

He decided to take care of this very quickly. "You didn't see the sign?" the instructor said.

"Sign?" Sabah asked.

"On the front door. 'No Soliciting'"

Sabah glanced at the red sign with white letters. "Oh! Yes, a sign, Yes, I did see it. Sorry, what does this mean?"

The teacher wasn't sure if Sabah was illiterate or the product of a highly effective sales training program.

He decided on the first option.

"It means no salesmen," he said.

"Oh, I see. Thank you." Sabah was always interested in new information. Now, in America, he'd become especially grateful for explanations on anything, at any time. "But I'm not selling anything."

"Okay, so what can I do for you?" the teacher asked, glancing back at his student who was, at this second, probably putting too much dye in her client's hair.

"My name is Sabah. I want to be a student."

The instructor looked at him for a few moments.

"Sally," the instructor called, "can you keep an eye on Kristine for a second, please?"

Another instructor, also dressed in a blue smock, nodded and approached the young student.

It quickly became clear to the instructor that Sabah was yet another one of those annoying immigrants. How did these people get the idea that they could have their visas extended simply by enrolling in his school as a student?

"That's not how it works, Sa … Sabah, is it?"

"Yes."

"You don't come here to get your visa. You get your visa *then* you come here. You got it?"

It wasn't quite as simple as Sabah had thought it would be, but the instructor had no more time for Sabah's bewilderment or confusion. He quickly wrote an address on a slip of paper and handed it to Sabah, as he had for dozens of others just like him.

"This is the address of the I.N.S. office and don't ask me what that stands for. I don't know. I just know that this is where you get your visa approved. So, good luck, okay?"

With that, Sabah was ushered out the beauty school door. He didn't go to the I.N.S. office right away. He didn't like the idea of any governmental office, even if it was in America. He would walk in and out of his hotel lobby several times over the next few days, postponing his trip to the I.N.S. office. He was looking forward to going there like a cancer patient looks forward to biopsy results in a doctor's office.

Now, his time was up. His passport had officially expired. He walked into the busy, governmental room. Even in America they were all the same. A little cleaner and newer, with better lighting perhaps, but still this room could have been anywhere, Mexico or Greece. He hated to admit to himself but, yes, even Iraq. He filled out a form and stood at a window, watching a woman behind a plate of glass. She quickly scanned his passport and forms. She stamped a narrow slip of paper and handed it back to Sabah, along with his passport and completed forms.

"Next," she said, looking around Sabah at the person behind him.

Sabah didn't count them but there were probably seventy to a hundred people in this room. They were sitting close to each other on long wooden benches. Sabah found a seat and waited for his number to be called. All these people were waiting for the next stage of processing, a one-on-one interview with an I.N.S. agent. Sabah glanced at the narrow strip of paper the lady had stamped. It was some kind of emblem and it was stamped in red. He hadn't noticed this before.

He looked to his right, then to his left, searching for other narrow strips and stamps. The person on his right had a stamp that was green. The person on the left had one that was blue. Sabah didn't like this. He didn't like the color red. Red meant stop. Red meant don't go any farther. Red could also mean the worst thing of all; it could mean go back.

Despite everything he'd told himself about America's magnanimity, their compassion and tolerance, the familiarity of this room was unnerving him. He was growing increasingly uncomfortable. His breathing became faster and more shallow. He'd always relied on his instincts and they didn't fail him now.

In the corner of the room he saw an exit sign. In an instant, he made one of the most important decisions of his life. He stood up and walked out that exit door, then out of the building. Had he stayed, like many others in that office on that day, he probably would have been detained and deported. Now, walking along a busy Los Angeles boulevard, listening to the din of rushing traffic, Sabah knew he was a fugitive.

CHAPTER TWENTY-EIGHT

★ ★ ★

Needed Friends And Borrowed Time

★ ★ ★

Knowing he was officially an illegal alien didn't make Sabah feel like a criminal. These were two very different concepts in his mind. As far as he was concerned, he was already an American. Those guys in uniforms just didn't know it yet. But in time, they would. Everyone would know. He would make sure of that. In the meantime, he would just follow his plan, as best he could.

He returned to the hotel from the I.N.S. office. It was early evening and the usual crowd was in the lobby. Though he hadn't actually talked to any of them, he felt like they were warming to him. The lobby continued to grow still and conversations were lowered as he came and went. But now, he would get an occasional nod of the head or a "Wassup, my man?"

Sabah wasn't sure if that was English slang or an entirely separate language. He had no idea what it meant but it sounded cool and he tried saying it to himself when he was alone in his room.

It was time for Plan B. Sabah picked up the phone in his room. It was of the wooden variety, the kind that hang on a wall with the mouth piece extending out the front and the ear piece hanging by a cord at the side. Sabah had called his brother George the first night he was in the hotel. Thank God George worked for an American telecommunications company based in San Francisco. Sabah could call him collect any time and talk to his brother for as long as George's work schedule would allow, which usually wasn't for very long.

But he'd never seen a phone like this, let alone used one. The first time he'd used it, he'd spent five minutes trying to talk and listen with the ear piece. Now his proficiency had improved, which was helpful, because he was about to call his father's friend, Farouk. Farouk was a manager at the Swiss Airlines offices at Los Angeles International Airport. He'd worked with Sabah's father many years earlier, for Swiss Airlines in Baghdad. Sabah had no idea what this man could do for him, if anything. But he wasn't exactly overwhelmed with options.

Farouk was happy to hear from Sabah and invited him to his office the next day. Whatever enthusiasm Farouk's warm phone reception had stirred in Sabah, it quickly gave way after a very sober encounter the following afternoon. Farouk studied Sabah's passport like it was a venomous spider. Fortunately for Sabah, Farouk was no newcomer to immigration, customs, or the people who worked in the airport branches of these offices. In fact, he'd been working with these people for over twenty years.

After a short trip deep into the bowels of the chaotic airport complex, surrounded by its log jam traffic and screaming jets, Sabah's visa was stamped valid for another twenty-eight days. Sabah looked at his new and improved passport. His first impressions were generally on target. He had been right about America. Things did happen fast here, including the rejection or validation of one's legal status. It was nice to know that he wasn't a fugitive anymore, but the various stamps on his passport were just ink on paper to Sabah. They had very little effect on his psyche.

Farouk offered Sabah a ride back to his hotel, which Sabah gladly accepted. It would sure beat the two hours and four transfers it had taken him to get here on the city buses. Sabah handed Farouk a business card for the hotel when they got in his car at LAX. Farouk looked twice at the address.

"Not sure that's the best neighborhood to be in," he remarked as he started up the car.

But it was only when they pulled up in front of the hotel that Farouk saw the whole picture. Sabah had his hand on the car door handle and was about to step out.

"Sabah, wait a second. This is where you've been staying?"

"Yeah, this is it."

"Oh, no, no, Sabah, you're gonna get killed here. Don't you know that?"

"What do you mean?"

Farouk was still studying the hotel, looking for some kind of positive identification.

"This might even be the same place. It was right around here, couple of months ago. Big shootout in one of these places. Five people got killed."

"Really?" Sabah said, appearing more impressed than afraid.

Farouk was becoming frustrated. "Sabah, you can't stay here! This place is full of pimps, whores, and drug dealers!"

"What's a drug dealer?" Sabah asked. He had no idea and he was genuinely curious.

Farouk stared blankly at Sabah, completely stupefied. Had this boy's naïveté crossed a line into mental retardation?

"Sabah, get your stuff. You're coming with me. Go ahead. I'll wait."

Sabah, well trained in his culture, had learned never to disrespect or disobey an elder, even if it was man he'd never met or, for that matter, a man his father hadn't seen for fifteen years. Farouk was still his elder. As safe and pleasant as this place seemed to Sabah, he would do as he was instructed and without question.

Sabah was up to his room and back down again in less than five minutes. He walked through the lobby a final time, but now with his suitcase in his hand. This was the visual cue that said the mystery guest was leaving. This was what made the old man speak up. The old man was one of them, usually sitting in the room's only rocking chair. He was a seventy-year-old black man with white hair. He wore suspenders and his pants were hiked up nearly to his chest. Sabah had noticed that he usually sat alone, smoking his filter-tipped cigars, minding his own business.

"Hey, young man," he called.

Sabah turned, startled that he'd been spoken to. He'd been here four days. Though he'd offered smiles and greetings in passing everyone, this was the first word anyone had spoken to him.

"Yes sir?" Sabah said, stopping in his tracks

"Com 'ere a second. I wanna ask you somethin'."

Sabah stepped closer.

"You see that guy over there?"

The old man was pointing to another lobby regular. Sabah had seen him before. It was the black guy with the unusual blue suit and chrome rimmed sunglasses. He was wearing a lime green suit today.

"Yes, sir, I see him," Sabah said.

"That guy and I have a bet. You know what a bet is?"

"I know what it is, yes," Sabah said.

"That guy bet me that you work for the Mexican mafia." The old man paused and looked Sabah squarely in the eye. Sabah had no idea what he meant or was referring to. He just knew that the old man's face was unflinching, almost paralyzed with seriousness.

Sabah said nothing. The old man continued. "Fact is, he says you're some big dude with them. But I don't think so. No, sir, I said. I told him you're a cop. Now, you tell me, who's right?"

A cop? The old man had to be kidding. And what was a Mexican mafia? He was either joking or drunk or something. Sabah didn't have time to figure it out.

"I'm a hairdresser," Sabah said.

"A what?"

"A hairdresser."

Now it was the old man's turn to wonder about Sabah, and in precisely the same way. Was this nutcase pulling his leg? For a moment the old man felt insulted, as if he were the victim of some practical joke or prank. But the earnestness that was Sabah's hallmark finally seeped its way through the old man's hard stare. In an instant, the old man realized that this weird, well-dressed, friendly youngster was telling the truth.

The old man let out a laugh that shook the entire lobby. Everyone in the room had already turned the moment he'd called Sabah over. If their interest had waned at all, the whole room immediately snapped back to attention. The laughter was so abrupt and wild they thought the old man might be choking or having a stroke. Maybe he'd even been shot.

"A *hairdresser*?" the old man asked when he was finally able to catch his breath.

"Yes, sir," Sabah said.

"You hear that?" the old man called over to the pimp. "The man is a *hairdresser!*"

Obviously, the old man thought something was funny, but Sabah didn't have a clue what it was.

He was confused as he walked out of the lobby and into Farouk's waiting car. It would be years before Sabah realized why the old man had been laughing so hard. For three days, in a hotel full of street hustlers, ex-cons, and gang members, Sabah had been the biggest bad-boy of all.

Sabah caromed and ricocheted his way into America, directed and re-directed during his first few weeks without a plan or roadmap. This was to be expected. Sabah was unfazed by the turbulence and unpredictability of his daily life. In fact, he welcomed it. Just being in America gave him so much hope and optimism there wasn't room for anxiety associated with lack of direction. He was simply too happy to be worried.

In Farouk's view, Sabah had been absconded and was being brought to a suburban safe house, far from the perils of an inner city war zone. His good deed, however, did little to alleviate Farouk's apprehension. He was a busy man with a family and a demanding job. He lived in Orange County and drove to and from work at LAX everyday. His driving commute was nearly a full-time job in itself. He really didn't need this added responsibility.

Farouk knew that Sabah had very little money. He was without friends, family, or other resources, and entirely without a plan. What was Farouk getting himself into? Had he just brought the equivalent of an abandoned puppy into his home? Was he going to have another mouth to feed for some indefinite period of time, years perhaps? And what about Sabah's legal status? Would he eventually be harboring an illegal alien, jeopardizing his own career and reputation?

Farouk considered the situation on the drive south. He took small comfort in knowing, at least, that he'd probably saved the poor kid's life. For all these reasons, Farouk, perhaps even more than Sabah, was delighted to receive George Toma's phone call. It came three days after Sabah's arrival.

If Sabah's American adventure made Sabah the equivalent to NASA's Viking spacecraft landing on Mars, then George had become mission control. As the only member of the Toma family with the capacity for daily, real-time communication, he was able to constantly monitor Sabah's functionality and orientation. It was perfectly clear to George that Spacecraft Sabah had no internal guidance system. Always the big brother, even from halfway around the world, George would take it upon himself to be that system.

It was the middle of the day in George's office when he received Sabah's collect call. George knew his brother's voice. He knew every nuance in it's timbre and inflection. Throughout their entire lives, George had collected information about his brother's emotional condition through these sources, often more than from words themselves. Words had always been only the data. It was George's role, now more than ever before, to accurately interpret that data.

The last thing Sabah wanted to do, in any conversation with George, was give him cause for concern. Especially since George would be immediately relaying updates to Sabah's mother and father. Saying anything that might worry them, or make them anxious in any way, was not an option for Sabah. George had spoken with Sabah several times since he'd crossed the border into America. Every report had been glowing and effusive, brimming with enthusiasm. But this one was different.

Sabah's words were the same but there was the slightest tension in his voice, a sense of urgency. George immediately deduced that Sabah was uncomfortable with the imposition he was creating on Farouk, but George didn't need to ask questions. Elaboration and explanations were unnecessary, not due to George's intuition but other opportunities. It was the right time for good news.

"Sabah, remember when I was in San Francisco, the place with the pool on the roof?"

"Yes, sure," Sabah answered.

"I talked with the guy I worked with there, my friend Nick. You remember him?"

Sabah remembered, yes. Nick was a Greek. That was all Sabah could remember but it was better than knowing nothing at all.

"He's on a project for a little while so he's not home. But he told me you're welcome to stay with his wife and kids in San Francisco for a few weeks. What do you think?"

"When can I go?" Sabah asked, his voice immediately brighter.

"Anytime. Right now if you want. Here, take down his phone number,"

And just like that, another link in the chain was forged. Sabah was grateful and relieved but not surprised. His entire adult life, extending into his American odyssey, had been on a kind of flying trapeze. The next bar had always been there. Sabah knew a certain phenomenon would always overlay his fairytale experience in America, namely his own uncanny aptitude for finding solutions in difficult situations, often at the last possible moment.

Farouk had given him more time. Now the next bar swept toward him, appearing out of a dark mist. Nick, a person he'd met only one year earlier in Baghdad, had given him a place to stay. And for an entire month. Right now a month was almost an eternity. Now Sabah would have all the time he needed to figure out his next move. It would come, again with George's help and guidance, and it would be the worst move of his life.

CHAPTER TWENTY-NINE

★ ★ ★

The Precipice

★ ★ ★

Nick was in Saudi Arabia when George spoke with him. He was very busy on a company project. He didn't have the time or energy for anything else, particularly any drama related to George's younger brother. Having Sabah visit for a week or two didn't represent a significant sacrifice on Nick's part.

"Who knows?" Nick wondered out loud to George. "Maybe he'll find a job, meet a girl, something. We'll let him hang out a bit and see what turns up."

Though Nick downplayed his generosity, George didn't take it for granted for a moment. The minute he hung up the phone with Nick, George was already making inquiries and doing research related to Sabah's long-term residential options.

Nick had been right in his assessment of Sabah's potential activities. Hanging out was about the sum of Sabah's experience in San Francisco. Sabah liked the city, though it was different than Los Angeles, or at least that part of Los Angeles Sabah had seen. It was colder, foggier, and it had more hills. Many of the buildings were older than those he'd seen in Los Angeles. Sabah noticed how well-preserved they were and how much pride was displayed in that preservation. There was something about them, something fundamentally different than the buildings in Los Angeles, but what was it?

Sabah also liked the little trolleys. They seemed quaint and friendly, a charming holdover from an America gone by. The buildings and these trolleys were related parts of that difference between Los Angeles and San

Francisco. This contrast was more subtle, perhaps, but far more powerful than weather or topography. Perhaps there were places in America where people not only remembered the past, but revered it as well. This divergence in values, symbolized in the architecture and transportation of these two cities, was both striking and puzzling. Sabah was beginning to understand something. America was a far more complicated place than he'd imagined.

Then it came to him. He knew what it was. He knew what San Francisco had that Los Angeles didn't have. San Francisco had character.

Even in 1976, living in San Francisco proper was an expensive proposition. Though Nick was a well-paid engineer with his company, he lived in a tiny two bedroom house near Broadway and Fillmore in the Pacific Heights area. In his wanderings around this fascinating variation of America, Sabah discovered a small market owned by a middle eastern man. It was a deli, coffee shop, and neighborhood gathering place for people from his part of the world. He was immediately drawn in by its familiarity. Though far more elaborate, it reminded him of the little café he and his father had started so many years before.

In the mornings, he would go there for his coffee and sit at one of several little café tables on the sidewalk outside the shop. One morning, an older man, close to seventy perhaps, was sitting at a table next to Sabah. The old man was holding a San Francisco Chronicle and glanced at Sabah over it's top edge. Sabah was looking at the man and smiled in response. The old man lowered his newspaper. White stubble covered his chin. He had a dark, deeply lined and weathered face. His teeth were long and uneven. He wore a keffiyeh and brown corduroy jacket.

"Where you from, son?" the man asked in Arabic.

"Baghdad," Sabah answered.

The man thought for a moment and finally said, "Then I don't have to ask what you're doing here."

"You don't have to," Sabah said, "but you can."

The old man smiled. "You got half a world away from the maniac."

"I was lucky," Sabah said. He seldom used the word. Luck was something he didn't believe in. But he used the word easily now, without thinking about it.

The man was looking closely at Sabah now. When he spoke again, his words were softer, more reflective. "Good for you. Good for you."

"And you? Where are you from?"

"Ramallah," the old man said.

"Israel?"

The old man looked at him as though from a great distance, across far reaches of time. "You could say that. Others might say Palestine."

"Which do you say?"

"I say I don't care. This is my home now."

Sabah had never heard anyone speak this way. Throughout his entire life, he'd heard only one thing, that the Jews from Israel were thieves and usurpers. The Jews had been taking Palestinian land and stealing the homes of people who lived there. This had been the constant cry of the Iraqi media both before and after the Baathist regime. It was the only doctrine Sabah had ever known. He had occasionally had Jewish friends throughout his life. Sabah knew that a person wasn't bad or evil simply because they were Jewish but Israeli expansionism was something else entirely.

The issue of land rights in Palestine had been the oldest, most polarizing argument within the Arab world, even more so for natives of Palestine. Sabah was very familiar with the vehemence and hostility this subject produced in Palestinians. This old man's indifference, so bluntly expressed, startled Sabah almost as much as a hard slap to his face.

"But, sir, didn't they steal your property, your home?" Sabah asked.

"Son, listen to me. They came to me and asked to *buy* my house. They weren't gonna steal it from me. I could have kept it. They told me they'd even help my family move to America. So I said okay. They did what they said they'd do, and that was that. And you know what? It was the best thing I ever did. Let me tell you something else. For as long as you live, for as long as your children live and even their children, those morons over there are gonna be killing each other. That's their choice. The Jews gave me a way out. It was a fair deal and I took it. And I thank God I did, every day."

Sabah had never known this about the Israeli Jews. But that wasn't what startled him the most, nor what made him disconnect from the immediate topic of conversation. The irony was crushing. All his life he'd heard the anti-Zionist rant: America was the big bully propping up their puppet country, giving Israel the military strength to stand up against the entire Arab world. Yet if he hadn't reached America, Sabah would have never known that at least one man, this man sitting next to him right now, had been treated fairly by Israel. How many others in America, or anywhere else in the world for that matter, were like this man? And how many people who never made it out of Iraq would never know what Sabah had learned at this very moment?

How big was a country that could allow this very conversation to be taking place? How good was that country? Freedom had always been an abstract ideal for Sabah. In his youth, he'd viewed freedom the way he viewed his own ability to leap from the ground and fly. He'd had no idea what either of the two would actually feel like but slowly, in Greece and now in America, the full force of freedom was ringing out in the smallest moments.

This old man was free. He was free to tell the truth only because he was in the land that had given him that freedom. Sabah looked at the old man, understanding his new world in a completely new way. How many more truths were out there, waiting to be discovered?

The old man must have recognized some process of illumination within Sabah because he said nothing. He simply smiled and sipped his Turkish coffee.

"They tell you a lot of garbage over there," the old man said, "but be careful. There's garbage here too."

Sabah suddenly refocused on the old man again. He'd been pulled back from his brief mental excursion by this odd, casual caveat.

"Son," the old man continued, "when you get to be my age you'll understand this. The older you get, the harder it is to know who the good guys are and who the bad guys are."

After another full day of urban exploration, Sabah returned to Nick's house still thinking about what the old man had told him. To Sabah, the words were cryptic and slightly ominous. He wasn't sure what they meant but he didn't particularly like the sound of them. Sabah definately knew who the good guys were and who the bad guys were, without a doubt. There was nothing in this world more clear to him than that. Maybe age had taken its toll and the old man was just missing a few marbles. And if "they" told lies in America, how would Sabah know who "they" were?

Sabah had been at Nick's house several days when the call came. Once again, it was from mission control—his brother George. Sabah could tell, right away, that an important development had come up. There was almost a shrill excitement in his brother's voice.

"You remember Dad's cousin, Hana?" George was saying.

The significance of the term cousin, in the Chaldean culture, can be easily lost in the simple frequency of its use. The idea of the extended family, for the average American, pales in comparison to the vast network of blood relationships within its Chaldean counterpart. This is never clearer than in traditional social gatherings such as a weddings, funerals, school graduations, or birthdays, each more closely resembling a family reunion than its comparable counterpart in the United States.

If this cultural trait is true in Iraq, it becomes exponentially increased as Chaldeans migrate. Within their colony communities, whether in Greece, America, or anywhere else in the world, their propensity for unity reaches even higher levels. Not one person is lost, forgotten, or unincorporated within their ever-expanding family network. A mother's aunt may have a cousin and this cousin might be as familiar to that mother's family as her own children would be to each other.

Unlike other minority sub-cultures within any dominant majority, the Chaldean survival instinct is not expressed in a demand for equal rights or self-defensive reactions against perceived or real aggression. It is found in one thing only: the depth of their loyalty and devotion to each other.

When George told Sabah he'd spoken with their father's cousin, Sabah knew who this person was. He'd met him and could identify him. Sabah knew he was personally related to him, somehow, but the exact connection was never analyzed. It didn't need to be. They were related and that was enough. He didn't need to know anything more.

"I remember," Sabah answered. "Is he still in Baghdad?"

"I think so. Anyway, he was talking with Dad a few days ago. Sabah, Hana's son is in San Diego!"

"*Really?*"

If George had said he was in San Diego himself, the information couldn't have created more excitement.

"Yes! He's been there a few years. He's got a job in a store. He told Hana he thinks he can get you a job there!"

"Without a green card?"

"None," George said.

"What's his name?"

"Faraj. You got a pen? Here's his phone number and address."

Sabah's American adventure, as riveting as every moment was, had just opened up in an entirely new way. The idea of arrival and all it suggested, the fullness of this concept was crystallizing with each passing second. At a rudimentary level Sabah understood arrival in America wasn't something you did all at once. It was done in stages. There was getting across the border. That was the first step. There was getting a visa extended. That was another. There was finding friends and material support. That was a third. Here was the fourth and, by far, the most important step: finding a job.

It would by no means be the last step, but at this time in his life, Sabah had no way of knowing that. There would be many, many more steps in this vague and elusive idea of arrival. So many that arrival would become an ongoing, moving target, permanently connected to his goals and dreams within his new world.

To arrive in America, to be *in* America, was seldom determined by those who came to America, but by America itself. To Sabah, and others like him, being in America meant to achieve in America, but achievement in what form and how much? These questions would occur to him only in the future, many years in the future, in a very different time and place, perhaps even in a different version of his own life.

For now, Sabah hung up the phone and ended his conversation with George. Now he was no longer just in America. He was on the precipice. It was all right here, right in front of him. He was going to have a job. If there was anything better than being in America, it was the promise of staying here.

CHAPTER THIRTY

★ ★ ★

The Promise

★ ★ ★

Sabah arrived in San Diego on a Pacific Southwest Airlines flight. It was early in the afternoon on a sunny day in March. Waiting at Lindbergh Field was a stocky, barrel-chested man, not much taller than Sabah but perhaps six or seven years older. Though not yet thirty, the top of the man's head was completely bald. An evenly trimmed mat of hair surrounded the bottom half of his skull. It wasn't yet three in the afternoon and the man already had a pronounced five o'clock shadow. His unkempt bushy eyebrows and hairy chest were an odd counterpoint to his baldness. The man looked like a demented Benedictine monk.

No, Sabah thought; not demented exactly. It wasn't so much a mental deficiency. There was a certain kind of intelligence about the man, but it was raw and brutish. Maybe it was the excessive chest hair beneath the unbuttoned silk dress shirt, or a lack of animation in his face. Sabah couldn't put his finger on it directly, but there was something distinctly simian about the man, if not reptilian. Sabah would find that, like himself, this was a man of goals and objectives. But whatever that natural dampener was in Sabah, that instinctive ability to soften himself in the presence of others as a means of attaining his goals, it was completely absent in this man.

Initially, for a very short time, Sabah was charmed by Faraj's directness. Sabah could forgive tactlessness if it was displayed by a good person. If there had to be a choice, Sabah would always choose too much honesty and directness, rather than not enough. Sabah put his suitcase in the trunk of Faraj's Chevy Impala.

"You like my wheels?" Faraj asked as they got in the car and drove away from the airport.

"Your car?" Sabah asked.

"Come on, man, you can say it. *Wheels.*" Faraj glanced at Sabah, offering something closer to a smirk than a smile.

"Okay, wheels, if that's what you like."

"Not what I like. You wanna be an American, you gotta talk like one. Don't you know that?"

It hadn't really occurred to him, but it seemed to make sense. Sure, why not? Sabah looked at Faraj. Faraj didn't seem to look at people soo much as he looked past them.

"Yeah, man, I dig your wheels," Sabah said.

"There you go. Now you got it" Faraj asked. There was an unnatural smile frozen on his face.

"Yes, for sure. It's big! It's great!"

"It's a piece of trash. I'm gettin' rid of it as soon as I can. You know what I'm gonna get?"

Sabah already had the feeling that most of Faraj's questions were going to be rhetorical, mostly used as a device to offer more information about himself. Sabah said nothing. He knew an answer wasn't required.

"Bet you can't guess. Of course you can't guess. You been here, what, a few weeks, right? How would you know. I'm getting a Corvette. Best car *ever.*"

Though his personal preferences were more closely connected to fashion than cars, Sabah could understand and even relate to Faraj's desire for material objects. What was foreign to Sabah was the force and ferocity of Faraj's desire. It seemed that if Faraj didn't get his Corvette in the next two minutes, he'd tear off his own head off and spit at himself. There was a raging, dangerous appetite in this person. Faraj wanted it all and he wanted it now.

Sabah had always been a discerning and astute observer. He was talented at piecing together new social situations of any kind and, if needed, instantly evaluating their threat level. Like many others of his generation, growing up in Baathist Iraq had only sharpened this ability. Still, Sabah was as open to new friendships as he was alert to danger.

Perhaps his overwhelming gratitude to Faraj diminished his

discernment. Perhaps he truly didn't believe that such maliciousness was possible from anyone within his own Chaldean community. Either way, he missed the early clues in Faraj's behavior which, otherwise, would have warned him of an imminent crisis. But then, even if he had recognized them, would the outcome have been any different?

Sabah's first job in America would be in a liquor store. This was not incidental or insignificant. The resurgence and renaissance of displaced Native Americans roughly coincided with the emerging Chaldean colonies in America. Like Native Americans, Chaldeans took the most direct route to financial stability. They catered to, and exploited, human weakness and vice.

Various tribes of Native Americans would convert their lands and sovereign nations into casinos and gambling meccas. Though perhaps less flamboyant than their fellow outcasts and companions in misfortune, the Chaldeans would prove no less effective in securing profits. The Chaldeans' overwhelming weapon of choice would be the liquor store.

From the airport, Faraj took Sabah to an apartment near 54th Street and El Cajon Boulevard. This wasn't the best area in San Diego, not like Faraj's own brand new neighborhood in Mission Valley. This section of the city, though affluent by Baghdad standards, was typical of most inner city American neighborhoods. It was gritty, seedy, funky, and dirty.

The apartment complex was a group of three separate two-story buildings, each with four units per building. The buildings were surrounded by an unpainted asphalt parking lot which was warped, cracked, or missing entire sections. The second floor walkways doubled as storage facilities. The walkways were crammed with children's bicycles, small barbecues, and plastic milk crates. Drying laundry and area carpets hung over the metal railings.

Had Sabah arrived at this place straight from Baghdad, it might have looked acceptable, even inviting. But he'd seen too much, both in Greece and America, to feel encouraged or even reassured by his new home.

"It's not a palace, but what can I say? Nobody got killed here lately." Faraj paused a beat. "That I know of."

Sabah could see that Faraj was entertained by what he considered to be his own wit and brilliant comic timing. He offered Faraj a courtesy grin. It was still very early in their relationship. He wanted to appear friendly and accommodating, as he would to any human being. Soon enough Sabah would understand that Faraj didn't fall into this category.

Faraj had arrived in San Diego in 1972, nearly five years before Sabah. This much could be said about Faraj: he was tough. He was one of the first Chaldean pioneers in the city. Decades later, their numbers would swell to nearly sixty thousand. San Diego would become the second largest Chaldean community in the United States, after Detroit. When Faraj arrived, there were only several hundred Chaldeans in San Diego.

With each new wave of Chaldean immigrants, opportunities for newcomers increased. The more people in their community, the more resources became available to its members. Conversely, the fewer members of any community, the stronger and more tenacious those first explorers had to be. Somehow, Faraj had survived. He'd gotten to America and stayed there, without the benefits or resources Sabah would have— resources exactly like Faraj himself.

No one had paved the way for Faraj. He'd done it on his own and now he was paving the way for others. But not in the way the George Tajirian had. Faraj was the polar opposite of George Tajirian. George's purpose in life was to help people. Faraj's was to exploit them.

Like others of his kind, Faraj laid traps covered in kindness. He'd done the same thing to his own brothers, Billah and Daud. Four months earlier, he'd brought them to America and set them up in the same apartment he took Sabah to. When his brothers had asked Faraj about the rent, as Sabah did, Faraj's answer was the same: "Don't worry about. I got it covered."

When Sabah explained his visa status, Faraj said he would take care of it. He would take Sabah to his attorney and Sabah's visa would be extended another ninety days. After that, who knew? Even Faraj couldn't make any promises when it came to visas, but that didn't prevent him from making promises of every other kind.

The night of Sabah's arrival, Billah and Daud came in from work sometime after eleven P.M. Though they would be Sabah's roommates, they didn't work at Paradise Liquor. They worked at another liquor store owned by someone called M. Faraj's brothers were near Sabah's age. Daud was slightly younger than Sabah and Billah was two years older.

They weren't at all like Faraj. In fact, they were so different that Sabah had trouble believing they were even related. They didn't seem brash, arrogant, or full of themselves in any way. They were just normal people, even the kind of people Sabah might have befriended back in Baghdad. He immediately sensed that they were more honest and approachable. He asked them questions he hadn't been comfortable enough to ask Faraj.

"It's true, Faraj's a little pushy," Billah was saying, "but he knows what he's doing."

"Are you saying you don't know how much you earn every week?" Sabah asked the brothers.

"Well, not exactly, no," Daud said.

"I told you," Billah said. "It all goes to savings for the store."

"The one Faraj's gonna buy?" Sabah asked.

"We're *all* gonna buy it!" Daud said emphatically.

"But you don't even see your paychecks," Sabah said. "They go straight to Faraj."

"Yes, they do," Billah said.

"And that doesn't seem a little strange?"

"Hey, he's our brother! What do you think? He's gonna rip us off?" Daud's voice had become louder and more shrill.

Sabah looked at Daud but didn't answer him. There was no doubt that it was a peculiar arrangement, but maybe Daud had a point. Even if Faraj was as bad as Sabah suspected, he couldn't be *that* bad. No one could make indentured servants out of his own brothers, not even someone as unlikable and shady as Faraj.

"Look," Billah said firmly. "Faraj brought us here. He got us jobs and a place to live. So you know what, if he wants to make us slaves, he can do it."

The conversation was over and shortly after that, the three new roommates went to sleep. Daud and Billah shared the one bedroom. Sabah was handed a blanket and left on the couch. The next morning at seven A.M., Faraj was there to pick up his brothers for work. Sabah gave him this much, the man always seemed to have a lot of energy, even at this relatively early hour.

"Sabah, I talked to my attorney. We're gonna need to come up with some more cash for the visa extension. How's your money situation nowadays?"

"I have enough," Sabah said, "and I can get more if I need it."

"From who?"

Sabah hesitated. Before he spoke, he had to review the potential risk of any information given to Faraj. He wasn't about to tell Faraj anything more than he needed to tell him.

"My brother, George," Sabah said.

"Well, unless you've got it, and I have a feeling you don't, you tell your brother you need a couple a thousand."

The look in Sabah's face told Faraj all he needed to know.

"I'm serious," Faraj added quickly. "He needs to send it."

The price was more than too high; it was extortion. Sabah knew it, but what were his options? Jump out of the car and run? Years later, there would be a new term for Faraj's activities. It would be called human trafficking. The victims of this barbaric practice are often unchained. Locked doors or guarded cells are unnecessary. Circumstances alone are sufficient to entrap and enslave. No one understood this better, or embraced the opportunity with more fervor, than Faraj.

He wasted no time with Sabah. With ruthless efficiency, Faraj emptied Sabah's pockets, the way a prisoner is stripped of personal possessions before his sentence begins. The check would be sent from George's office in San Francisco. When it came, it would be signed over to Faraj. Even before he handed it over, Sabah knew he'd never see any part of the money again.

Now it was seven thirty in the morning and Faraj was pulling into the parking lot of M's Liquor Store. This store was within a mile of Paradise Liquor, but Sabah would only realize this weeks later, when his new surroundings had become more familiar. All the windows of the store, as well as the glass front door, were covered by bars. In the weeks and months to come, Sabah would reflect on how appropriate this was. These liquor stores looked more like a prisons than businesses.

M's Liquor and Paradise Liquor were both located in Logan Heights, perhaps the original home of all San Diego gang activity. For Sabah, going to work meant being in the middle of a turf war between black and chicano gang members. A brand new red sports car was in the parking lot outside the store.

"M's here," Faraj announced to everyone and no one.

"Who's M?" Sabah asked.

"Mudar," Daud explained. "We call him M. He owns the store."

"And lots of others," Billah added quickly.

His glance at Sabah suggested this was all anyone needed to know about M.

"That's his car?" Sabah asked.

"One of them," Billah said.

"What kind is it?"

"Come on, man," Faraj said. "That's a Corvette."

M was close to Faraj's age, but this had no influence on the nature of M's relationship with Faraj. His accent was weaker than Faraj's. He sounded like he'd been here much longer. In fact, he'd arrived five years before Faraj. At this time in San Diego, in the earliest era of Chaldean colonization, it might as well have been five decades. If Faraj was a pioneer, M was a godfather.

Woven into the fabric of his demeanor were strands of CEO, mob boss, field marshal, and perhaps even a bit of patron saint. There was a distinct weight and gravitas in his bearing, proportionately reflecting his additional years, and the immeasurable dues he'd paid within them.

Everything about him was just a little more American than Faraj, or for that matter, any other Chaldean Sabah had ever seen. He dressed well, in a suit jacket and slacks. Physically, he was a diminutive man. He was only five foot six and maybe a hundred and fifty pounds. But Sabah could see right away that M was small the way Napoleon was small. This was a man to watch yourself around. He had a thick black moustache and black hair combed neatly back straight over his head.

Billah and Daud quickly passed M and disappeared into the store's backroom. M acknowledged them with a glance and nod of his head.

"So. The crew's growing, huh, Faraj?" M said. He was standing at the cash register, thumbing through receipts and cross-checking them with another sheet of paper attached to a clipboard.

"Hey, just tryin' to keep up," Faraj said, grinning.

M didn't glance up from his notes. "That's good. Just don't try to get ahead. So, who's your buddy?"

"This is Sabah. Sabah, M."

M looked up and, for the first time, straight at Sabah. It was a cursory glance, nothing penetrating or overly critical. M gave Sabah all the attention he was worthy of, and nothing more.

"Welcome to America's Finest City," M said.

Sabah had no idea this was San Diego's unofficial slogan. Nor could Sabah have known that the irony in M's voice was due to their present location, San Diego's most notorious ghetto. Sabah only sensed that he was, in some indirect way, being used as the butt of a dark and ugly joke.

"Thank you, I'm happy to be here," Sabah said, and smiled.

M continued making notes for another second, then looked up and put down his pen. He walked around from behind the counter until he stood next to Faraj and Sabah. M called back to the storeroom.

"Billah, Daud, you guys wanna come out here a second?"

Billah and Daud reappeared in moments. Now the four of them, Faraj, Sabah, Billah, and Daud, were gathered in front of M like a small platoon. M paused and collected himself. He took a moment to look at his assembled troops.

"Okay, so here's the deal," M said. "Faraj said he needed another guy so I let him bring you in. You watch Faraj. You do what he says. He's a sharp guy. You can learn a lot from him. As for you, we'll see. I told these guys already; you do a good job, you work hard, we'll be fine. You follow?"

"Yes, sir, very well," Sabah said.

He'd never been spoken to this way by any member of his Chaldean community. It was so peculiar he didn't have time to feel frightened. Who was this person? What kind of man was this? It couldn't be possible but, for a moment, Sabah was looking at the very people who had driven him out of his own country. He was looking at a Baathist.

But that couldn't be. This was America. There were no people like that here and if anyone here was remotely like a Baathist, it certainly wouldn't be a Chaldean, a person who had fled Iraq for the same reasons Sabah had. Sabah tried to make sense of this. Finally, he determined it was much simpler than all the fuss he was making. It had to be. Faraj and M were just idiots, that was all. Whatever else might come with that, Sabah was sure he could deal with it.

Later that afternoon, Faraj and Sabah would start their workday at Paradise Liquor. But not before Faraj paid a visit to Victor. Victor had recently opened a market. It was a Chaldean custom to pay respects by signing some form of currency, a dollar or five dollar bill, then offering it to the new store owner for posting on a wall. Though Faraj arrived at Victor's market under the auspices of this homey tradition, his real motive was far more self-serving. Faraj had come to Victor's to flaunt his newly acquired human capital.

Sabah had no idea he'd become a status symbol in Faraj's twisted view of reality. His transparent, honest nature didn't allow him to grasp the unlimited creativity of Faraj's exploitation. All Sabah could see at that moment was the kind, genuine face of another human being. It came in the form of this man, a man named Victor.

Within the ugly seed Faraj had carried into that moment, in the darkness of his selfish motives, something glorious and beautiful would emerge. Sabah would often reflect on this irony, many years in the future. Though it was something Faraj had never intended, or could have possibly foreseen, he had introduced two men who would become best friends, collaborators, and business partners. In fact, aside from his wife, Victor would be the most important partner Sabah would ever have. It would be some time before Sabah would see Victor again, but the two would both remember each other very well.

CHAPTER THIRTY-ONE

★ ★ ★

The Abyss

★ ★ ★

Sabah's gross miscalculation could be traced back to the words that once moved so casually through his mind: "Whatever else might come." Days turned into weeks and weeks into months. The ninety day extension on his visa had long since expired. Each week, Sabah's unseen pay check, like Billah's and Daud's, went directly to Faraj.

M would appear sporadically, sometimes once a week, sometimes twice, other weeks not at all. But each time M made his rounds at Paradise Liquor, Sabah noticed Faraj's behavior would tweak the slightest bit. During these visits, Faraj would become, if possible, even less likeable. Obviously M was Faraj's mentor, if not his idol.

Faraj reminded Sabah of those wild pack dogs roaming the streets of Baghdad. Late at night, especially, everyone had to be cautious. It was common knowledge that the beasts were both predators and a complete wild card. If you were unlucky and just happened to be at the wrong place at the wrong time, you could be dead.

Yet, within that savage group, Sabah had once seen one of those usually aggressive and vicious dogs suddenly begin to crawl and whine. As the pack's alpha male approached, the dog turned completely over on its back in an ultimate sign of submission and surrender. Sabah noticed Faraj's attentiveness and self-restraint during M's visits. He was quick to laugh at M's jokes. His entire disposition was milder around M, more servile, obsequious. In all this Faraj reminded Sabah of that filthy, groveling dog. It made him sick to his stomach.

Strangely, it seemed when M did come in the store, he would make it a point to seek Sabah out. He would ask him how things were going. Sabah knew M didn't have to extend this courtesy. On the rare occasions they were all together in the same place and at the same time, Sabah noticed M didn't make this effort with Daud and Billah. He would acknowledge Faraj's brothers if they happened to cross paths, but he offered them nothing more. With this small amount of additional attention, Sabah realized M had taken notice of him, perhaps even respected him for some reason neither of them could easily identify.

It was true, Sabah had always been a hard worker. This habit ran deep. His work always seemed to take on a life of its own, completely independent of the kind of work it was or who he was doing it for. Whether it had been for his father in their small cafe, at the Tokalon salon, the construction company, or even Jaqueline's place, regardless of the people he was with or the circumstances, his work ethic was constant. Sabah would never accept money for anything less than all he had to give. He continued to do this even now, when he never even saw the money he earned.

But something had changed. Now, in addition to his own standards, there was another reason for his consistently hard work. As it is for so many sad and lonely people, people without friends or hope, Sabah had started to find solace in this final refuge. Sometimes all a person has left is his work. In those dark and empty days, Sabah was never idle. This was, first of all, because he had integrity. After that, if there was room for anything else, Sabah used his work as a form of escape.

Even a person with feelings as coarse as M's recognized dedication when he saw it. But something more than this impressed M. There was some mysterious and untouchable quality in Sabah. There was something about him that neither M nor Faraj could recognize or name. It was like a forgotten word on the tip of one's tongue. It hovered so near while being annoyingly evasive.

Sabah had something M and Faraj understood but only in principle, as an abstract and theoretical idea, like that fundamental level of math neither had ever mastered. That thing they saw in Sabah, but could never name or recognize, was honesty. What they were looking at was the truth.

Sabah's first twelve months in San Diego were, and would remain for all time, the most difficult year of his life. And the first six months were the most difficult period of that year. So many harsh realities and conditions simultaneously conspired against him. It was as though multiple natural disasters occurred at the same moment. An earthquake would be bad enough, but what if, at the same instant, he had also fallen victim to a hurricane, tsunami, avalanche, and global pandemic? The probability of this convergence was so remote that such a crisis would seem absurd, even comical. Yet, within Sabah's soul, an event of this magnitude was occurring every day.

In a real way, Sabah's life was other people. It always had been. To say he was gregarious was an understatement. His inquisitive and curious nature could only be completely satisfied in direct, meaningful contact with other people. He loved and needed people, but the lifeblood people provided was being drained away in both his domestic and work environments. They were the only two places he ever went and both had become two parts of the same prison cell.

He was a trusting person. The only people he'd ever encountered who were completely incomprehensible were the Baathists. He'd left his home, family, and friends and traveled halfway around the world to escape those monsters. And for what? So that his own people, his own Chaldean people, could treat him the same way? The irony and horror of this realization drove him to start smoking cigarettes. He also began drinking almost every night after work.

His American dream had been turned inside out. It had been stolen from him and shattered. His dream of freedom had become a horrible nightmare from which he couldn't awake. He had come to America for *this*? His thoughts began turning to old friends, home, and particularly, to Jaqueline. Had it only been a few short months ago that they had sat together by a bonfire outside her townhouse, sharing a bottle of wine, holding hands and watching the moonlight reflected on the sea? If it had been possible, he would have returned to her in a second.

He thought of how kind she had been to him, how much she had loved him. For the first time in his life, Sabah had wandered into that most destructive human quagmire, self-pity. This is the place where fight escapes us. We surrender, as all prey eventually do, to the predator's inescapable jaws. We are the victims of our own numb indifference. We begin to view our lives with a listless detachment, as though standing outside ourselves, watching someone else being slowly destroyed.

Sabah couldn't have said exactly how long he was in this state. He wasn't counting the number of days, weeks, and months any more than he was taking notice of the world around him. He had long since stopped noticing the details of his world. He was no longer engaged in his lifelong, systematic process of organization and classification. His insatiable curiosity, along with his all-consuming need for new information, had been lost. That essential part of Sabah which had drawn him, so many years before, to the Al Batiwen Tea House and the world of knowledge was dormant and close to death.

In their occasional phone calls, George tried to be encouraging. In conversations with George, Sabah had difficulty disguising even the mildest disappointment. Concealment was an unnatural act for Sabah, and something he'd never been good at. After several months, George heard something in Sabah's voice he'd never heard before. It was despair and the sound tore George's heart.

He knew his brother was in America illegally by now, and had been for many months. He knew Faraj had, basically, been holding Sabah hostage. He knew his brother was alone and lonely. George tried to sound positive and upbeat. He kept telling Sabah that someway, somehow, better days were ahead. He would get his green card. He would get away from Faraj. But now George couldn't listen to himself any more.

Going back to Iraq would have been so easy. All Sabah had to do was walk into the nearest I.N.S. office and say, "Hello, I'm Sabah Toma." He would have been on a flight to Baghdad within days, if not hours. But then what? It would have been a prison transfer, nothing more. He would have moved from one cell to another.

Even Jaqueline wasn't an option any longer. Sabah had called her from Los Angeles to tell her the truth. He still cared for her. He owed her that much, at the very least. He had hoped she would understand. Perhaps she would reconsider and even join him in America, but her response was precisely what he didn't want. Only one thing was important to Jaqueline; Sabah had lied to her. Sabah loved another woman and her name was America. He had gone to her. Jaqueline had been betrayed and Sabah had made his choice. The moment they hung up, Sabah knew. The door was closed on any future they might have had together.

Who knows what the lasting consequences of such circumstances would be on most men? Perhaps we can only see them in the lives of actual prisoners. Sabah's life would be held and controlled by Faraj for more than four years. That is a long time for any man. It is an especially long time for a young man only twenty-four years of age. Could any man emerge unscathed and undamaged from such an experience? Perhaps very few.

Many years later, in a different time and place, Faraj would point Sabah out in public gatherings, long after Sabah's prominent, even dominant, position within his Chaldean community had been firmly established. At those festive occasions, when life was celebrated in so many ways by these closely knit people, Faraj's voice could be heard above the crowd.

"Look at the guy. I made him the big shot he is today. He owes it all to me."

Sabah would put his arm around Faraj and smile at him. He'd even kiss the man on the cheek and turn to anyone listening. Sabah would lift his glass as a toast and say the same words again and again, always confirming Faraj's claim.

"It's true. Every word of it. It's all true."

The legend of what Faraj had done, not only to Sabah but to many others, had been carried to every corner of the San Diego Chaldean community by that point. Everyone knew who Faraj was. Sabah's public displays of affection for Faraj, his magnanimity and forgiveness, would become woven into the legend itself. How could a man be so kind to someone who had stolen four years of his life?

For Sabah, the answer was simple. Faraj *was* telling the truth. He *had* made Sabah who he was, but not remotely in any way Faraj could understand. Like the people Faraj had introduced to Sabah, those handful of people who would be so vital to his future success, Faraj had unintentionally and inadvertently given Sabah the greatest gift he would ever receive.

Faraj had created the environment and circumstances that would become the greatest crucible of Sabah's life. Without ever knowing it, Faraj had forged the refiner's fire that would transform Sabah. If Sabah had met Faraj as a crude iron sword, he left Faraj as a chromium blade. In passing this test, Sabah would acquire a permanent brilliance of character impossible to attain any other way. But, like many epic battles, when outcomes remain so exhaustingly elusive, Sabah would only rise above the crushing weight of his unhappiness, one day and one choice at a time.

Sabah's thoughts turned to his friends and family in Baghdad many times during this period. It was so tempting, like standing at the top of a tall bridge or building, closing his eyes, and falling over backwards. He might still be in a jail, but at least he'd be in a jail with people who loved him, and people he loved.

Finally, as he had that night in Greece during that fateful conversation with Ramsey, Sabah saw his mother's face. He saw it as he'd seen it the moment he'd said goodbye. She hadn't believed he would succeed. She hadn't believed he could save himself or any one else in their family.

"Was she right?" Ramsey had asked.

The words echoed through his mind, as clear and loud as if Ramsey were standing right beside him.

Never, Sabah answered. She'd been wrong then, and on this, she would always be wrong. If it took the rest of his life, he would prove that to her.

A decision had been made. It wouldn't be his only decision. It would be one of ten thousand more over the months and years to come. Each one of those decisions and choices, as in the life of any man, would determine who Sabah Toma was and who he would become.

During one phone conversation with George, Sabah spoke quietly but with an intensity of resolve that almost frightened his brother. "Tell everybody I love them. And I want you to tell Mom something. Tell her just like this. Tell Mom I will see her in America."

CHAPTER THIRTY-TWO

★ ★ ★

Reawakening

★ ★ ★

With the fragility of a grass blade pushing up through spring soil, Sabah slowly rejoined a world that had never gone away. In one tiny expression after the next, a moment of eye contact here, a small smile there, offering whatever help he could in the midst of his own helplessness, Sabah made the choices that would restore him to his own life.

As human beings, we tend to honor courage and valor in their most dramatic forms. Perhaps this is as it should be. We honor the policeman or fireman who saves a life by putting his own at risk or the war hero who is killed or disfigured for his country. Our debt to the bravest among us can never be repaid, not in the depth or our gratitude and not in our memorials, not even in unfailing memory itself.

Yet how often do we forget or overlook courage of another kind, courage less visible but just as real. What courage is there in a man who gives love and compassion when he is surrounded by both? When a man is blessed with abundance, how much courage does charity require? When one is shown friendship, how much courage does it take to be a friend? If there is a currency in Heaven, it is not earned by this kind of courage.

For the first time in his life, Sabah was completely alone and without hope. He was unloved and had lost his ability to show love, in any form, to anyone. Perhaps this was exactly what had happened to Faraj and M. Perhaps they'd failed their own personal Gethsemanes. Overcome by years of intense longing and isolation, perhaps their own moral compasses had been destroyed, their true purposes lost forever. Sabah would never know.

All he knew was that it wasn't going to happen to him. They wouldn't defeat him. Whoever and whatever M and Faraj were, he was going to be everything they weren't.

As a young boy, Sabah had a friend who owned a dog. The dog was the boy's closest friend and companion. For years, Sabah had never seen one without the other. One day Sabah had been walking with his friend when the dog wandered away, into a busy street. There was a horrible screech of brakes and a yelp. Sabah and his friend saw the dog, alive, but trapped beneath a car. Sabah's friend instantly reached under the car to save his dog. A moment later, Sabah heard a vicious snarling and his friend cried out.

His friend pulled his hand out from under the car. His own dog had bitten him. He was bleeding so badly he had to go to the hospital. Sabah's friend had ten stitches sewn into his hand. Ironically, he'd been more seriously injured than his own dog, who'd suffered nothing worse than a few oil stains.

For some reason, the memory came back to Sabah clearly now. How could that have happened? The dog had loved his friend and his friend loved his dog. They were as close as any two living things Sabah had ever seen. Then Sabah knew. There came a point for any creature, animal or man, when pain becomes so all-consuming it makes any kind of connection or contact impossible.

Sabah knew he had become that dog. For the past six months, his pain had blinded him to the smallest gestures of humanity. But it was over now. He knew his suffering would continue, but his life would continue as well. He would make sure of that.

Sabah found little comfort in his roommates, Billah and Daud. Partly because of his state of mind since arriving in San Diego, but mostly because neither were of genuine interest to Sabah. It soon became clear that Faraj was to Billah what M was to Faraj. They were all on some kind of ladder, a horrible status structure that was as unfamiliar as it was repulsive.

From the cars they drove to their designer jeans, from the food they ate to the kind of women they would or wouldn't be interested in, social status was the single thread that simultaneously connected and separated them. Every day, Sabah saw chronic malcontent and anxiousness etched in their faces. There was never a moment of peace for any of them. They never had enough and the more they had, the more they wanted. Billah wanted to be Faraj. Faraj wanted to be M and who knew what M wanted to be. They were all on their way somewhere, though none of them had any idea where that was.

Sabah, on the other hand, had reached his destination. He wasn't on their ladder and he never would be. For Sabah, there was nothing beyond being in America. To reach America and to live here had been his dream for as long as he could remember. Now, he only wanted three things. He wanted to be free in America; this meant to have a green card and then, eventually, to become an actual citizen. Finally, he would save his family from Saddam Hussein by bringing them to America.

The fog of despair slowly began to dissipate in Sabah. Though he was far from the lively and cheerful person he'd once been, a certain amount of peace returned to his life. It showed in his face and in his eyes, which were gradually becoming reflecting pools, filled with patience. The pulse of hope, though faint, had returned. There was a future again. Somehow, some way, everything would be all right. Sabah believed it again. Hope is a hearth, a fireplace within us. It draws others toward us where they might find comfort from the cold and darkness within their own lives.

Perhaps this was why, against logic and reason, Faraj began to seek Sabah's friendship. Unlike his brothers, Faraj was a smoker, drinker, gambler, and womanizer. Sabah and Faraj had some things in common but hardly enough for either to experience anything like a mutual rapport. Faraj's interest in socializing with Sabah was more closely related to the fact that every Chaldean in San Diego hated Faraj. Perhaps Faraj also misinterpreted Sabah's mellowing disposition as a growing acceptance of Faraj's dominant role within their world.

For whatever reason, Faraj would take Sabah out for drinks or dinner once or twice a week, usually to a belly dancing restaurant named Haji Baba's. It was near Faraj's apartment in Mission Valley. Faraj was particularly partial to a certain dancer there. In fact, he'd been trying to make her a conquest for years. Sonia was a voluptuous, blonde haired American girl, exactly the kind of woman so many middle eastern men, Faraj included, fantasized about.

Beyond his adolescence and throughout his entire adult life, Sabah never lacked the company of women. He was a good looking man, first of all. But more than this, he had always been happy with or without women.

The physical expression of love never represented to Sabah, as it did for so many men, a kind of remedy from an ongoing fever. A lack of opportunity for intimacy didn't shroud Sabah in a cloak of desperation. There was too much to life, and too much life within him, for this to be so.

Sabah had his own interpretation for his success with women. He traced it to his days in the Tokalon Salon and his thorough training from Baligh, Mazhar, Faraj, and Rashid. He'd learned about women from the masters in this field. He'd also been exposed, routinely, to so many beautiful women there. He'd shared their unguarded feelings and thoughts so intimately and over such a long period of time that, as an adult, he was actually more comfortable in the presence of women than men.

However, like so many other essential traits, he'd lost this vital part of himself during his first year in San Diego. In some ways, he'd become like so many of his male peers. He began to long for the companionship of women. But his longing was woven into a far more complicated fabric of longing for so many things. In fact, nearly everything.

As he slowly reemerged, women began to take note of him again, as they always had. But now women approached him like hummingbirds in the early morning. The real Sabah, the Sabah who had always been and always would be, was reopening like a blossom in the morning sun. That blossom's nectar, perceived only by the delicate sensitivity of a woman, was making Sabah visible and attractive once again.

Faraj had been away only for a few minutes, first to the bathroom, then to speak with some people he knew at the restaurant's bar. He was re-telling a recent exploit when he noticed something. It was something he didn't like. Sabah was sitting at their table, near the stage, where Faraj had left him. But now, Sonia was sitting next to Sabah. For as long as he'd been coming to Haji Baba's, she'd never sat down next to him like she was, right now, with Sabah.

That would have been unsettling enough, but she suddenly threw her head back in a full, hearty laugh. Her long, smooth blonde hair cascaded like a perfect waterfall around the back of her chair. Faraj had never seen her laugh like this, with such unguarded spontaneity. Without another word to the guys at the bar, Faraj walked toward Sabah and Sonia. As he approached, the music began again and Sonia stood up, continuing her entertainment for a group at another table.

"What did she say?" Faraj asked, sitting down next to Sabah.

"Nothing," Sabah smiled and continued watching Sonia as she danced.

"Tell me!"

Sabah shrugged. "You know, just the usual chit-chat."

"What?" Faraj asked again, now with a threatening shrillness and urgency. Sabah turned and looked directly at Faraj.

"She asked me if I wanted to see where she lived," Sabah said.

Faraj's face went rigid. "Perfect. That's perfect."

"You wanna loan me your car?" Sabah asked. "You're close enough to walk home, right?"

"What does that have to do with anything? Are you kidding me?"

"She asked if I could give her a ride home."

"No way," Faraj growled. "If she wants a ride, we'll both go."

For reasons Sabah could never completely understand, Sonia accepted Faraj's offer. Now, sitting in Sonia's living room, Faraj and Sabah waited in an uncomfortable silence. Sonia had gone into her bedroom to change her clothes. If his reemergence in the world was beginning to attract women again, it was also attracting Sabah to women. He could definitely use the kind of attention Sonia seemed more than willing to offer. Sabah was quietly deliberating on the best way to get Faraj out of her apartment when Faraj suddenly stood up and began walking out of the living room.

"Wait here," Faraj said and left the room. Somewhere in the apartment, Sabah heard a door open and close. Faraj reappeared five minutes later.

"Let's go," Faraj said.

"What happened? Is she okay?" Sabah asked.

"Sabah, move. Now!"

Of course the evening would end like this. Faraj had always taken everything he could and left Sabah with nothing. This was just one more thing torn away in his typically brutal way. Sabah never did find out what happened that night. If Faraj had forced himself on Sonia in any way, she never mentioned it. Sabah was fairly confident that whatever else Faraj was, he wasn't a rapist. It was more likely that Faraj had insisted on going with Sabah and Sonia simply as a preventative measure. If he couldn't have something, especially something he wanted as much as Sonia, Sabah sure wasn't going to have her either.

CHAPTER THIRTY-THREE

★ ★ ★

The Rise and Fall of Faraj

★ ★ ★

Armed with a year and a half of paychecks collected from Sabah, Billah, and Daud, Faraj was ready to elevate himself. Somehow, Faraj had convinced M and Hussein, another of his acquaintances, to co-sign on a loan. He became the owner of his first grocery store, the Happy Town Market.

Sabah considered the possibilities. Perhaps his new position as a store owner might appease Faraj's obsessive need for status. He might calm down a little, even become a bit more human or, at the very least, a more palatable employer. It was a false hope and, on all counts, Sabah couldn't have been more wrong.

The moment he became an official market owner and CEO of his own world, Faraj distributed his first memo in the form of an opening day speech. There would be a new policy, effective immediately. Employees of the Happy Town Market would work eighty hours a week. Billah and Daud, in the same position as Sabah, asked no questions and made no complaints.

It was like that first morning in Faraj's car, when he told Sabah he needed two thousand dollars. They were all in a speeding car, every day of their lives. What were they going to do, jump? The only choice was to stay in the car and keep going, with a faint hope that they might someday reach an actual destination.

In fact, Faraj's new work edict hardly made any difference to Sabah. When one's entire life is a prison, does it matter if a work week is forty, sixty, or eighty hours long? For the next year, seven days a week, ten to twelve hours a day, the Happy Town Market would be Sabah's world.

As the new management, meaning mostly Daud, Billah, and Sabah, established themselves in the community, profits increased for Faraj. With increased financial security, Faraj soon upgraded his residence. He remained in his Mission Valley neighborhood but moved into one of the brand new, fancy "apartment home" complexes, the kind with a gym, swimming pool, jacuzzi, clubhouse, and even billiard tables. This was a much more suitable situation for a man of his stature.

Not as a demonstration of generosity or kindness, but purely financial expedience, Faraj moved Sabah and his brothers into his new two-bedroom apartment. There was no sense in paying for two places. Faraj knew communal living had its disadvantages. There wouldn't be as much privacy. But what his new roommates represented in terms of money saved was too tempting.

By this point, Faraj wasn't able to view people as anything other than dollar signs. Every decision involving other people, including his own brothers, was based and calculated on one simple idea: how much money would they make for him or how much money would they cost?

The added creature comforts associated with the move were welcomed by Sabah and Faraj's brothers, but they did little to alleviate the fundamental emptiness created by their bondage. Still, it was nice to not be in a ghetto. The building was filled with pretty, young, single American girls. Faraj's third floor unit had a perfect view of the pool, where they could see those girls in their bikinis. Unfortunately for Sabah, Daud, and Billah, only Faraj was home frequently enough, particularly on weekends, to not only enjoy that sight but participate in it.

At this time in Sabah's life, it would be hard to say if his interest in women was an expression of his natural life force or a remedy for chronic pain. Was he responding to his genetic programming or desperately trying to anesthetize himself? It's possible both could have been happening at the same time. In any event, another element of his neighborhood, like his new home and community, was a new nightclub. It was called Flannigans, so close to their new home, it was separated only by a parking lot.

It would have been easy to call Flannigans Sabah's second home. Easy, that is, if he'd had a first one. First or second, it became more of a home to

240

him than anywhere else he'd been in America. As with most fashionable clubs, Flannigans' novelty and sexiness would dissipate over time, along with its seductive aura of trendiness. Its power to attract the beautiful people would diminish. Eventually it would be completely abandoned, discarded by that eternally changing, insatiable mistress, fashion.

But now, it was in the throes of its white hot genesis. Sabah had arrived just in time to not only participate, but be one of its locals, a regular, permanent fixture. It was perfect. He didn't have a car, he didn't have money, but he did have walking access to the busiest, most popular bar in San Diego.

Resilience, like so many other qualities of youth, is taken for granted by the young. When Sabah wasn't at the Happy Town, he was at Flannigans. But he wasn't grateful, even for a moment, for his stamina. He'd only had four hours of sleep per night for a full year. Flannigans was his escape and refuge, a daily haven from Faraj's prison.

Sabah's own fortitude and upgraded domicile, which featured a nightclub living room, lifted him somewhere above agony but far below well-being. The slow burning embers of hope, not completely extinguished, were supplemented by the ample dalliances so conveniently provided by Flannigans. His life became bearable, rather than horrible, as it had been in his first year. Still, without a plan or means of escape, Sabah's next several years could best be described as a kind of hibernation.

He wasn't asleep but he wasn't fully awake. He was simply waiting, like the Israelites, for his time of deliverance. Finally, Sabah's liberation from Faraj would arrive, not due to his own efforts but to the implosive power of greed itself.

Four years had passed since Sabah's arrival in San Diego. One day, Faraj walked into the storage room of the Happy Town Market with a large cardboard box. He set it on a counter where Sabah was working.

"Here's another one. Crumple them up a little more after you cut them. Make them look more used."

For months, Sabah had been taking coupon inserts out of newspapers. Copies of the local newspaer would arrive by the thousands. Faraj had given Sabah the job of cutting and separating every coupon from every insert. Sabah would cut and neatly organize them. Piles of coupons numbering in the thousands, even tens of thousands, accumulated in the Happy

Town storage area. Sabah had no idea why he was doing this, but he was doing it every day. Billah and Daud were cutting coupons also, both at the market and at home. Perhaps the odd, repetitive procedure was connected to the responsibility of store ownership. Who knew? Faraj never gave explanations, he only gave orders.

Sabah never made a connection between this strange new work duty and the move to the Coronado Cays. The Cays were an affluent private neighborhood across the street from the ocean, built right on the San Diego harbor. Each multi-million dollar home featured a private dock, usually occupied by a yacht larger than Faraj's Mission Valley apartment.

The day they moved in, Faraj stepped to the middle of a large empty room. The room featured a bank of floor to ceiling windows and a white marble floor. Faraj opened his arms and gestured out the window. Rows of large boats gently rocked in a tidal sway.

"Will this do?" he asked, smiling.

"What'd you do, rob a bank?" Billah asked, clearly stunned by what he was seeing.

"Almost," Faraj said. "Actually, the store's doing better than I thought. Better than I dreamed! See? I told you I'd take care of you guys, huh? Huh?"

Billah, Daud, and Sabah didn't know that, in addition to themselves, lots of other people were cutting coupons. Faraj had purchased two more stores, one a market and another liquor store. At the same time Sabah and Faraj's brothers had been clipping and organizing coupons, all of Faraj's other employees had been doing the same thing.

Faraj and six other confederates, mostly Chaldean store owners, were returning coupons on items that were never sold and collecting the cash back from dozens of different companies. Faraj's cut of the enterprise was nearly twenty thousand dollars a month. It was fraud. It was illegal and Faraj's house of cards would eventually collapse, bringing Faraj down with it.

But not before Faraj could attain that ultimate symbol of status, a pretty young wife nearly half his age. He flew back to Iraq while Billah, Daud, and Sabah took care of things at Happy Town. He returned with his bride and began his happily ever after in the Coronado Cays with his wife, brothers, and Sabah.

On the day of Faraj's return from Iraq, a U.S. Postal employee in the

San Diego community of National City noticed something for the first time. An unusually large number of coupons were being repeatedly mailed from the same location. It was the beginning of the end for Faraj. It would also be a beginning *and* an end—the beginning of Faraj's imprisonment and the end of Sabah's.

Within weeks of Faraj's return from Iraq, Sabah saw a change in Faraj. In some way, perhaps noticed only by those exposed to him as often as Sabah was, Faraj was softening. He seemed brighter and more cheerful. He was smiling and laughing more. Sabah and Faraj's brothers assumed his wife had everything to do with it.

"Amazing what a woman can do for a guy," Daud said while they were working in the market.

"It's not that," Sabah said.

"What then?"

"I don't know." Sabah thought about it for a moment. "Maybe, for the first time, he cares about somebody other than himself."

Sabah had been impressed with Faraj's young wife from the day he met her. She wasn't just young and pretty. She was kind and sweet, caring and compassionate. She was everything Faraj wasn't and everything he needed most. Sabah knew that the time was right for a conversation with Faraj, a long overdue conversation. Sabah had rehearsed it many times, but before now, he'd always feared it would fall on deaf ears.

It was a late spring evening. Faraj and Sabah sat on the moonlit porch of the Coronado Cays home, drinking red wine and smoking cigars. They'd finished a good meal prepared by Faraj's wife. Now they sat quietly, saying little. But unlike other past silences between them, this one was comfortable.

"Faraj," Sabah began, "Have I done a good job for you?"

Faraj glanced at Sabah, but not with shifting eyes or a momentary tilt of his head as he generally did. Instead, he turned and gazed directly into Sabah's eyes. The two men looked at each other for a moment.

"Yes. You've done very good," Faraj said.

"I've helped you. Things are better now, right? I mean, you've got a good business, a nice wife. You seem ... happy."

"Things could be worse." Faraj shrugged and smiled. He lifted his cigar and took a drag. The large ember tip grew brighter. He studied Sabah another moment.

"What's on your mind?"

"I think it's time for me to go," Sabah said.

"Go where?"

"Back to school, to get my license."

"You mean hairdressing?"

"Yes."

Faraj said nothing but Sabah didn't look away.

"Sure," Faraj said at last. "Why not? When?"

"Any time that's good for you," Sabah said.

"We need to find somebody to replace you. That's not gonna be easy you know. You don't find a Sabah every day, right?"

Sabah smiled. "I guess not, no."

"Can you give me a couple a weeks?" Faraj asked.

Give him a couple of weeks, Sabah thought. He'd given him five years, if given was the right word. Can a man give anything when no choice is involved? Sabah simply returned Faraj's smile.

"Sure, I can do that."

Sabah never did know if Faraj was telling the truth or maneuvering for additional time to tighten his binds. He would never know because the next day Faraj was indicted. The case received more than it's fair share of city-wide media coverage. Faraj wasn't just a participant in a band of fraudulent store owners, he was their ringleader and mastermind. In newspapers and even on local television broadcasts, Faraj became the poster child for business fraud and corruption. He had gained a level of fame and notoriety exceeding his wildest dreams, in a way he'd never imagined.

Between his arrest, post for bail, impending court date, and ongoing meetings with attorneys, Faraj wasn't able to maintain his usual focus and iron fist control over his employees. After Faraj's release from a fifty day jail term, without fanfare or further discussion, Sabah left. He quietly moved out of the Coronado Cays and, finally, out of Faraj's world. Faraj was out on bail at that time and had gone to his attorney's office to fill out some papers. By the time Faraj returned home, Sabah was gone.

Sabah wasted no time. Immediately after Faraj's indictment, he enrolled in a Chula Vista beauty college. The school was in southern San Diego near the Mexican border. Sabah called a young Syrian named Nazar, a Happy Town customer. Nazar was living in an apartment near the beauty college. It was small, a two-bedroom with walls that had been patched and repainted dozens of times, always in the same boring shade of beige. From the acoustical "cottage cheese" ceilings, stained fabric curtains, cheap vinyl bathroom floor, even the Salvation Army furniture, everything about the place said cheap, generic, temporary, and transient.

The first time Sabah saw it he beamed with delight. It was a palace. Though he'd just come from a place eight times the size and a hundred times the quality, it had been a gilded cage. Now he'd be sleeping on a foam mat in a tiny box of a room. Instead of the sound of ocean waves lulling him to sleep every night, there would be a four-lane boulevard with non-stop traffic just a few yards outside his window. But none of that mattered because for the first time in over five years, he would be free. As free as an illegal refugee in America was allowed to be, in any case.

For Sabah, beauty school was more of a formality than an education. In fact, he could have easily been one of the instructors. Here was another kind of freedom. He was free from study. His license was acquired with little more than simple attendance. This left Sabah ample time and energy to pursue other means of income.

At some point in the past, Sabah had met Baja. Baja was a Muslim and a swap meet veteran. He'd made a career of selling whatever he could at these American versions of the Middle Eastern bazaar.

He advanced Sabah reams of Jordache jeans which Sabah, in turn, could sell at slightly marked up prices. While he was at beauty school, and for some time after, Sabah could be seen on weekends at the Spring Valley swap meet.

Though he didn't know it at the time, he was doing far more than just earning enough money to stay alive. At this place, daily interacting with thousands of people from all walks of life, Sabah was receiving a crash course in Sales 101. He was unaware of the skills he was developing, skills that would lead him, step-by-step, to a life he'd always believed he'd have and, at the same time, a life he never could have imagined.

Halfway through Sabah's state-required eight month course at the beauty college, Faraj's court date arrived and Sabah received a call from Faraj.

"Hey buddy, how's things?" Faraj asked.

"Good, great," Sabah said. Though he was firmly beyond Faraj's clutches now, he was still conditioned to answer Faraj's questions as he always had, quickly and with the least amount of information.

"Good, good. School's going good?"

"No problem. What do they say? Easy as cake? No, simple as pie. See, I'm finally speaking American."

Faraj laughed. "You got it! But hey, uh, you know my court date's next week."

"I know,"

"Well, the thing is, my attorney, he was looking at the notes I asked you to send me, about the whole situation, you know?"

"Right."

"Well, he told me he thinks you should testify."

There was a long pause.

"Faraj, you want *me* to go into an American court room? I'll be in bigger trouble than you!"

"No, not at all! My attorney told me, it's not a big deal. He says you'll be fine."

"How does he know?"

"Sabah, please," Faraj said. There was something in his voice, a desperation and fear that Sabah had never heard there before.

"Listen to me Sabah. I'm in trouble, really, really bad trouble. You know my wife's expecting. I can't leave her. Who knows what they'll do? Sabah, please. I need you to do this one thing. Just this one thing."

At that moment, Sabah realized: *Faraj's fate is in my hands.*

He could easily say no. He probably should say no. Faraj had, after all, exploited him and left him a veritable prisoner in his own life for five years. Faraj had shown him misery and darkness such as he'd never experienced before, and after all that, he seriously expected Sabah to help him?

And yet now, with Faraj's life in his hands, Sabah found that he could not hate the man. There simply was no room in his heart for it. All Sabah could feel for him now was pity. And with that, the five year cycle was complete. Passing through the refiner's fire, Sabah had fully returned.

He would agree to testify. He would risk deportation, along with his own imprisonment or execution in Iraq, not because he loved Faraj, but because he loved everyone else.

"Okay, Faraj," he said quietly. "Where do I go?"

"I'll have my attorney call you," Faraj said, "and he'll … He'll, um …"

His voice cracked and there was a rustling sound, as of someone hurriedly covering the mouthpiece with his hand. For a few moments, all Sabah could hear was the muffled sound of Faraj weeping.

"Thank you," Faraj choked out after a while. "Thank you."

"It's okay," Sabah said. "We're gonna be okay."

★ ★ ★

Sabah was familiar with governmental offices of every type, but he'd never entered a courtroom before, anywhere. He was afraid, and for good reason. If the prosecutors had done their homework on Faraj's supporting witnesses, they would know that Sabah was a fugitive, wanted by the I.N.S. But the angels were looking after Sabah in that courtroom. The prosecutors cross-examined his innocent involvement with Faraj's coupon scheme, but his immigration status was never questioned or discussed.

Later, Faraj's attorney would attribute Faraj's sentence, in large part, to the testimony Sabah had given. Faraj could have gone to prison for a number of years. Instead, for his part in the scheme, Faraj was given his freedom and released from the courtroom. It was a blessing and a gift that Faraj would not forget and, in years to come, Faraj would return that favor to Sabah in nearly equal proportion.

CHAPTER THIRTY-FOUR

★ ★ ★

The Birth Of A Salesman

★ ★ ★

As soon as Sabah graduated from beauty school, he realized hairdressing in America was not the same as it was in Iraq. He had a hint in the ratio of male to female students at his school—one man for every twenty women. He was offered a job in a salon very close to the Hotel Del Coronado. Coronado, an upscale community by San Diego standards, would have provided a relatively affluent clientele. But the lucrative prospects of the community were offset by the environment of the salon itself.

For Sabah, personal evolution and growth were synonymous with working in a beauty salon. Now, however, his co-workers would no longer be able to dramatically expand his understanding of the world, as his good friends at the Tokalon Salon had done. Perhaps due to his age and experience, he was no longer able to view any salon co-worker as a mentor. Sabah was no longer an impressionable youth, though he was just as inquisitive, just as eager to grow and evolve. Now, he needed a new kind of mentor.

It was true. He was older and more mature. But more than this, he'd become like water. He was beginning to conform to the shape of his new vessel. America was that vessel now. America provided his new horizons and America would be the mentor that would help him reach them. The simple truth was this: being a hairdresser was no longer enough. He didn't know what he wanted in terms of his life in America. He only knew that it was something other than hairdressing. Whoever he was, wherever he was going, whatever he could be, America had forever changed Sabah's view of his world and himself. He was the verge of a new era in exploration.

Perhaps due to sentiment as much as pragmatism, and also as a child of poverty who could never have too much protection from future misfortune, Sabah would renew his beautician's license every two years for the rest of his life. And perhaps there was another reason, something closer to the covenant he'd made with God, for when the fruits of his hard work and choices began to abundantly manifest. His constant prayer had remained the same, "God, if I'm not grateful, if I don't help others, take it all away from me. Take it all away today."

Finally, Sabah renewed that license so he would always remember, no matter who he became, that he would forever be a person of no greater or lesser importance than a hairdresser.

Though much changed in his life after his liberation from Faraj, one thing remained the same: Sabah's sense of duty to his family. He hadn't forgotten, even during his darkest moments with Faraj, the reason he'd come to America. He was here to help them follow. Now it had become even more urgent. A letter had arrived with news of his brother Wally. The Syrian branch of the Baath party was at odds with the Iraqi branch. Like gangs battling against each other in cities across America, the two branches of the Baath party were sworn enemies. Wally was being detained and tortured in Syria as a spy for the Iraq Baathists. He was neither a spy nor a Baathist but it didn't matter. He had been in the wrong place at the wrong time and his life was in peril.

In desperation, Sabah consulted an immigration attorney. Could Sabah do anything to help his brother come to America? The attorney leaned back in his chair, took off his glasses, and gave Sabah a long, searching look.

"Let me ask you something," the attorney said. "Are you in the United States legally right now?"

Sabah dropped his gaze. "No."

The attorney sighed and reflected for a moment. He was considering his next words carefully. How could he say them in a way that this young person with limited English skills would understand and remember what he was about to say?

"Sabah, I'm not going to charge you anything. You don't owe me anything for seeing me today, okay?"

"Yes, okay, thank you," Sabah said, looking simultaneously grateful and slightly confused.

"There is nothing you can do for your brother," the attorney said. "I'm sorry, but that's the truth."

Sabah nodded his head, but said nothing.

"But here is something you can do. I want you to listen to me very carefully and remember what I'm about to say. Will you do that?"

"Yes, I'll remember."

"First, take care of yourself. Then take care of your brother and your family. You understand?"

Take care of himself. For weeks after meeting the attorney, Sabah considered what, exactly, that could mean. Obtain his citizenship, of course, but it was something more than that. Until this time, he'd viewed assistance to his family in simpler terms. He would gain his citizenship, somehow, and in doing so he would be able to help them gain their own. Sabah began to see, now, that there was much more to the process. Taking care of himself first. The idea slowly grew in his mind. He started to think of the ways, means, and financial resources he would need to bring his family to America. For the first time, he began to think about money.

Without knowing it, Sabah had already formed the basis for his own unique approach to sales and capitalism. He'd done it while working at the swap meet. In barter and trade, Sabah attained what the world said could not be attained, the perfect practice of a laissez-faire marketplace. He did this every day he worked in the patchwork beehive of the swap meet.

He would begin his day by visiting every other vendor at the meet. He'd make purchases to supplement whatever else he'd brought with him to sell. He would, in turn, re-sell the very purchases he'd made, marking the price up. At the same time, he would sell to other vendors who, in turn, would mark up what they had purchased from Sabah. He was often questioned, even criticized, for his practice of the second policy.

Friends visiting him at the swap meet would witness, first hand, Sabah's generous trade policies. Sometimes, in the stall right beside Sabah's, a vendor would be selling products Sabah had just sold him, at double the price. To so many critics of his business practices, it was like throwing money away. And they didn't hesitate to let him know what they thought.

Sabah was unfazed. They just didn't understand. He'd made his money. Let someone else make theirs. If they made their money the same way he did, he was connected to them by something more powerful than money itself. They were friends, partners, and companions in the same process. They were all buying and selling and making a profit. It was as simple as that. For the rest of his life, as his portfolio of real estate properties grew, he would never forget this simple guiding principle learned at a swap meet: live and let live.

"Just come in and talk to them. I'm telling you, Sabah, this is big."

Billah had phoned Sabah to tell him about the new job he'd found. Sabah wasn't the only one who had escaped Faraj. Billah had done the same thing, but where could undocumented and unskilled workers go in America? Where could they find a job that would provide anything close to a living wage, let alone a respectable income?

At that time, there was at least one place in San Diego. That place was American International Marketing, a small life insurance agency in Mission Valley.

It was a commissions-only pyramid operation. Commission percentages accrued as more senior employees and managers took overrides on newer agents. It was exactly the kind of organization most American-born college or business school graduates wouldn't be caught dead in.

For Sabah, however, it was exactly what he was looking for, and the world of American Insurance Marketing, or AIM, would be like a completely new dimension in his American experience.

As with any other job he'd ever had, Sabah arrived early on his first day at AIM. He was dressed in a new suit and tie, one of three he'd acquired in a barter with Baja, another vendor at the swap meet. Sabah had never lacked for confidence or ease in any social setting, but the sight of so many desks, phones, typewriters, fax machines, not to mention thirty other men in suits, overwhelmed him.

There was a great deal of chatter in the room. So many conversations were happening simultaneously, and each one seemed to have its own history and special significance. Sabah was meandering around introducing himself, trying to connect with one clique or another, when he heard a man's voice rise above the din of group.

"Gentlemen, agents, may I have your attention please? For those who don't know me, I'm Sam Dolenzio. First time agents, welcome to American International Marketing."

Sabah like the sound of the word "agent." It was what he was now. He didn't know exactly what it meant but it suggested that he was something more than anything he'd ever been. It sounded official, professional. It made him feel refined. Mr. Dolenzio was the President and owner of the company. He was standing by a bank of windows overlooking the parking lot of the office building.

"I'd like you all to take a look down there," Mr. Dolenzio said. "Do you see that silver car over in the corner, parked all by itself?"

Sabah pressed against the window until he could clearly see a brand new Mercedes SEL in the parking lot. It was a newer version of the same car he'd seen so many times before in Iraq. It was the official livery car for the highest ranking members of the Baath Party.

"You see that car down there? That's my car. Some people might call that a status symbol. You all know what a status symbol is, right?"

Heads nodded. There was a murmur of general acknowledgement throughout the conference room. Sabah was slightly uncomfortable. He didn't know what it meant. He would try to understand it in context with everything else Mr. Dolenzio was saying.

"People might say, 'Look at old Sam. Thinks he's a hot shot with his big Mercedes, showin' off like some movie star.' Some of *you* might have said the same thing. Am I right?"

A ripple of chuckles quickly subsided as Mr. Dolenzio's sharp eyes searched the room.

"Sure, you can admit it. Why not? It's only natural. I might have said the same thing myself when I was your age, ninety years ago."

A wave of laughter rolled through room again.

"But you know what I see when *I* look at that car?" At that instant, no one in the room was listening more closely than Sabah, and no one wanted to hear the answer more. "I see the proof that I'm as good as I think I am. And you know what? I like that. When I'm driving on the freeway and

252

I look at that emblem, I say to myself, Sam, you smooth operator ... you are good!"

Mr. Dolenzio stopped and looked at the car again. When he glanced back around the room, the eyes of everyone in it were on the car.

"And here's what I want for every person in this room, right now. I want the exact same thing for each and every one of you. And you can do it. Just like me. I want each of you to have a car just like that. Or a Cadillac or a Porsche or whatever. It doesn't matter. I just want you to have that one thing, whatever it is, that you can look at and say to yourself, I deserve that. That's mine because I'm good."

Sabah was filled with a dizzying euphoria. He was a brand new peer in this distinguished fraternity and their patriarch was offering the sermon. Sabah couldn't have been more impressed if God Himself had been standing in front of the group. He made a silent, sacred vow to himself to learn everything this man wanted to teach him and to do it exactly as he was told.

The first thing Sabah was told to do was to learn how to sell, and not from Mr. Dolenzio himself, but from a man he viewed as *his* mentor. That mentor came in the form a thirty day video training program, shown in the AIM conference room during Sabah's first month. That mentor was a man named Tom Hopkins. There never was, or ever could be, a candidate more ready to benefit from this training than Sabah.

Tom Hopkins spoke simply, using easy to understand words and phrases, many of them from the Bible. Sabah instantly grasped every word that was said. It wasn't just that Tom Hopkins was speaking a kind of English Sabah could completely understand. It was as though Tom Hopkins were speaking a language especially designed for Sabah. But his instant, complete acceptance wasn't simply due to the ease with which he grasped the concepts. Sabah was untainted by cynicism of any kind, particularly the sort which can be an unpleasant byproduct of the American higher education system. Sabah's naiveté and childlike faith, still alive and even vibrant after a life that would have extinguished them both in most other men, were his most valuable assets.

He questioned nothing and consecrated himself to do exactly as he was instructed. For some, such blind obedience leads to disaster. For Sabah, it was the beginning of a miracle.

CHAPTER THIRTY-FIVE

★ ★ ★

The Fullness of Time

★ ★ ★

Sabah's sales territory was in National City, near his old workplace, Happy Town Market. Armed with his brochures, triplicate forms, and Tom Hopkins cassette tapes, Sabah began his door-to-door sales crusade. He did this in addition to his work at the swap meet. Though he'd been free from Faraj for almost a year, his work hours remained the same. Between the beauty school, the swap meet, and AIM, Sabah had been working seventy to eighty hours a week since leaving Faraj.

For many people, the idea of working as a door-to-door salesman is horrifying. After all, if there's anything worse than one of those annoying sales people, surely it's *being* one of those sales people. It's a job anyone can do, and anyone does do. Armed only with indestructible enthusiasm, any uneducated bumpkin can jump in and try to make their fortune by bending the will of another human being to their own. The least sensitive among us, even when unemployed, starving, and destitute, shiver at the prospect of this kind of work.

But Sabah knew nothing of these things. He was the definitive case study on how personal experience affects perception. He was much like the proverbial farm boy who, after a lifetime of getting up every day at four A.M., joins the Marines and is delighted to sleep in until five. Sabah never viewed his work based on what it was. He saw it only in terms of what it wasn't.

He wasn't a slave anymore. He wasn't working to make someone else rich or to make *their* dreams come true. He wasn't running on an endless treadmill or navigating a maze like a laboratory rat. Now he was working for himself and all he could feel was the joy of his new freedom. Slammed doors, apathy, and even outright hostility were big improvements in his overall working conditions. Far from being discouraged, he accepted each rejection with gratitude and moved brightly on to the next.

But enthusiasm alone does not make an effective salesman. It took Sabah about six months before he began to see through the fog of that mysterious phenomenon known as the sales pitch.

He began to feel his own unique rhythm. His approach became more informed, assured, and effective. He became familiar with common objections and developed completely reassuring answers for all of them. And he did all this without changing his one most vital asset: himself.

He had always been likeable for reasons completely unrelated to his skills as a salesman. In fact, as a salesman, Sabah's personality was not at all shaped by the contrived, external mechanics of salesmanship. He was untainted by the salesman's general impulses toward ingratiation or feigned modesty. Just the opposite occurred. His sales skills were imbued with the honesty and transparency that had always served him so well in every other aspect of his life. Within six months, Sabah was one of the most successful agents at American International Marketing.

After a year with AIM, however, Sabah began to feel a restlessness similar to his experience in the Coronado Beauty Salon. It was as though, in some way he couldn't clearly identify, he'd reached an ending point. He began to be nudged by his instincts and tugged by a familiar yet mysterious force. He wasn't being pulled away from anything but toward something else. The big leagues were calling.

The local John Hancock office had about as many agents as the AIM office, but Sabah could tell that this was, as the Americans said, a whole new ball game. If corporate offices and professional appearances were a kind of seductive veneer to Sabah, then this new environment had a higher sheen and luster in that veneer. The interior design and décor were more contemporary. In the reception area, matching chrome chairs with black leather straps faced each other around a black, polished coffee table.

There was no harsh overhead florescent lighting as there was at AIM. Halogen lights were carefully positioned on ceiling tracks, directing beams at features within the office area. Sabah took them each in individually: a company logo on the wall behind the desk, a painting, and on the coffee table, a tall simple vase with a bouquet of fresh long-stemmed flowers. It was all so minimal and understated.

Sabah introduced himself to the receptionist and moments later, a short, bald-headed man, perhaps forty years old, walked into the office lobby.

"How ya doin'? I'm Frank." He extended a hand to Sabah. Sabah felt the firmness in his grip and returned it.

"So, you finished the shrink quiz?" Frank asked.

Sabah handed the completed form to Frank. "I put the checks by the boxes, yes."

Sabah didn't know it was called a "shrink quiz" and, in fact, had no idea what that meant. Whatever its purpose, it had been a strange test. It had just seemed like a lot of the same questions being asked, over and over, in slightly different ways. He wondered if it was some kind of trick, or if the people who'd written the quiz just thought he was stupid. Or maybe they were stupid.

"Good, good," Frank said. "Well, come on back and let's talk."

He led Sabah down a hallway lined with eight and a half by eleven inch photos. Each photo had the same inscription: "Salesman of The Month."

"Nice looking people," Sabah said. He was already imagining what his own photo would look like.

Frank's office was a corner suite overlooking the large Highway 805 bridge span across the length of Mission Valley. Sabah sat down on a cream-colored leather sofa while Frank took a matching chair.

"So, Toma … It is Toma, right?"

"Sabah Toma."

"Sabah? You're first name's Sabah?"

"Yes, sir."

"Funny. I thought it was Toma Sabah. Sorry. So, you're from where? India, Iran?"

"Iraq."

"Really? I flunked geography. Where is it?"

"Well, it's kind of in the Middle East, I guess," Sabah said, smiling.

"Right. Wherever. Could be Egypt for all I know. The question is, can you sell?"

"I think I can, yes."

"You *think* you can?" Frank asked.

"Well, I don't like to brag. I did okay at AIM. Mr. Dolenzio helped me. He taught me a lot."

"Sabah, you wanna know my philosophy on modesty? Forget modesty. It doesn't pay. If you got it, you got it. So, do you got it?"

Sabah looked at Frank, stunned for a moment, then broke into an easy, genuine smile.

"I got it," Sabah said.

"I thought so," Frank said, and grinned at him.

For the next forty five minutes, the two men shared a conversation that was more like a reunion than a job interview. At one point, Frank picked up the completed psychology test, a standard requirement for all new John Hancock employees.

"You know what this is?" he said. "A joke. A complete joke. I'm supposed to get the results on this before I hire somebody."

Frank tore up the test and put the sheets in a wastebasket next to his desk.

"You're hired."

Within three months, Sabah would have his photo on that long row of photos, not once, but every month for the next year. No one worked harder and no one earned his success more than Sabah did.

In time, though he was still without citizenship, Sabah would not only become a member of the union at John Hancock, he would become the local chairman.

Life was good and getting better all the time. His combined income from the swap meet and John Hancock didn't allow Sabah an extravagant lifestyle, but he was earning enough to hire a new attorney. Here was another cog in the revolving wheel of legal and governmental officials perpetually spinning throughout his life. This one was a man by the name of Jason Blix. Through his involvement with Sabah, Blix would gain both a notorious and legendary reputation within the entire community of California immigration attorneys.

Blix's counsel to his young client was for Sabah to find a nice American wife as soon as possible. Sabah wondered why he'd paid for this advice. This wasn't information he didn't already have. In fact, from the earliest stages of his relationship with Blix, Sabah wondered if the man actually knew what he was talking about. Even so, Sabah took him at his word. He kept his eyes and attitude open for a suitable candidate.

At home in Iraq, things were getting worse. Saddam Hussein's tyrannical oppression was manifesting itself in new ways every day and Sabah's mother could wait no longer. Sabah had been gone for seven years and he still wasn't a U.S. citizen. It was true, he'd managed to stay in America and that was a miracle in itself. But without being a resident, he couldn't sponsor anyone in his family. If anyone else in the Toma family came now, they would have to come as Sabah had—any way they could.

Mrs. Toma made the trip to Greece with her youngest son, Sam. Like Sabah's trip, it was a risk. There was no guarantee she would get a visa from Greece to America. For some reason Sabah never understood, his mother easily obtained American visas for both Sam and herself. Perhaps things had become more lax at the American Consulate in Greece. Perhaps escalating rumors of Saddam's brutal and nightmarish regime had converted the typically legalistic, law-abiding Consulate staff members. Maybe they'd become more charitable and humanitarian. Or maybe Sabah's mother had the face of a saint. And who could deny the pleas of a saint begging to see her long lost son?

Whatever the reason, Sabah found himself standing at San Diego's Lindbergh Field in the summer of 1981, waiting to see his brother and mother for the first time in over seven years. He couldn't help fidgeting as he stood there, putting his hands in his pockets then down at his sides, his entire being buzzing with hope, excitement, and an inexplicable anxiety.

Finally, the gate opened and a stream of people poured out. His gaze flicked from one face to another, searching—

And there she was. With one hand holding onto Sam's arm, Sabah saw his mother before she saw him. She seemed to be shuffling more now, moving more slowly, looking slightly more frail than when he had last seen her. He could see that dazed, disorientation in her eyes, which had been so much a part of his own first days in America, but unlike himself, there was something that could not be overpowered in her gaze. Her thin, parchment skin held eyes that were in awe but equally alert. She was searching for him. Her silver hair tightly pulled back, showed her smooth forehead moving sytematically from side to side. Then he appeared to her and a journey of 10,000 miles was complete.

There was a heavy feeling in the back of his throat and he wondered if he might cry, but all the while he was smiling. She didn't smile or display any kind of strong physical reaction. She simply kept walking steadily toward Sabah even as he ran to meet her.

He'd wanted to greet her as a man, to show her all that had changed in him over the last seven years, but it was as if the intervening years all melted away as he drew near her. When he finally stood in front of his mother, all he could do was wrap his arms around her and embrace her, and be held tightly in return.

After a few moments, he felt and heard her sigh. "Thank you, God," she whispered. "Thank you, thank you. I prayed for you. Every day, I prayed for you."

As people continued to stream past and around them, Sabah and his mother held each other in the middle of that busy airport. Finally his mother pulled away and looked at his face closely, intently+.

"You're a man now," she said, and in those simple words, Sabah heard a lifetime of warmth, love, and pride.

Sabah hugged his little fourteen-year-old brother and the three started to make their way out of the airport.

"I was a man when I left," Sabah said.

"Yes, but not like now. You're different. You're stronger now."

Sabah said nothing but smiled at his mother. He was in the presence of the one person who knew him better than anyone else in the world. Who was he to disagree or question her in any way?

Mrs. Toma had come to America for two reasons. One, of course, was to see Sabah. The other was to leave Sam with Sabah. His mother would only visit for a month before she returned home to her husband in Iraq. But Sam would stay, under Sabah's protection, guidance, and supervision. It was a responsibility Sabah accepted gladly and without hesitation. If he couldn't get his family here all at once, he would take them one at a time, and do whatever he could for each of them.

★ ★ ★

Patrice was a regular vendor at the Spring Valley swap meet, the same one Sabah had been working at every weekend for nearly two years. She was a local San Diego girl, close to Sabah's age, but her swap meet style was very different from his. She arrived early each morning and quietly set up her tables. With care and precision, she neatly organized her sales space.

She carefully unfolded her freshly ironed table covers and draped her tables. She would gently tug at the covers and stand back from the table to make sure they hung with even, balanced precision. She meticulously arranged and stacked her collection of high quality pens and writing instruments. Then she would sit or stand quietly and wait for customers to arrive. Her sense of order, sweetness, and gentility enveloped her vending space in an aura of peace and safety. The key to her sales style was her genuinely kind, non-threatening disposition.

She'd noticed Sabah many times. He was, after all, one of the most mobile vendors at the meet. He'd often passed her space while saying hello to his swap meet friends. She'd seen him barter and trade, buy and sell, with nearly every regular at the meet. In fact, she may have been the only vendor he hadn't yet tried to make a deal with. If Sabah was a bee flying around the swap meet, Patrice was the nectar. More than anything else, Patrice was a patient woman. This would prove to be her greatest strength and asset.

For the month Sabah's mother was in San Diego, he was with her every moment he wasn't working and even some of the moments he was. He even took her to the swap meet, where she stayed with him all day. Sabah knew their time together was limited. Once she left, he had no idea how many more years would pass before they saw each other again.

Her departure flight was early on a Sunday morning, well past the time Sabah would have been open for business at the swap meet. He and his brother Sam took their mother to the airport, but this goodbye wasn't like that day so long before, when they'd parted in Baghdad. She didn't say the words, but Sabah knew. The day was coming closer for all of them. Sabah knew it and he knew his mother knew it. Sabah had survived in America and he would help Sam do the same.

Now, it wasn't a matter of *if* the Toma family would be together again, but when. Still, this mutual, unspoken conviction did little to remove the pain of the moment. Sabah held his mother. His final words to her were a promise that he would do his best for Sam.

Sabah and his brother drove directly to the swap meet from the airport. Sabah welcomed his young brother's assistance in unloading and unpacking the heavy cardboard boxes filled with Jordache jeans, women's cosmetics, and whatever else he happened to have that day. Patrice noticed Sabah's late arrival and the appearance of his new, young assistant. She also noticed that Sabah didn't immediately begin his rounds this morning. He wasn't buying his usual assortment of items for re-selling throughout the day. Was it because he was late? Why was he late at all? The expression on his face was slightly different than usual. He looked more serious, even a little sad perhaps. Always a careful observer, Patrice was curious as to what these things might mean.

Sabah quickly spread out his wares and told Sam to watch the stand. He wouldn't have time for his usual thorough pre-opening reconnaissance of his co-vendors. But, despite the lost time and late hour, he couldn't resist at least a cursory review of the day's opportunities. On this particular day, of the hundreds of vendors sprawled out over acres of asphalt, Sabah happened to find Patrice.

Patrice, always an avid reader, glanced up from her book and saw Sabah studying her neatly arranged row of Mont Blanc, Cross, and Parker pens.

"I think I have one that would fit you nicely," she said.

"How do you know I can write?" Sabah asked.

They smiled at each other. Sabah introduced himself and Patrice shook his hand warmly. They were both swap meet veterans, skilled in their own ways at the art of sales and trade. Though, at this moment, neither of them knew just how unique this negotiation would be. Later, Sabah would think how interesting it was that on the very morning he'd said good-bye to his mother, he should share a first hello with his wife.

CHAPTER THIRTY-SIX

★ ★ ★

The Most Important Partner

★ ★ ★

Throughout his life, Sabah had more than his fair share of relationships with women. They'd come in many forms, from the briefest affairs to more substantial, long-term companions. Even in his darkest days with Faraj, women had provided relief. At the very least, they were a momentary escape. He'd had nearly anonymous encounters at Flannigans and more meaningful, longer term connections. In fact, he'd met more than one or two American women who would have married him had this been his preference.

But he hadn't married them, even though he'd known it would be his fastest route to citizenship. So, why hadn't he? Was it because, somewhere in his heart, his idealized view of love and marriage simply didn't allow him to marry for that reason?

Other women he'd met, the American women he might have married, had been different. They hadn't just wanted to help him get his citizenship. They'd deeply cared about him, even loved him, and would happily have shared their lives with him. He may have cared for them in return, but he hadn't loved them, and no matter how desperately he wanted to become an American citizen, he knew that it would be impossible to build a marriage on a foundation of his own self-serving interests and selfishness.

In the days and weeks after meeting Patrice, some long-running cycle in Sabah, perhaps a pattern as long as his life itself, was interrupted. The firmly established rhythms of his relationships with women began to lose their syncopation and familiarity. His growing friendship with Patrice was carrying him into new and unknown territory. The final wall Sabah had created for himself, the barricade that had prevented the idea of marriage, let alone the act of an actual wedding ceremony, began to erode piece by piece.

For Patrice, the process wasn't nearly as complicated. If Sabah's life had been, in large part, shaped by his instincts, he'd now a met a woman who surpassed his own exceptional abilities. In fact, the day Sabah approached her stall at the swap meet was a day Patrice had known would eventually come. She'd been looking forward to it. As far as dating and marriage were concerned, Patrice wasn't at all affected by ambivalence or confusion. In terms of men, she knew what she wanted. She recognized the qualities she was looking for as soon as she saw them. Inside a genuinely warm and tender exterior, she was a woman of precise judgement and calculation. Well before Sabah knew he would marry Patrice, she knew she would marry Sabah.

The weekend after they met, Sabah stopped by Patrice's space again to say hello. The conversation flowed naturally and easily between them.

"You're working at John Hancock?" Patrice asked, looking startled. "Now?"

"Yes, I am," Sabah said.

"Do you know Debby?"

"The receptionist?"

"Yes."

"Of course."

"She's my good friend!" Patrice exclaimed.

It was another piece added on to something that had been building within Sabah. He'd already found out that Patrice was his neighbor. She lived across the street from him, within walking distance of his Chula Vista apartment. It made perfect sense that such an important person in her world should be so unexpectedly connected to his own.

They began to see each other outside the swap meet. Sabah would spend time visiting Patrice at her apartment. But it was at the swap meet that Sabah found himself bringing up a subject he rarely mentioned to women. He'd felt comfortable with Patrice from the moment he'd met her. Now, he didn't share the truth with her as much as it emerged naturally and of its own accord.

"You know I'm from Iraq," Sabah began.

"You told me, yes," Patrice said, straightening a few pens on her table. "And I've been in America seven years."

"Yes, I know."

Sabah took a breath. "I'm not a citizen yet," he said, keeping his eyes on Patrice to gauge her reaction. "I'm here illegally."

Patrice gave him a soft smile. "I know."

"You do? How can you know?"

"Debby told me."

Sharing this information with Patrice had consumed so much of Sabah's concentration that he'd completely forgotten the obvious connection to Debby. Just then, one of Patrice's customers approached her with a question. Sabah needed to get back to his own work. The conversation would be resumed later in the week.

For Sabah, the mention of his immigration status to a woman was far more significant than a mere admission of criminal activity. It was a kind of code he used for another message of greater importance. That message was this: "If you're at all serious about pursuing a relationship with me, don't take another step until you know what you're dealing with." Their reaction could tell him much, if not all he needed to know about his prospects with that woman.

She might be taken aback, uncomfortable. She might be disappointed and withdraw. She might even be shocked or, like Patrice, she might be completely unaffected, as though Sabah had just mentioned a hobby or favorite kind of food rather than his immigration status. Her simple and casual acknowledgement was both encouraging and slightly unnerving. Who was this person? How did she really feel about him? And did he feel the same way about her?

★ ★ ★

Patrice and Sabah had been dating for several months when Patrice was given notice by her landlord. Her financial situation was month to month. She was a single woman who was, like Sabah, at the cusp of thirty. Facing a sudden eviction notice, Patrice was in a panic.

Sabah made the suggestion that he, Sam, and Patrice should find a place together. Sabah and Patrice had already been virtually living together for the past couple of months, Sabah spending more time at Patrice's apartment than he did at his own. Getting a place together would be far less expensive than living on her own as she had been her entire adult life. For Patrice, it was a reasonable option, especially considering the fact that she didn't have any others. She agreed and a place was found in their neighborhood.

A week before their moving date, Patrice heard a knock at her door. She opened it and Sabah stood there, like he had a hundred times before over the past few months. But his expression was different now. For days they'd been preoccupied with logistical issues related to the move, but the look on his face didn't seem connected to those minor details. There was something denser and more concentrated about him. For a moment Patrice thought he might have reconsidered and changed his mind.

She ushered him inside. "What is it, Sabah? You look like someone died."

Sabah halted in the middle of the room and said nothing for a moment. Hesitation was something Patrice had never seen in him and she became even more concerned. Her apartment was already in the depths of packing and deconstruction prior to the move. She pulled a cardboard box off a kitchen table chair.

"Sit down, Sabah," she said, but still he didn't move. "Please," she added and pulled up a chair herself.

They sat together and Patrice said nothing more. After a moment, Sabah took in deep breath and let it out.

"It can't be that bad," Patrice said. "I *hope* it can't be that bad." She was smiling and keeping up a brave front, though she was trembling with apprehension.

"I've been thinking," Sabah began.

"Good, thinking is good," Patrice said.

"I think we should get married," Sabah said.

For a moment, all Patrice could feel was relief. At least he wasn't reneging on the apartment agreement. A moment later, the words Sabah had said, as well as what he hadn't said, began to register. This man hadn't even told her he loved her. What was she hearing? Was this a marriage proposal or a business proposition?

"Marriage?" she said.

"Well, we'll be living together anyway and it just seems to me, well, it seems like the best idea."

She knew his story and she believed it. His entire life had been a hope against hope, a risk placed on top of a risk. He'd arrived in an unknown world in search of something he might never find. He'd fought a very hard fight, and continued fighting with undiminished energy every day. But what impressed her most was his hope. It never flickered or grew dim, even for moment. It brilliantly burned in him every moment of his life.

Perhaps this was why Patrice had fallen in love with him. If pressed, she would say that his immortal optimism, even more than his honesty, savage work ethic, or undampened sense of humor, had transformed her simple admiration into love. Yet, in the seven months they'd known each other, she'd never told him how she felt about him. And he had never told her. Like Sabah, Patrice lived her own life on the principle of hope.

"You haven't told you me you love me, Sabah," Patrice said.

Sabah looked blankly at her. Her words were not spoken as an indictment or accusation but as a heartbreakingly simple fact. Sabah said nothing because the idea didn't entirely fit into his construction of the arrangement. He liked her, very much. He cared about her. They could apply for his citizenship and the process would take about a year, once started. He'd already worked out the plan in his own mind. He would be true and loyal to her. He would be respectful. Together, they would help Sam and, in their own way, they would be a family. Love would grow out of that. Why, Sabah thought, did love always have to come first?

"Sabah, look at me," Patrice finally said. "I love you. I think that's how a man and woman should feel when they get married. And I think they should say it to each other."

Sabah said nothing. Patrice stood up and walked to a window, overlooking the busy boulevard. She stared out into the traffic for a moment before she spoke again. With her back to Sabah she said, "But you're not any man. And I'm not any woman." She paused again. A final curtain had been pulled away. Nothing seperated them now, no illusion, no pretense, no dreams.

Patrice turned to face Sabah again. When she spoke now her words were filled with an infinite calm and tenderness.

"Sabah, look at me." She waited for his eyes to meet hers.

266

"You think you've got courage? You think you take risks? You think you're the only one who takes off into the great unknown with no security, no guarantees, no promise of anything? Sabah, you just asked a woman to marry you and you don't even know who she is. I *invented* risk. I take chances with my life in ways you can't imagine. You know I've actually thought, maybe it's the risk taker in both of us that makes us understand each other so well. I never asked if you love me. And I'm not asking now. I told you I love you because I think it's the right thing to do. Honestly, I don't know if I *want* to know if you love me or not. But this is what I want you to know. I hope, too, Sabah. I take risks, too."

Patrice paused again, but her eyes remained unwaveringly fixed on Sabah's. She needed to make sure he understood exactly what she was saying. His focus and silence satisfied her and, after a moment, she continued.

"So, you say you think we should get married. Are you asking me to marry you, Sabah?"

"Yes," Sabah said.

"Then ask me."

"Ask you to marry me?"

"Yes," Patrice said.

"Well, I thought I did."

"No, you didn't. I'd like to hear the question. Please."

Sabah, slightly perplexed and off balance, stared at Patrice for a moment. She was seated again, leaning toward him, her hands clasped together on the table. There wasn't a hint of irony or antagonism in her voice. At that moment, she looked as serene as he had ever seen her.

"Patrice, will you marry me?" Sabah asked.

Patrice leaned forward even closer and took Sabah's hands in her own, still looking directly into Sabah's eyes. "This is why you know nothing about real risk, Sabah. My answer is yes."

CHAPTER THIRTY-SEVEN

★ ★ ★

Blix's Interview

★ ★ ★

The wedding ceremony took place in a tiny rental wedding chapel in Chula Vista. It was perfunctory, at best, attended only by Sabah and Patrice themselves. The moment was approached in the same way other tasks were. Though the wedding was memorable for both Patrice and Sabah in terms of its ceremonial significance, in the end, it was just another item on the long "to do" list of their lives. The lists were not identical. Sabah and Patrice may not have wanted, or wanted to do, exactly the same things. But their lists were handled in exactly the same way, with relentless persistence and unwavering faith.

Even more than Sabah, Patrice was a person of strong religious conviction and devotion. Unlike the man she married, who had remained comfortably within the confines of his Chaldean faith throughout his entire life, Patrice was a convert, and an unusual convert at that. Raised in a devout Lutheran home, as an adult Patrice had converted to Catholicism. Her faith was not a product of her culture or upbringing, as Sabah's was. Her faith was a choice for which she had paid a price. Other than martyrdom itself, the highest levels of religious zeal and purity of faith are always found in the convert, particularly when persecution, in the form of estrangement from friends or family, is involved in that conversion.

In this regard there was, for Sabah, something immediately familiar and comforting about Patrice. He'd been raised on this kind of devotion. Growing up, he'd seen it every day in his mother. It wasn't an unbalanced fanaticism demanding to be noticed, listened to, and agreed with. Like Mrs. Toma, Patrice displayed a very personal, quiet, and steady kind of faith, a faith that whispered and tiptoed. It was a constantly moving faith but never drew attention to itself. It was a faith that was never distracting or disconcerting. In short, it was a faith that felt like home.

Though his own faith in God was deep and exerted a profound influence on his life, he hadn't been a regular church-goer since his childhood. This changed when he married Patrice. Without prodding or pleading, or even an actual invitation as far as he could recall, Sabah began regularly attending Patrice's church.

With Patrice's help, Sam was enrolled in a private Catholic school near their new apartment in San Ysidro. At the same time, Patrice found a relatively well-paying job as an administrative assistant in a large law firm. Sabah would come home from his grueling days of door-to-door work for John Hancock and find a hot meal being prepared on the stove or in the oven while Patrice sat at the dinner table patiently helping Sam improve his English reading and writing.

The apartment door would open and Patrice would look up and smile at Sabah. Sabah saw that smile along with a clean home. He would take in the savory aroma of a roast or stew slowly cooking. He saw his little brother learning and growing. For all these things, Sabah would feel grateful. He'd never lived with a woman before. Also, he'd experienced nothing like a home or family for over seven years. He was feeling something he'd never felt in America, or even in Iraq, since the rise of the Baathists. How long had it been? He would have to go back to when he was a little boy, that innocent little boy who had thought a thief was an actual monster. After many years, Sabah was finally beginning to feel a sense of belonging and security.

Within a very short time, the three of them, Patrice, Sabah, and Issam, had created a very peaceful and smoothly operating home. Everyone had their duties and roles. Everyone was working. There was trust between all of them. They were relying on each other and thriving on the safe, nurturing conditions always found in homes that are truly alive. Within the first two months of their marriage, the time came to meet Fredrick Blix at the I.N.S. offices in downtown San Diego. Sabah and Patrice approached the meeting with excitement and overflowing optimism.

It was going to be simple now. They just needed to bring their wedding certificate and apply for Sabah's citizenship. They both knew the entire process could take about a year, but they'd grown much closer, even in the small amount of time they'd been married. Now it was no longer something Patrice was doing for Sabah, in exchange for something he might or might not do for her. His citizenship was now a shared event in two lives which were slowly and miraculously becoming one. Patrice was as excited to submit the application for Sabah's citizenship as Sabah was, perhaps even more so.

Patrice watched Sabah as he dressed for their short trip to the I.N.S. office downtown. She didn't ask him why he was ironing one of his few dress shirts or why he was polishing his shoes or carefully removing whatever small amount of lint was on his suit jacket lapel. She knew why. As he had on his first day of arrival in American, or the day of their marriage, Sabah groomed himself with the amount of detail proportional to the importance of the event. Today they would take their first step on Sabah's road to becoming an American citizen. Any bureaucrat or governmental functionary he met on the way would know that, for Sabah, reaching the end of that road would be the greatest honor of his life.

Quietly, Patrice put on her own makeup and one of her more expensive dresses, one she ordinarily wore only for midnight mass at Christmas. Sam was at school and the apartment was quiet. They turned and looked at each other.

"Ready?" Sabah asked.

"I'm ready," Patrice said.

Twenty minutes later, they entered the reception area of the I.N.S. office located near the County Courthouse on Broadway in downtown San Diego. A man in a gray suit, red tie, and white shirt stood waiting for them, holding a large briefcase. He had a slightly disheveled, off-center appearance. His loose, uneven tie was skewed too far to one side. His slightly crumpled suit jacket was long overdue for dry cleaning. The cuffs on his slacks were a quarter inch too long. He'd either recently had a bad haircut or was several weeks overdue for one. Any one of these elements might not have been noticeable or noteworthy but, collectively, they suggested a man who lived his life in haste and without attention to detail.

"Good morning, Mr. Blix," Sabah said.

Blix took Sabah's hand. "Good, right on time. How are you, Sabah?"

"Great. Perfect. Mr. Blix, this is my wife, Patrice."

"A pleasure, Patrice. We only have a few minutes, so let's make sure we've got the game plan. They're gonna call us up and ask for the certificate. You have it, by the way?"

"Of course, right here," Sabah said, handing the marriage certificate to Blix.

"Now, there might be some questions, probably not, but there might be. It's pretty cut and dried at this point. But, if there are questions, I'll handle them. Okay?"

"Sounds good to us, right, Patrice?" Sabah asked, smiling.

"Lead on," Patrice said.

They sat down and waited several moments. Their quiet conversation was interrupted only once by a clerk's voice, calling out a name. They watched an Asian couple stand up and walk toward one of two windows.

"Toma. Sabah Toma." Another clerk's voice broke the stillness of the room.

Instantly, Patrice, Sabah, and Mr. Blix stood up and approached the clerk's window. Blix briefly explained the purpose of their visit as the clerk sat motionless. Finally she nodded.

"Certificate, please," the clerk said, and Blix handed her the wedding certificate.

The clerk, an overweight black woman perhaps in her mid-forties, took the slip of paper and placed it carefully in a small stand so it could be more easily read in an upright position. She adjusted the stand at the same moment she swiveled her low-rise office chair and faced the fluorescent green characters on her computer screen. It was all done as a single motion, as though it had been performed just this way ten thousand times before.

For several moments, the computer screen flickered and scrolled. One page of DOS text replaced another, then the woman suddenly leaned forward, looking at something more closely on the screen.

"You are Sabah Toma?" she asked, adjusting her glasses and looking straight at Sabah.

Blix had told him not to answer questions, but this one was so direct it would appear rude if he didn't answer. He hesitated and quickly glanced at Blix.

"He is," Blix said.

"Spell that, please," the clerk said. Blix began to say the letters.

"Are you able to spell your own name, Mr. Toma?" the clerk interrupted.

"Yes, ma'am," Sabah said.

"Spell your name, then, please."

"Last name, T – O – M – A. First name, S – A – B – A – H."

Sabah watched as each green letter appeared on the computer screen, followed by a single, steadily blinking cursor. The clerk leaned forward again, reading something on the screen.

The clerk took her reading glasses off and swiveled around in her chair again. She looked at Sabah with lifeless eyes. For reasons Sabah could not remotely begin to identify, he felt sick to his stomach.

"Mr. Toma, you're not an easy man to find. We've been looking for you a long time." The woman's head abruptly turned to her right. "Mr. Saronna, could you join us a moment, please?"

A uniformed officer, complete with holstered pistol, appeared next to the woman. He was tall and in his late thirties, with short cropped hair and a weightlifter's body.

"Mr. Saronna, this is Mr. Toma. Would you kindly place him under arrest?"

"What?" Blix nearly shouted, shocked as much as both Patrice and Sabah.

"Mr. Toma is scheduled for deportation, and has been for well over two years."

"Wait, wait. Wait a second!" Blix exclaimed, even as Saronna was placing handcuffs on Sabah.

"Look, the man is married, employed. He's done nothing wrong!"

"Maybe not, but you sure have," the lady answered. "I have no idea what you were thinking, bringing him here."

"Sabah, what is this?" Patrice asked, holding his arm as the officer began leading him out of the room.

"I don't know, I don't know," Sabah said.

"Please," Blix continued, all but begging now. "Don't do this. You can't do this."

"Counselor, the man has been in this country under a visa that expired seven years ago and you're telling me I can't do this? What kind of attorney are you? Tony, take him out of here. Now."

In one nightmarish, fractured moment, Sabah was gone and Patrice stood alone in a formerly quiet reception area that had now grown deathly silent. Though in a state of complete disbelief, Blix was sufficiently coherent to reassure Patrice. They would get him out on bail. He couldn't be deported without a hearing. He'd be all right. Patrice didn't know if she was listening to an enemy or friend. All she knew, for sure, was that just moments before, Sabah had disappeared behind a very plain looking office door. She didn't know where he'd been taken and she didn't know when she would see him again.

CHAPTER THIRTY-EIGHT
★ ★ ★
Heroes Likely And Unlikely
★ ★ ★

Patrice was a sensible woman, with a better general understanding of the law than the average person. After all, she did work in a law firm. Though she was, fundamentally, a woman of faith, she was also a realist. She knew that, behind the Norman Rockwell view of a land bound by principles such as decency, generosity, hard work, and freedom, America was like any other country: divisive, selfish, and filled with a diversity of people often at odds with each other.

Patrice knew there was only one final power in America holding everything and everyone together. That power was the law. Sabah had violated the law and now he was paying the price. Blix had only been the trigger or mechanism for what was, perhaps, an inevitable consequence of that violation. Sabah had been a fugitive. The law, with its inexorable persistence and flawless memory, had made its claim on him.

She saw all this in her mind as clearly as the text from one of her cookbooks, but in the end, these thoughts gave her no comfort at all. She and Sabah lived in the community of San Ysidro, wedged squarely against the Mexican border in the southernmost part of California. Patrice couldn't help thinking that half the people in their neighborhood were probably, at that very moment, in the United States illegally. Out of them all, why did Sabah have to be taken? He probably worked harder than many others who'd arrived in America the same way.

In fact, the very quality that had first attracted her to Sabah had been his pride and self-reliance, his sense of absolute responsibility for his own destiny. If ever a man had come to America with the goal of taking nothing and earning everything, that man was Sabah. Yet America had taken everything from *him*. America had rejected the very man who loved her the most. It wasn't fair, it wasn't just, and it wasn't right.

At least once a week, Patrice and Sam would make the two hour drive to El Centro. A bond had been placed and a bail set of fifteen thousand dollars. They didn't have a tenth of that saved and had no idea where they could get the rest. Until they did, Sabah would wait in El Centro for a court hearing that would end, in all probability, with him being placed on a flight directly out of the country.

Before that hearing arrived, after nearly three months in the center, Sabah was summoned from his cell block. He was led through a series of locked doors to the detention center's administrative office. As he entered the room, a short-haired white woman with thick glasses and no makeup was leaning over her desk, writing something on a piece of paper. She looked up at Sabah, said nothing, and went back to the form. She continued writing for another moment then looked up again.

"Toma?" she said finally.

"Yes, ma'am," Sabah answered.

"Looks like you're getting outta here." She turned the paper around with one hand and held out a pen for Sabah in her other.

Sabah stared at her. "Really?"

"Bail's been paid," the woman responded. "Sign it."

All Sabah could think was, *How can this be?* Who could have done it? He'd received no information from Patrice. He'd had no clue at all that this was going to happen.

"Who did this?" Sabah asked.

"I have no idea, but, I got a feeling, whoever it is, it's your new best friend."

Sabah signed the form and handed the pen back to the woman. The form was still resting on her desk. She reached out her hand to pull it away.

"May I see it one more second, please?" Sabah asked.

The woman studied him for a moment, then nodded. Sabah looked at the form again, trying to find an answer. And there, neatly typed in one of the many rectangular boxes, was Faraj's name. It didn't make sense and it made perfect sense. It was bizarre, shocking, and almost funny. Sabah slid the form back to the woman.

"Thank you," he said, even as he mused on how strange and wonderful life could be.

The day he returned to San Diego, Sabah went to Faraj's new home. Faraj was no longer in the Coronado Cays. He now lived with his wife and son in Tierrasanta, a more modest and unassuming middle-class community in the center of San Diego. Together, they went to a bank where Faraj co-signed a fifteen thousand dollar loan for Sabah. Faraj had re-paid a debt to Sabah. They were now both able to say that they'd helped the other stay out of jail. Debt payments aside, money was always money to Faraj. The fifteen thousand bail certainly was not a gift of gratitude. It would be repaid. In fact, Sabah repaid it within a year.

Between his growing salary at John Hancock and Patrice's law firm job, they were able to give Faraj over five hundred dollars a month. If getting out of Faraj's debt wasn't Sabah's highest priority, it certainly was Patrice's. Despite Faraj's generosity and apparently loyalty, Patrice didn't share Sabah's tolerance for those who mistreated her, or anyone she loved.

Faraj's benevolence would be expressed in more than just paying Sabah's bail. Sabah's court hearing was coming up in only a few weeks. Clearly Jason Blix was not the best option. Faraj, no stranger to attorneys himself, suggested a man who might help Sabah. Faraj said he was the best immigration attorney in San Diego. He was expensive but, considering the consequences of an unsuccessful court appearance, he would be worth every penny. His name was Lynn Goldberg and for once, everything Faraj said was true.

Faraj knew Mr. Goldberg through M. M was actually a closer friend of Mr. Goldberg but, typical of Faraj's general approach to everyone he met and social situations in general, he relished his power in providing Sabah access to a man of Mr. Goldberg's importance and stature. Mr. Goldberg's office was located just a block away from the federal courthouse in downtown San Diego. As soon as they walked in, Faraj's brashness and bravura instantly made Sabah queasy.

"Hey, Lynn, how's it going?" Faraj said, with his typical swagger and misplaced intimacy.

Mr. Goldberg's office wasn't like Blix's. It was clean, perfectly organized, and completely functional. Everything about it said experience, discipline, and maximum efficiency. From the way reams of folders, manilla files, and papers were crisply ordered on his large, sturdy walnut desk to the reassuring complement of the newest office equipment including an Apple Macintosh computer, fax machine, and full color photo copier, Sabah sensed this man accomplished more in one day than most attorneys did in a week.

Mr. Goldberg, a strong, fit man, was in his late forties. Though Sabah knew he was a busy and important attorney, he couldn't help feeling as if he were looking at one of his professors at Baghdad University. Mr. Golderg possessed vast amounts of knowledge but, unlike so many powerful people in the fields of business and law, he didn't wield this knowledge as a weapon. He had a gentle and unassuming bearing, and was the kind of man Sabah had all too briefly encountered before leaving Iraq. Like Sabah, Lynn Goldberg never looked down on another human being. Perhaps it was this shared quality of character that made the two men instantly familiar and recognizable to each other.

Though it was a relatively warm Friday afternoon, Mr. Goldberg was wearing a Brooks Brothers navy blue camel hair blazer with gold buttons. Sabah noticed the graceful drape of his tan Super 100 virgin wool cuffed slacks and his bright white button-down dress shirt with extra starch. A silk tie with thin red and yellow stripes was accented by a simple pearl tie clasp. The man was immaculate, which would have been impressive in itself, but was particularly reassuring to Sabah because he seemed, in every way, to be the exact opposite of Jason Blix.

The moment they entered his office, Mr. Goldberg stood up behind his desk and walked toward Sabah and Faraj. Faraj continued babbling for another moment, but Mr. Goldberg didn't even glance at him. His gaze was fixed steadily on Sabah.

"This is Sabah, the tough case I was telling you about. I thought you might like a special project. Sort of keep things interesting, you know? We all need a challenge, right?"

Faraj was offering his cold, shark-like smile to Mr. Goldberg. To Sabah's relief, and probably Mr. Goldberg's, Faraj soon excused himself and the two were left alone.

Sabah assumed he would have, perhaps, a half hour at most with Mr. Goldberg. Since coming to America, he had become well-acquainted with the relationship between time and money. He was acutely aware that time meant money. For some people, including Mr. Goldberg, that time meant more money than it did for others. Sabah knew he was in the presence of man who, through his own intelligence, diligence, and hard work, had converted his time to extraordinary value. He felt humbled by the privilege of simply being in this man's presence.

"Your hearing is next Tuesday at ten A.M.?" Mr. Goldberg asked.

"Yes, sir."

"That doesn't give us a lot of time. So, let's get started."

Mr. Goldberg took a notepad out of his drawer and crossed one leg over the other, poising a Cross pen over the notepad. Sabah wasn't sure what to do.

"Where would you like me to start?" Sabah said.

"The beginning is always a good place," Mr. Goldberg said, offering a small but friendly smile.

So, Sabah began to recount his story from the moment of his arrival in America. For the next several hours, Lynn Goldberg did almost nothing but listen and take notes. He interrupted Sabah only a few times, with questions that didn't seem particularly pointed or even relevant. Then he would politely ask Sabah to continue. It was nearly four in the afternoon when Mr. Goldberg carefully made a final note and put down his notepad. He looked at Sabah, then stood up and looked out his office window. The office was facing west and Mr. Goldberg could see, beyond the other downtown high rises, large portions of the harbor in the distance. His back was turned to Sabah.

"It's getting to be the good time of day," Mr. Goldberg said. "This time of year, I can see the sunset over the harbor. Dawn and twilight, my two favorite times in the day."

He stood still for another moment then turned and faced Sabah. The two men looked at each other in the quiet and calm of the office.

"If I listen to my head, I won't have a thing to do with this," Mr. Goldberg said flatly, as though finishing a conversation he'd been having with himself. "But if I listen to my heart, I have to help you."

Sabah said nothing. He didn't want to disrupt such delicate and precise deliberations. He already knew this man's decision-making process was absolutely unique and essential to whoever or whatever he was.

Mr. Goldberg sat down again and rocked several times in his high backed, black leather office chair. "Something isn't right here," he said after a few moments.

He reached for the phone on his desk. "Hi, Mary, it's Lynn. Is Chuck in? Does he have a minute? Okay, tell him I'm on the way." Mr. Goldberg put the phone down, stood up, and started walking toward his office door.

"Let's take a walk," he said to Sabah.

Their destination was less than a block away and Sabah suspected he knew which Chuck they were going to see. As secure and confident as he felt with Lynn Goldberg, it was possible that they were, at that moment, heading toward the last place in San Diego Sabah wanted to go.

"Mr. Goldberg, I hope you don't mind, but … about who we're going to see. Is this, by any chance, Chuck Karpinski?"

Mr. Goldberg turned and gave him a slightly surprised look.

"You know him?" he asked.

"Well, not personally. I know who he is."

Sabah, and every other fugitive from the I.N.S. in San Diego, knew exactly who Charles Karpinski was. He was the chief federal prosecutor for immigration in the city. More than knowing who Karpinski was, Sabah knew Karpinski knew who *he* was.

"He's a colleague. I just want to see what he can do for us," Mr. Goldberg said.

Sabah knew what Karpinski *couldn't* do. As much as he'd like to, he couldn't immediately throw Sabah in jail. It was the good side of the law. Sabah was free on bail until the date and time of his court appointed hearing, which wasn't for another four days. Sabah could walk right into the den of the lion but, no matter how hungry the lion was, it would be chained. Even so, as he walked with Mr. Goldberg, keeping up with the man's energetic pace, Sabah approached their destination with considerable trepidation.

Even in 1983, the issue of illegal immigration in San Diego had exploded like an uncontrollable virus. One might fairly ask how a man of Mr. Karpinski's standing should be so familiar with Sabah Toma, just one man out of tens of thousands of cases pouring into his office. The answer could be attributed to several key factors. First, Sabah Toma was, at that time, the only Iraqi in San Diego marked for deportation. Second, the I.N.S. disaster with Blix had already attained a kind of legendary, even mythic status within their tightly connected community. It had been told and re-told dozens of times at every lunch table or happy hour frequented by Karpinski.

But more then these things, the combination of Sabah's evasiveness, along with his relatively high profile within the community of illegal immigration, had been an ongoing source of irritation and even embarrassment to Karpinski. His office had designated Sabah as a target. He was someone who needed to be deported as an example to the public, to show the department's organizational and operational competence. When Goldberg had called, the last person Karpinski expected him to be with was Sabah Toma.

"Lynn, you know I can't give you any information. Blix's his attorney of record."

"Can we get him on the phone?" Mr. Goldberg said.

A moment later, they could hear Blix's voice on the small black box on Karpinski's desk.

"Hey, Blix, Chuck Karpinski. I have Toma here in my office. He's got a new attorney with him, Lynn Goldberg."

"He's got what?" Blix asked. They could all clearly hear the surprise in his voice.

"Let's see," Karpinski continued, glancing at his wristwatch, "It's now four forty. Goldberg will have a messenger there by five to pick up Toma's files. Have them ready to go, please."

Karpinski hung up. Sabah realized the urgency Karpinski was displaying was self-serving. As far as Karpinski was concerned, the faster he could get Sabah ready for his deportation hearing, the better. Mr. Goldberg and Karpinski shook hands, though Karpinski and Sabah parted without this courtesy. As Sabah was about to leave the office, Karpinski called after him.

"Toma. Ten A.M., next Tuesday. Federal building. Be there." Karpinski barked the orders, looking and sounding like a Marine Corps drill instructor.

No one was better than Mr. Goldberg, but even he wouldn't have enough time to make his best preparations for the hearing. It was the one thing Sabah and Mr. Goldberg didn't discuss that day. It was the one thing they couldn't discuss. It was also the one thing they both knew, as surely as they knew how much they already liked each other: next Tuesday, federal court was the last place on earth Sabah Toma would be.

CHAPTER THIRTY-NINE
★ ★ ★
The Refugee
★ ★ ★

The decision wasn't entirely unprecedented. Sabah had done something like it once before, in Hollywood during his first month in America. It was the day he'd sat in the I.N.S. office and seen the red stamp on his form. It was the day he'd intentionally walked out the exit of that building and disappeared into the anonymous masses. He'd felt it then, but it had been a much smaller, more diluted version of what he was feeling now.

When he'd walked out of that Hollywood I.N.S. office, he'd walked out a wanted man. But the fusion of feelings he'd felt than, the combination of remorse, guilt, frustration, and anger, had been nothing more than a twinge. In the months and years that followed, Sabah's self image hadn't included the idea of being a refugee or someone fleeing justice. With or without his citizenship, he viewed himself as an American. In fact, he behaved more like an American than most Americans do. Income tax was withheld from his John Hancock checks. He had a credit card and checking account. He was married and devoted himself to his home and family.

Patrice was troubled, but unlike Lot's wife, she wasn't capable of looking backward. They'd been married a relatively short time, and Sabah had been incarcerated for half their married life. Now, in just a few days, their lives would change again. Her husband would officially be in hiding. Patrice knew this meant Sabah couldn't live with Sam and herself. Patrice's friend Debby, the receptionist at John Hancock, arranged for Sabah to meet her parents. They didn't live far from Sabah and Patrice.

Debby's parents, Mr. and Mrs. Miller, agreed to take Sabah in

281

temporarily, though Mr. Miller was more amenable to the idea than his wife.

For Patrice, Sabah's absence was far more than a nuisance or logistical inconvenience. His flight from the I.N.S., both of them now hiding and living life under the shadow of the law, was in direct conflict with other fundamental forces shaping her character. Like tectonic plates colliding against each other, responding to pressure from the center of the Earth, primal forces began to violently converge within Patrice.

Her life with Sabah was creating constant instability and friction. He was the most honest, decent man she'd ever known, yet he was now forced to live in hiding. She would be an accomplice in his concealment. Patrice had been raised on one guiding principle: tell the truth. Always tell the truth. This code of conduct had been so deeply ingrained in her, and practiced so consistently throughout her life, that she was almost physically incapable of lying, deception, or misrepresenting herself in any way. Now she was required to do all these things in order to protect the man she loved.

The decision for flight was equally damaging to Sabah. He'd made so much progress in just the past year or two. He'd started to see himself as an entrepreneur, businessman, and capitalist. He'd become a fully functioning member of the free enterprise jamboree called America. Now he was a criminal, hunted by the very nation he was most desperately trying to succeed in.

Sabah and Patrice had suspected from the start that his flight from deportation might lead them down a road like this, carrying these heavy consequences along with it. But in the end, it was unavoidable. Deportation was not an option. Certainly it would mean their marriage, along with their individual and shared dreams, would end. But far worse than that, for Sabah, deportation to Iraq would mean death.

The name Saddam Hussein and all it represented, the totalitarian regime he controlled, the casual executions occuring by the thousands sweeping through Iraq at that time were, as yet, unknown to the vast majority of Americans, including many Americans within the legal and judicial systems. Years later, perhaps, a person in Sabah's position might have appealed for mercy from the courts regarding his deportation, based on the most extreme and violent retribution from the Iraqi government. But now, simply to say that deportation to Iraq would mean death was, as far as most American courts were concerned a desperate and disingenous ploy by the defendant to avoid that fate.

Sabah had left Iraq on a two week visa and never returned. That was strike one. In Sabah's absence, Iraq had been at war with Iran. By edict of Saddam Hussein, any Iraqi man of draft age who refused to fight in that war would be executed. That was strike two. In his legal battles to stay in America, Sabah had signed a form seeking asylum as a political refugee. He'd cited Saddam Hussein as a tyrant and corrupt dictator. Sabah had every reason to believe this form had been sent to an Iraqi embassy, if not directly to the current Iraqi government. That was strike three.

Those facts in themselves would make his forced return to Iraq a death sentence. But even more chilling was the attitude of the Baathist regime itself. Sabah knew them very well. He'd personally known many men in Iraq who'd been tortured or killed for far less than his own offenses. For the Baathists, Sabah's life had no more value than a fly's. He would be shot on site at Baghdad Airport without the slightest hesitation or moral compunction. This was who the Baathists were. This was what they did. But it was 1984. At this time in America, if you weren't working for the CIA or some covert branch of the state department, you probably didn't know who Saddam Hussein was. Finally, if you were an I.N.S. agent, Sabah Toma would be the last person on earth who could enlighten you.

As expected, agents came to the home address Sabah shared with Patrice and Sam. Deeply suppressing her revulsion toward the moment and all it required of her, Patrice listlessly answered the agents' questions. She treated these men the same way so many others had treated Sabah when he appeared at a front door selling his John Hancock policies. Shrouded by indifference, she responded only with the amount of information precisely required to satisfy the question.

But the agents didn't stop at Sabah and Patrice's home. They went to the John Hancock office with such regularity that Sabah began to take his completed policies to work, not during the day, but at night after office hours. Lynn Goldberg would continue working on Sabah's case. Between the debt they were paying Faraj and Mr. Goldberg's legal fees, Patrice and Sabah were exhausting their entire monthly income. In addition, because Sabah was unable to live with them, Patrice was now taking care of Issam on her own. More than anything else, the uncertainty of their future hung over them like a guillotine blade, ready to fall with a swift and final judgment. It was a debilitating time for Patrice and Sabah, testing them both as individuals and as a married couple.

Finally, with Sabah's fate far from certain, the length of road ahead undetermined, and Issam's own student visa expired, it was decided that Issam should be relocated to Wally's home in Canada. By now, one of Sabah's younger brothers, Wally, was living near Toronto with his family. For the time being, Issam would be safer and more secure with Wally. In the worst case scenario, should Sabah's deportation actually occur, at least Issam would be safe.

Patrice, a sensitive and empathetic woman, noticed the anxiety on Debby's mother's face during her occasional visits with Sabah at the Miller residence. Despite Mr. Miller's rugged individualism and selfless determination to assist Sabah, Patrice saw the cumulative pressure Mrs. Miller felt in harboring a fugitive. She spoke with Sabah about it. It had now been over three months since Sabah had missed that important hearing. The worst seemed to be over. Sabah seemed to have once again disappeared into the faceless sea of refugees. It felt like he had rejoined that mighty, invisible river of untargeted, undocumented non-citizens struggling their way through America.

Sabah and Patrice found another place, even closer to the border. So close, in fact, that almost every day, they saw new refugees climbing across that international fence, making their way through a no man's land of marshes and fields just outside their apartment window. Patrice and Sabah redoubled their efforts, yoking themselves to a common goal. Somehow, through a vague and hazy hope, they saw a better life and encouraged each other toward it. But neither of them were the kind to wait for that better life. Together, they would create it.

A new swap meet had opened in what seemed to be a better and more promising location. It was the Kobey Swap at the San Diego Sports Arena. Together, they purchased a permanent space at the meet. What they'd been doing for years, separately, in Spring Valley, they now began to do as a team. It was a new swap meet but Sabah approached it with the same passion and fervor as he had the old one. While Patrice stayed to watch their merchandise, Sabah would scour the vast expanse of the meet, looking in every crack and crevice for items he and Patrice could mark up and re-sell.

One particular morning, Sabah saw a neon sign. It was a beer sign with a single word on it: "Bud."

He thought this might be worth a try and bought it for fifteen dollars. He re-sold it that same day for fifty. Encouraged by this, he began a regular search for neon signs at the Kobey meet, particularly beer signs, which seemed to be popular among the meet attendees. Sabah almost immediately realized he'd stumbled on to a gold mine. He couldn't sell neon fast enough or mark it up too much.

Soon, he was purchasing old, non-working neon signs simply for the base and transformer components. Working in his San Ysidro apartment with a Mexican neighbor and acquaintance who was also a refugee, Sabah would refashion these signs with a new inscription. He put the word "Open" on the signs. His total investment for the sign components and his neighbor's work was less than thirty dollars. Sabah would personally carry these signs to stores and shops in downtown San Diego, selling and installing them for ninety-nine dollars each.

In the meantime, Patrice and Sabah had started positioning their van more carefully in their rented slot at the Kobey swap meet. The neon beer signs were dull and lifeless when unlit, but in the darkness of their van, powered by a portable generator, the signs burst into life like an electric flower field. People passing by would ooh and aah at the beautiful, vivid colors. They were gold, pure gold, and Sabah couldn't keep up with the demand. He soon became known as the neon guy and, to a few swap meet regulars, he was "Mr. Neon." Within months, this source of revenue would rival and even exceed both their day jobs put together.

Sabah and Patrice fought back. In the process they forged ties with each other stronger than ever before. They'd both re-emerged into the world again. Patrice was free of the funk generated by what she considered to be her own dishonest and deceptive behavior. Sabah had risen above the temporary sense of inadequacy and self defined role of second-class citizen. Though a friend of Sabah's, Steve, had no idea his timing was so fortunate, it was the perfect moment to ask Sabah for help.

Steve was a member of the fledgling Chaldean community in San Diego. Like Sabah, he was also a hairdresser. Sabah's success at the Kobey Swap Meet, though far from making him wealthy, had not gone unnoticed within the Chaldean community. There were, at most, five hundred

Chaldeans in San Diego at the time. To Patrice, it seemed like each one of these Chaldeans knew the business and personal life of every other one. Though caring and compassionate, Patrice was also a private person. This aspect of the Chaldean culture was one she could never be completely comfortable with.

Steve had found a beauty salon for sale in La Mesa and asked Sabah if he would co-sign on a loan. In the year since Faraj had co-signed the repayment loan for Sabah, Patrice and Sabah's financial situation had improved significantly. With individual incomes at John Hancock and the law firm now supplemented by their neon revenue, they'd been able to repay Faraj in full, make their retainer payments to Mr. Goldberg, and actually save some money.

Sabah was not only happy to help Steve, he was grateful to God he was able to so. It was a sunny mid-week morning when Patrice left Sabah and drove to her work. They'd been having coffee and reading the morning paper. Patrice thought it might be a good time to expand the neon business by purchasing a small workspace downtown. Sabah liked the idea and told Patrice he'd look for a possible location right after he took care of his business with Steve. The office was very close to downtown, so he could do both.

"Call me if you find anything," Patrice said as she closed the door and left.

Sabah picked Steve up at his home in El Cajon and together they entered a small escrow office on Fifth Avenue just blocks north of downtown. Steve, an enthusiastic person by nature, was ecstatic as he and Sabah walked up one flight of stairs to the second floor office. Within a half an hour, the loan was signed and Steve held the paper in his hand. His eyes were wide as he studied the paper. He slowly shook his head.

"Sabah, thank you," he said, stepping forward to embrace his friend.

Sabah returned the hug and patted Steve on the back. "No problem, my friend, no problem."

He opened the office door and they walked back down the stairs to Sabah's car.

"I don't believe it," Steve said. "You know what I am, Sabah?"

"No, what are you?"

"I'm not just a hairdresser anymore. I'm a business owner. I own a business."

Sabah smiled. "That's right, you do."

"I have to get some business cards!" Steve exclaimed as they got in Sabah's car.

"That would be a good idea," Sabah said.

"I wonder, should I have one of those, what do they call them … logos? Should I make a logo?"

While Steve bubbled on, Sabah turned on the engine. He glanced over his right shoulder, making sure no one was behind him as he started to back out of the parking lot. Before he'd gone more than a few feet, however, another car skidded to a stop directly behind and perpendicular to him. It was only a foot or two from the back of Sabah's car, blocking his exit and forcing him to quickly apply his brakes. Steve's head hit back against the headrest.

"Easy, Sabah! You gonna save me and kill me in one day! Who are those guys?"

Sabah had been watching two men in suits quickly get out of the car blocking his own. Now, Steve also noticed them for the first time. In a coordinated approach, they separated and walked to either side of Sabah's car. Steve had no idea who they were. They could have been gang members or thieves.

"Sabah, what's going on?" Steve asked quickly.

One of the men was tapping on Sabah's raised side window.

"Lower the window, please," the man said.

"Sabah, don't," Steve said, even as he noticed the second man standing outside his own window.

"It's okay," Sabah said.

But he knew that it wasn't okay. Nothing was okay. He knew exactly who they were. Sabah rolled down his window. A badge pinned inside a wallet flashed in front of his eyes.

"Officer Kaufman, I.N.S. San Diego. Are you Sabah Toma?"

"I am," Sabah said.

"Out of the car, Toma. Game's over."

Less than ten minutes later, Sabah was standing handcuffed in the San Diego Metropolitan Correctional Center in downtown San Diego. The game *was* over, but only Sabah understood exactly what that meant.

CHAPTER FORTY

★ ★ ★

Judgement Day Begins

★ ★ ★

Sabah was allowed one phone call. It was to Patrice. She picked up the phone at her work desk. Instantly, her face went white and her entire body constricted. The nightmare was back.

For the next month, she resumed her weekly trips to El Centro. A hearing date hadn't been set. All she and Sabah could do now was wait. Almost two months before his trial, for reasons Sabah never understood, he was transferred back to the MCC in downtown San Diego.

During the few brief phone conversations and personal visits Sabah had with Patrice during this period, he did his best to appear cheerful and optimistic. They'd recently celebrated their first wedding anniversary. Sabah had taken the occasion to consider how remarkable his partner was and how blessed he'd been by finding her.

The immigration issues alone would have been sufficient for many women to at least reconsider, if not terminate, their most sacred vows. But Patrice hadn't complained, not even once. She'd shouldered his burdens when he was a prisoner. She'd rejoiced with Sabah in his freedom. She'd been a partner in every sense of the word, living month after month with Sabah on potato salad and eggs while they created a future together.

For Sabah, Patrice was now far more than the chief component of reasonable life plan. Her judgement had been consistent and sound. Her good sense—common, business, and otherwise—had seeped into every aspect of Sabah's own decision making process. He'd grown to rely on her as far more than support, guidance, and emotional sustenance. Her presence and value in life had now transcended his own tribulations.

Whoever he was now, whatever he was to become, he could not seperate that reality from this remarkable woman.

One week before the court date, Sabah received a visit from Lynn Goldberg. He wasn't carrying a heavy briefcase or stacks of folders, as he had so often in the past. Instead, he held only a single, thin leather notepad folder. He sat down across from Sabah in the visiting area of the MCC and opened the folder. He lifted a single sheet of paper and slid it across the plastic table toward Sabah.

"Do you remember Blix giving you this form?" Mr. Goldberg asked.

Sabah studied the piece of paper as carefully as he could, but he knew as soon as the question was asked that his answer would be no. He'd signed so many forms, almost always without reading them. Even if what he was signing was explained to him by an attorney, Blix or otherwise, he would barely understand the explanation. In all his years in America, Sabah had simply signed what he was told to sign, trusting his lawyers to do whatever was necessary to help him.

"I'm sorry, I don't," he said.

"It is your signature, correct?"

"Yes," Sabah said.

"Sabah, this is a consent form. You gave the court permission to do something they never could have done without your permission. Blix shouldn't have given you this. You never should have signed it."

"What does that mean?" Sabah asked.

"It means our chances just got better."

Sabah's face brightened. Mr. Goldberg never spoke in terms of probabilities or chances. He approached the world, and his work, only in terms of what was and what wasn't. His choice of these words now, and the excitement with which he'd said them, made Sabah realize just how well the man concealed his own opinions. Mr. Goldberg would never give any client, including Sabah, false hope or a misplaced sense of security. On the other hand, he would never say or do anything that would cause a client more anxiety than their circumstances had already created.

His role as a counselor was as simple as it was precise. He wasn't being paid to provide encouragement. He was being paid to think, as carefully and completely as a man can think. Whenever Sabah saw Mr. Goldberg, he had the impression that this gentle, soft-spoken man was assembling an infinitely intricate jigsaw puzzle. Listening to this, reading that, comparing this information with something else, and all the while waiting for that one final piece that would drift down like a single autumn leaf, fluttering perfectly into that final empty space.

Perhaps, Sabah thought, this sheet of paper was that leaf. He had no way of knowing, but the look in Mr. Goldberg's eyes gave Sabah a sudden lightness and buoyancy.

"Sabah, I need to ask you something," Mr. Goldberg said.

"Sure, what is it?"

"How many people do you know? How many people do you think you can get in the courthouse next week?"

Sabah wasn't sure why the question was being asked, but that wasn't unusual. He generally didn't understand why Mr. Goldberg asked anything. Sabah simply answered as accurately and honestly as he could.

"I don't know. Twenty, thirty maybe."

"Good. I want you to call your wife. I want you to have her get as many of those people in that hearing room as she can possibly get. Can you do that?"

"Sure."

Sabah hadn't been told whether he would actually be in attendance at the hearing or not. Unknow to Sabah, the two prosecutors, led by Karpinski, had been working behind the scenes to avoid that possibility.

In fact, they had constructed a very tightly choreographed sequence of events. The hearing would be at ten A.M. At exactly eleven twenty A.M., Sabah and Tony Saronna, the same bailiff who'd originally arrested him during the Blix debacle, would both board a jet at Lindbergh Field. Tony and Sabah would fly first to LAX, then to Athens, Greece, where Sabah would be put on a final flight to Baghdad. Tickets had been purchased and schedules had been cleared.

Unlike Mr. Goldberg, the prosecutors did think in terms of probabilities and percentages. In their view, Sabah's chances of conviction were one hundred percent.

The evening before the hearing, Sabah stood by himself in a corner of his cell. Through the narrow window slit rising vertically from floor to ceiling, Sabah could catch a small glimpse of the sunset. It was a late autumn day. The winter clouds were more prominent now. There, beyond the harbor and the tip of Point Loma, pillars of amber and golden sunlight found their way through dark, billowing clouds.

He had seen many sunsets before, and in beautiful places, but Sabah thought he'd never seen a sunset as beautiful as this. It was so beautiful it nearly broke his heart. He thought of home, but what home? His home as a young boy, in Baghdad? The little apartment he shared with Patrice in San Ysidro? Somehow they became blended together in one idea, one image. He wanted to be both places at once but couldn't be in either. He began to cry. He was as afraid as he'd ever been in his life. To every other prisoner on his floor, this was only a jail. For Sabah, it was death row. It was very possible, even probable, that in less than two days he would be dead.

He didn't look around to see if there were other people in the cell at that moment, or if those people were taking note of him in any way. It didn't occur to him to look. Either way, he didn't care. He knelt on the floor of his MCC cell, lowered his head, and prayed. There was no one else who could help him now. When he finally lifted his head, the sun had set.

★ ★ ★

It was nine forty-five AM on the morning of the hearing. Sabah was in his cell, certain he wouldn't be appearing in court. If he was going to appear, he certainly would have heard by now. He hadn't yet shaved or showered. He'd barely slept the night before and from the moment he'd woken, he was exhausted. He thought of the night, so long ago, when he'd been taken in by the Baathist police. The same kind of powerlessness was draining him now. He was barely able to think, let alone sit upright on his bunk, waiting for his fate to be decided. Somewhere deep within himself, he knew it was best to try and prepare for that fate, whatever it might be.

At exactly ten thirty A.M., as Sabah was sitting motionless on his bunk, imagining what might be happening in court, a key turned in his cell door lock. Tony Saronna stepped inside. Sabah looked up at him in a gray fog of despair and confusion.

"Toma," he said. "Let's go."

Sabah stared at him, uncomprehending. "Where?"

"They want you in court," Tony said.

Overriding Sabah's surprise, apprehension, and anxiety was another sharp feeling of alarm, the emotional equivalent of a knee jerk reaction. Even now, in his darkest hour, Sabah thought of his appearance.

"I haven't showered … my clothes …!" he exclaimed to Tony.

"Toma, what you look like is the least of your problems. Come on. They want us *now!*"

From the fifteenth floor of the MCC, Tony and Sabah took an elevator to a private tunnel below street level, connecting the prison to the courthouse. Tony and Sabah stood alone, descending in the elevator. Sabah was trying to make himself as presentable as he could, but it was a pointless endeavor. In the end, he sighed and settled for standing up as straight as he could. He glanced down at his handcuffs and folded one hand on top of the other.

"You know, I've never been to Greece," Tony said.

"It's nice," Sabah said.

"Is it? I know it's bad news for you. But it's sure good news for me."

"I'm glad for you," Sabah said.

By now, they'd arrived at the rear entrance of the court room. Tony was still leading the way, guiding Sabah with one strong hand wrapped almost completely around his upper arm. Tony paused at the door and looked at Sabah.

"Ready?" he asked.

Without waiting for any kind of reply, Tony swung the door open. Sabah would describe that moment, much later, as a kind of blast furnace. There was so much to take in during that first split second he couldn't process and separate what he was seeing from what he was hearing and feeling. The room itself wasn't particularly large. It had a maximum capacity of sixty or seventy, with an additional separate section for a jury.

What he was seeing didn't make sense. Was he in the wrong room? Was there a mistake? Were these people waiting for another case? Every seat in the room was filled, and some seats were occupied by two people.

At the same instant, Sabah was hearing a discussion, or was it an argument? The words were sharp-edged and heated.

"Your honor, we've already exceeded room capacity. I don't think we can get any more in."

The man speaking was one of two prosecuting attorneys. He was standing next to Karpinski.

Sabah's head turned quickly to the right. There, seated on a tall, regal, and stately dais finely hewn in polished walnut, was a man in a black robe. His name was Ed Shwartz and he was a Federal Court judge.

Sabah immediately discerned that Judge Shwartz wasn't exactly glaring at the prosecutor but he wasn't being particularly cordial either.

"I don't think I need to remind you this is a public hearing," Shwartz said mildly. "Let them take the witness stand seats."

By now, Tony had led Sabah into the center of the courtroom, toward Lynn Goldberg's desk. Looking past the spectators jamming the courtroom, Sabah noticed the glass wall at the back of the room. Just beyond that wall, he could see a hallway and reception area. In that area were at least another sixty or seventy people, pressed against the glass. The double doors at the court entrance had remained open and two bailiffs were standing in their frame, holding back the crowd of people trying to get into the court.

The bailiffs maintained tight control of the group and carefully escorted fifteen more people into a section containing twelve seats.

"All right," Judge Shwartz said. "Bailiffs, could you now please close the courtroom doors?"

Sabah's handcuffs were removed. He sat down next to Mr. Goldberg, completely confused and disoriented. Mr. Goldberg turned to Sabah. Sabah had never seen a more serene expression in his life. He offered Sabah an almost imperceptible nod and the faintest of smiles. Whatever was happening in the courtroom, so far, was good. Sabah could see it in Mr. Goldberg's face.

"Mr. Goldberg, what's happening?" Sabah whispered. "Why are these people here?"

The faint smile tugged at Mr. Goldberg's lips again. "Why? They're here for you, Sabah."

CHAPTER FORTY-ONE

★ ★ ★

Judgement Day Ends

★ ★ ★

Patrice, accompanied by her family and two dozen family friends, had been the first to arrive in court that morning. Sabah looked for her in the crowded room. Eventually, his eyes found hers, already gazing back at him. At least fifty feet away from each other, they shared an intimate and complex conversation without words. With only her eyes, Patrice told him everything he needed to know: she loved him and she always would. No matter what, she would always be there. Sabah nodded to her. The message had been received. He understood, and he needed her to know that he understood. She nodded back.

Sabah glanced around the rest of the courtroom and, at last, realized this wasn't a crowd of strangers at all. There was his manager and some agent friends from John Hancock. There was Debby the receptionist. There were Mr. and Mrs. Miller. There were some of his friends from his time at AIM. There were even some swap meet regulars. Daud and Faraj were there too. He recognized many other faces, some more intimately connected to his life than others, but all of them bringing back a distinct moment in time, or a vivid memory of a shared experience.

Each one of these people gazed back at Sabah as he looked at them. Each one, in their own way, with the stamp of their own unique personality, sent Sabah the same silent message. The message, though perhaps not quite as powerful as Patrice's, was no less poignant and clear. In every face he looked at and every glance he shared, the message was as consistent as it was unambiguous. Silently, in perfect unity, the entire room said, "I love you, Sabah."

Sabah was overwhelmed by a feeling of humility unlike any he'd ever experienced before.

He was so overcome with emotion that he lost track of the proceedings in the court room. When he managed to compose himself, he saw that Mr. Goldberg was presenting a document to Judge Shwartz. It was the same document Mr. Goldberg had shown Sabah at the MCC, the one he'd said Sabah never should have signed. Mr. Goldberg stepped away from the judge's bench and looked out into the room. It was completely silent. In another moment, he turned back to the judge.

"Your honor, in addition to that document, I'd like to mention just a few things about my client. First, he's been paying taxes to the federal government for over four years. He has a reputable job with an established company. He's been married for over a year. He's never been found guilty of any illegal activity. Your honor, the man's *driving* record is perfect. I'm sure the court wouldn't have time for the character witnesses who would love to testify on his behalf. Every person in this room, some immigrants and many non-immigrants, all people of stellar reputations in their own right, would be proud to tell you who Sabah Toma is. And I am proud to join them. Your honor, Sabah Toma is an honest, decent, hardworking man who asks nothing of America other than to call our country his own."

Mr. Goldberg continued on but not at all in a bombastic oration. He spoke simply, in a way both the judge and every other person in the courtroom, regardless of age or education, could easily understand.

The prosecutors, of course, had a very different version of Sabah, whom they characterized as a bond-busting fugitive who'd broken nearly every rule in their entire immigration book.

What Sabah didn't know, and would only find out later through Patrice, was what had happened before he'd arrived in the court room. Judge Shwartz had looked at Lynn Goldberg and asked him where his client was. The prosecutors had objected to the need for Sabah being in the court at all.

Anticipating this, Lynn Goldberg had requested a writ of habeas corpus. The fact that the hearing was being held in a federal court at all, rather than at an immigration court, was due to this request. The writ wouldn't have been applicable in a standard immigration hearing. Mr.

Goldberg wanted Sabah in the court and if he had to bring him to federal court to do it, so be it.

This, however, placed Judge Shwartz in a delicate position. Typically, it wasn't his role as a judge to rule on immigration cases. Judge Shwartz, as well any other person directly involved with the American system of jurisprudence, understood perfectly well that the I.N.S. was, in effect, a separate state within the government. Whether his final ruling was due to wariness and a private reluctance to disrupt some established harmony between his own court and the I.N.S., no one would ever know. Judge Shwartz, however, did ask Mr. Goldberg one pointed and specific question.

"Mr. Goldberg, does your client currently qualify for the pending Immigration Reform and Control Act?"

"He does, your honor," Mr. Goldberg said.

The act, sponsored by the Reagan Administration, was proposing the legalization of illegal immigrants who had entered the United States before January 1, 1982. The Act was already moving swiftly through the House and Senate. Immigration and federal courts across the country knew that a big change was coming, and within a relatively short time. In fact, the act would be signed into law by President Reagan on November 6, 1986—less than two months from the day of Sabah's hearing.

Sabah would recall, during that fateful day, Judge Schwartz glancing at him several times. Each time it was a piercing gaze, but Sabah never turned away from it. He was afraid, but not of this judge. Now, after Mr. Goldberg had answered this particular question, Judge Shwartz looked at Sabah once again. Reflecting back Sabah would wonder, what had Judge Schwartz been thinking at that very moment?

Was he contemplating life's mysterious relationship between time and events? Was he momentarily marveling at the eternally unpredictable and numerically incalculable consequences of their strange interplay? Two months, that was all this young man needed. Was that what Sabah was seeing in the rugged face of this large, bald-headed man sitting so high above him?

Shwartz began to offer a closing statement to the hearing, prior to his decision. Some of it Sabah could understand, some it he couldn't, but his final words were perfectly clear:

"I'm going to refer this back to John Williams in immigration court for further review. Mr. Toma, you're dismissed."

The words rang in his ears for a long moment, and a lifetime seemed to pass before he realizhed what they meant.

Further review. Further review meant that there would not be a decision today. And if there was not a decision today, there would not be a flight to Greece and then on to Baghdad.

He wasn't leaving America today. He wasn't going back to Iraq. He had been given the gift of time, though how much of it he couldn't be sure. But did it matter? For today he was safe, and the knowledge of that safety rippled through his body in a relief so powerful it made him feel weak.

Mr. Karpinski and his co-prosecutor reacted with violent protestations to the ruling. In fact, they were so incensed that Judge Shwartz told them to either quiet down or be physically removed from the room. The rest of the courtroom, those who fully understood what was stake, let out sighs of relief and their own silent, private thanks to God. In the commotion, Tony Saronna quickly collected Sabah and led him out of the court, but not before Sabah could share a glance with Lynn Goldberg.

"We did good," Mr. Goldberg said. "But I'm not done here. I'll see you soon." He was looking a little relieved himself, but not at all surprised.

Tony guided Sabah back and down through the enclosed, windowless corridors and stairwells of the courthouse. He said nothing to Sabah for a few minutes as they walked, but Sabah didn't notice the silence. He was completely preoccupied with one, single, glorious thought: he wasn't going to the airport. Anywhere else he might be going, including his cell at the MCC, was going to be a vacation.

"Well, Toma, you really messed me up," Tony finally said, pushing the ground floor elevator panel at the MCC.

"I know," Sabah said, and he couldn't help smiling. "I'm sorry about that."

"Yeah, Greece woulda been great." He was watching the floor numbers blink on and off as the descending elevator approached.

"You'll get there," Sabah said.

"Maybe. Who knows?" Tony was quiet for a moment, a thoughtful look on his face. "Hey, you wanna know somethin'?"

"What?"

"In a weird way, I'm kinda glad I'm not goin'."

"Why's that?" Sabah asked.

"All those people in there today. I've never seen that many in a court room. I was just thinkin', maybe they know something I don't."

When Sabah looked at him, Tony offered a single, terse upward tilt of his head. "You're okay, Toma," he said.

For another moment neither spoke. Sabah found himself blushing slightly. Embarrassed, he quickly changed the subject.

"What happens now?"

"Well, if they allow a bond to be posted, you'll be outta here. If not, who knows? You could be here or El Centro for a few months till the next hearing."

As the elevator door opened, another bailiff approached Tony and Sabah.

"Tony, you just got a call from the clerk in Judge Shwartz's room. They want you to call."

Tony stepped away and picked up a wall phone near where he'd been standing with Sabah. Sabah couldn't clearly make out the conversation. It was short, and when it was done, Tony walked the few steps back to Sabah.

"The judge is going to let you post bond. Things are lookin' up for you, Toma," he said with a smile.

Sabah's journey to citizenship in the United States was not marked with the certainty of an athletic competition. There was no single, final moment of victory or defeat. Nor was there such a moment, as in all great stories, when a final climax was reached. In Sabah's American story, the hero did not prevail in a single moment, nor was the villain defeated, killed, or forever banished. The crowd did not erupt in joyous throes of ecstasy nor did a ship sail off into a tranquil sunset. His journey was far more subtle and nuanced.

Together and alone, Sabah and Patrice crossed individual thresholds of hope and promise, which lifted them up like invisible streams of air, higher and higher into a perfect day.

Sabah's bail wasn't small change this time. Now, it would take someone very special to help him and, for the moment, Sabah and Patrice had no idea who that someone would be. In the meantime, Sabah was transferred to a San Ysidro holding facility for the weekend. Perhaps because he was so relieved by his own personal circumstances, Sabah was able to quickly return to his naturally generous and charitable disposition.

Long before, during his first week with Faraj in San Diego, Sabah had been introduced—or, more accurately, shown off by Faraj—to a supermarket owner. The man's name was Victor. Victor was six or seven years older than Sabah. He was one of those established members of the Chaldean community who had been in San Diego from the very beginning.

The day they'd met, there was nothing Victor could do for Sabah, other than be as kind to him as he could. Sabah had no idea, those many years ago, what life with Faraj would be like. But Victor had known. Had Sabah been slightly more observant that day, he would have recognized Victor's face held both compassion and pity.

But Victor had never forgotten Sabah. Over the years, they'd seldom met. When they did, it was usually at large Chaldean celebrations and parties. They would say hello in passing at these events and always Victor would ask how it was going with Faraj. In all the time Victor had known Sabah, not once had Sabah said a bad word about Faraj. Sabah had never complained nor demonstrated anything remotely close to self-pity. To Victor it was more than impressive; it was astounding. Here was a man, Victor thought, with the patience of Job and the work ethic of Hercules. He reminded Victor of his own brothers and himself, raised in a small Iraqi village, working almost non-stop since their pre-teen years.

Even so, Victor and Sabah had never been particularly close. They hadn't worked together or socialized often.

In the end, Victor helped Sabah not because of who Sabah was, but because of who Victor himself was. Not every man comes home to his wife and says, "Everything was fine at work today and by the way, I've mortgaged the house to pay a jail bond for some guy I've met five times." And not every wife would accept this decision without question. This was who Victor and his wife were.

There was no loan this time, no co-signing of contracts. Victor knew people, he knew Sabah, and he knew that the loan of sixty thousand dollars would be repaid. That was all there was to it.

Mr. Goldberg took Sabah to an immigration office in Kearny Mesa several weeks after the hearing with Judge Shwartz. In general, these offices were always busy places, but on this day the line reached outside the building and halfway down the block. The word had reached the streets about Reagan's Immigration Act and thousands of qualified illegals were applying for citizenship before the bill had even been signed.

It was another one of those little minor victories for Sabah. He walked into that building with nothing. He walked out with a White Card which held the eventual promise of a Green Card. He was getting so close but there was one final obstacle. Karpinski had appealed Judge Schwartz's ruling on Sabah's case and Mr. Goldberg would need to go the Ninth Circuit Court of Appeals in Los Angeles the following month to see if the judge's decision would be overturned or not.

Before the case even reached the court, President Reagan signed the bill and, according to the Federal Government, Sabah gained legal status in the United States. He was not a citizen, but he was no longer a refugee or a criminal in hiding. Mr. Goldberg phoned Sabah from the court in Los Angeles as soon as the decision was made. The judge had, in fact, overturned Judge Schwartz's ruling. Karpinski had been vindicated but it was an empty, hollow victory. The court was not in a position to overturn a bill passed by the Congress and signed by the President of the United States.

Only then, that night, sitting together in their little San Ysidro apartment, did Patrice and Sabah fully realize it was finally, and forever, over. A Green Card would come, swearing in ceremonies would take place, but right now, at this moment, on this day, Sabah Toma became an American.

PART III

THE AMERICAN

CHAPTER FORTY-TWO

★ ★ ★

Mr. Neon

★ ★ ★

Since his arrival in America almost ten years earlier, a cloud of varying size and density had hovered over Sabah. It was something he'd done his best to ignore. The cloud had compelled him to live in a constant, splintered state of denial. His single, unwavering response had been to transform himself into something like a work horse. As he plodded forward, pulling the weight of his own life, Sabah had outfitted himself with permanent and invisible blinders. He'd needed to do this because the cloud wasn't something he could afford to think about. What he hadn't realized, throughout his entire American journey, was how many *other* things those blinders had prevented him from seeing.

For ten years, his work and general circumstances had consumed him. He'd had very little time, if any, to consider how he'd feel as an actual American citizen. Even if he'd had had the time, luxury, or inclination to fantasize about this day, he couldn't have imagined how much his world actually would change.

He'd had a vague premonition that it would be the most wonderful moment of his life, but nothing had prepared him for what he was now experiencing: an overwhelming sense of buoyancy and exhilaration. But his legal status in America brought something even more than this. His attitude was affected, in a more subtle way, by a shift in his perspective. He was seeing America, and his relationship to America, in a completely new way. It was as though, for ten years, he'd been looking at a seventy millimeter film version of America broadcast on a small television set.

In a matter of weeks, even days, that image had taken its proper place

on a movie palace screen. The borders of the image had been expanded to
their full, proper, and intended dimensions. There was no more cropping
or awkward framing. He was seeing America as it was intended to be seen,
by all free citizens, as a complete visual composition full of power, grace,
and unimaginable opportunity. For the first time, Sabah knew the sky,
that big, blue, beautiful American sky, truly was the limit.

Despite these dramatic internal transitions, for some time after
obtaining his White Card, Sabah's work habits remained unchanged. The
force and weight of these habits were something like a very heavy train or
ship that had been moving at full speed. Stopping such a vehicle or vessel
isn't a sudden process. Sabah and Patrice continued their respective work
as usual, she at the law firm, Sabah at John Hancock. Together, they went
to their weekend stall at the swap meet. But a clock was ticking in Sabah.

Though not a superstitious person, nor one inclined to interpret events
as omens auguring good or bad fortune, Sabah awoke from a dream one
morning and immediately took action. He went to the nearest printing
shop and had business cards made up. The cards simply said "Mr. Neon."
It was a name given to him at the swap meet, occasionally and casually,
along with "the Neon Guy." But in his dream, he'd felt a perfection
connected with the name he'd never felt before.

Victor, the man who had offered his home as collateral for Sabah's
second bond, and one of two people, along with Lynn Goldberg, responsible
for Sabah's freedom, had only a vague idea how Sabah was supporting
himself. The only thing Victor knew for sure was that, without fail, a
substantial check arrived every month from Sabah and Patrice. Victor had
never been concerned about Sabah's ability to pay him back. He'd always
been a good judge of character, and besides, he honestly considered charity
to be its own reward.

Still, even by Victor's standards, what he'd done for Sabah was
considerable. His home, after all, had been put up as collateral for Sabah's
bond. With each passing month, Sabah's debt continued to be paid back
right on time and in amounts well ahead of schedule. Victor's trust and
confidence in Sabah quickly grew. The feeling of familiarity they'd
immediately shared so many years before, when Faraj first introduced
them, hadn't diminished in the least. In fact, it had only grown stronger.

What they recognized in each other, beyond word, thought, or simply being Chaldean refugees from Iraq, was the similarity of their life journeys. Like Sabah, Victor had been working since he was a young boy, perhaps ten or twelve years old. It had been the 1960s, and Victor had worked in the hamburger stand his family owned. It was one of the few hamburger stands in Baghdad at the time, if not the only one.

Like Sabah, Victor had not been taught about the value of a good day's work or the importance of having a strong work ethic. For both these men, work had always been something far more fundamental than that. Work was not something you did to get ahead, it was something you did to survive. Survival in the Iraq of their childhoods, particularly in their oppressed Chaldean community, required such massive amounts of work there was no time to consider how else time might be spent. Unlike Americans who viewed work as something they did with or in their lives, for people like Victor and Sabah, work was life itself.

As Sabah paid off his bond debt, Victor and his wife were living in relative comfort compared to Sabah and Patrice. Victor's home was perched high on a hill overlooking Mission Valley in central San Diego. Well into the first year of his repayment, Victor and his wife invited Patrice and Sabah to their home for dinner. It was past dusk. Patrice and Victor's wife chatted in the kitchen while Victor and Sabah sat outside on the wooden patio. They gazed down on the twinkling grid of city lights in the valley below. The din of the city with its freeway traffic was far enough away that even this sound seemed tranquil and calming, like wind chimes in a gentle breeze.

"Beautiful," Sabah said, staring out at the valley while sipping his red wine.

"Nice, isn't it?" Victor asked, but not in a way that required an answer.

When Sabah glanced at Victor, he saw look of appreciation and contentment on the other man's face.

"But you see it all the time," Sabah said.

"And I thank God every time I do," Victor said, without a trace of irony. He suddenly turned and looked straight at Sabah. "Really, I do."

Sabah was struck by the man's humility but said nothing more. The two men, though having spent a relatively small amount of time together, sat in a comfortable silence for another few moments.

"I like your home very much," Sabah said.

"I'm glad you do, especially since you're helping me keep it." Victor flashed Sabah a mischievous grin.

Sabah laughed. "That's right. We both are, Patrice and I."

"Absolutely. We're all in this together."

How could Victor say that? Sabah asked himself. Victor's financial circumstances were far beyond Sabah's. How could they be *anywhere* together? There was something about Victor that Sabah found both mysterious and accessible. Here was a man who owned real estate and supermarkets. He had a nice car and home, all the creature comforts Sabah had been taught to associate with the "American Dream."

Yet Victor didn't appear to be connected to the external manifestations of his success. His attitude and behavior weren't in any way defined by them. It was as though Victor was living in the middle of someone else's dream, seeing and appreciating his own life exactly the same way Sabah did.

Victor was so different from M, Faraj, or so many others trying to succeed in America. Sabah couldn't sense their restlessness in Victor. He had none of their anxiety or anxiousness.

Sabah had noticed it in so many other natives and immigrants alike, that constant need for all things newer, bigger, better, or faster. But Victor wasn't waiting for anything. He didn't want anything more than what he had and he already had far more than he'd ever wanted. Yet this didn't mean he was satisfied or complacent in any way. It was his orientation to success that most intrigued Sabah. He didn't need something more or something better, the way some other Chaldeans did, as though he was constantly suffocating or being seized by a fit of claustrophobia.

For Victor, the whole thing, America and all it offered, was just a fun pastime, a hobby. This patio, this home, his cars, his businesses, whatever these things were to Victor, they had nothing to do with his life, whatever and wherever that was. Sabah sensed all this without at first being able to put his impressions into words. All he knew for sure was that he liked this man very much.

"How did you do it?" Sabah asked.

Victor glanced at him but said nothing. He knew exactly what Sabah meant.

Sabah meant that work couldn't be the only explanation for all Victor had attained. Many people worked hard, immigrants and naturalized citizens alike. Yet there was never a guarantee that hard work would result in wealth. What Sabah was asking was this: how had Victor transformed his work into the relative affluence which Sabah, at this very moment, was surrounded by? Victor sipped his wine for a moment then spoke.

"You know what I think's crazy?" Victor said. "This whole thing in America about work. I mean, how many times you heard it here, 'Find your passion,' 'Follow your dream!' You know? And that other thing they always say. What is it? 'Do what you love, and you never work a day in your life.' Have you heard this one?"

"I have," Sabah said.

Victor shook his head. "It's all a buncha garbage."

Sabah laughed out loud. It was true. It was exactly what Sabah thought but he'd never heard it expressed like this before.

"It's true," Victor said. "These people talkin' like that, they're all fulla garbage."

When Sabah's laughter had subsided, Victor went on. "You know, I love America. This is the greatest country in the world. No question. But Sabah, wow, we got a bunch a morons here. So many people, young people especially, wasting their lives looking for something or *someone*. Like there's some big mystery to happiness. Or that other word, what is it? Fulfillment. Everybody in America want's to be *fulfilled*. It makes me crazy. You work, that's it! You plan, you build, you grow, but the main thing is you just keep working."

"True, absolutely," Sabah said in emphatic agreement. It was as though the words had come out of his own mouth.

"Find your passion! What is that? Did you grow up in Baghdad thinking, 'I have to find my passion?'"

Sabah shook his head and laughed out at the absolute absurdity of the suggestion.

"When we were kids, the only thing we wanted to find was food. Right? You know what I'm talking about."

"Completely," Sabah said.

"So, how did I do it? One day at a time, one year at a time, making some money, saving some money, helping when I could and sometimes even when I couldn't." Victor paused and looked out over the valley again. "You'll do it too. You'll get there. Sabah, there are so many ways to make money in this country. I mean just today, for instance. I've been trying for a month to get a sign made for my new store. I've been calling this guy who makes neon for a month! I can't get even get him to come in and give me a bid. There's a business! How busy is this guy that he can't call me back after a month!"

The expression on Sabah's face pre-empted Victor's mild diatribe and prompted a double take from Victor.

"What?" Victor asked.

Sabah unzipped the brown leather aviator jacket he'd purchased just a week earlier at the swap meet. He reached inside the breast pocket and pulled out his worn wallet. From within the wallet, he pulled out a business card and handed it to Victor. Victor looked at it, then back up at Sabah.

"What is this?"

"My card," Sabah said.

Victor looked at him in blank disbelief. "You make neon signs?"

"Well, I buy them, repair them, re-sell them."

"I thought you sold insurance," Victor said.

"I do. I do both."

"Can you make me a neon sign?" Victor asked

"Not really," Sabah said.

"What do you mean not really? You either can or can't."

"I'm not a bender. A neon bender."

"A what?"

"It's a special skill. An art. You know. It takes a lot of experience to do that."

Victor leaned back in his chair and took another sip of his wine, staring at the valley lights for another moment. Then, abruptly, he swiveled in his chair to face Sabah and set down his wine glass.

"Sabah, how'd you like to be partners?"

Even not understanding exactly what Victor was talking about, Sabah could think of nothing more appealing. And once it was explained to him, he realized that Victor's proposal was a very simple one. He and another business partner of his, a man named Fauzi, would put up the money to open a small store in downtown San Diego. It would be a neon sign store where all the work would be designed and built on site. Sabah wouldn't need up front money. He would be a "sweat equity" partner, running the shop and developing the business. Sabah would need to take a crash course on building neon signs, but Victor would cover the training costs which, at five hundred dollars a week for three months, wasn't exactly small change for Sabah. With a single handshake on Victor's balcony, the business began.

Within four months, Mr. Neon was open. The company was born in a ground floor, eight hundred square foot space located in a seedy, dilapidated section of downtown San Diego. It was 1986 and America's cities were on the verge of transformation. The explosive growth of suburban America from the fifties through the seventies had reached a critical mass. Suburban sprawl throughout the country had reached its apex. Cities were poised to collapse in on themselves with one massive contraction. Americans were on the cusp of a renewed love affair with their urban cores and San Diego was no exception. A renaissance was about to begin.

Mr. Neon was right in the heart of this forsaken, seedy urban wasteland. It was a neighborhood dominated by ramshackle monthly hotels, boarded up windows, tenements, and trash covered sidewalks. Downtown was a place most San Diegans had no reason to visit. It was dirty, disheveled, and disreputable. Mr. Neon was at ground zero in a neighborhood called "The Gaslamp".

CHAPTER FORTY-THREE

★ ★ ★

The Investor

★ ★ ★

"If you can sell a piece of paper, you can sell anything."

This was what Sabah's trainers and managers at AIM and John Hancock had always told him, and it was true. Perhaps the only other door-to-door marketers greeted with less enthusiasm than a life insurance agent are Mormons or Jehovah's Witnesses. But it wasn't simply that Sabah now had a physical product to promote, namely the neon signs he was designing and building on his own. That would have been a refreshing change of pace in and of itself.

The real excitement of his new job was that he no longer had a boss. He was over thirty years old, and he had never experienced this before. For the first time, Sabah wasn't working for anyone. He was working for himself and there never was a person more perfectly suited to be his own employer. Every aspect of his personality had prepared him for this moment. His self-discipline, determination, and ambition had now perfectly aligned with his innate love for freedom. Every moment of his life had become an opportunity to build equity in himself.

Of course, Victor and Fauzi had given him this opportunity. They'd provided the means for Sabah to build and grow his business, but these men were partners. This also was a completely new experience. Working with other people, instead of for them, completely changed the dynamic of his workplace. Decisions needed to be made. Gathering and processing information, deliberation, representing his opinion when he was in agreement or disagreement with his partners; all of this contributed to Sabah's growing sense of self-confidence in his work and in the neighborhood surrounding it.

By the end of his first year at Mr. Neon, Sabah had visited every business in downtown San Diego not once, but several times. He'd become better known than many of the other small business owners and merchants who'd been there far longer, eking out livings in their rundown little neighborhood.

On each marketing foray, Sabah carried the golden lessons of his sales mentors with him. One of the most important lessons was the power of listening. A good salesman listened with great care and attention and Sabah was an expert salesman.

As he listened, Sabah quickly recognized a recurring theme. It seemed, with each passing week, that one simple idea was being expressed more and more frequently. His clients, company executives, and fellow business owners throughout the downtown area were all saying the same thing: change was on the way.

Not just a small change, but a very big change. Though it wasn't going to come overnight, and some couldn't hold on long enough, among everyone Sabah spoke with, the consensus was the same: don't go anywhere, you're sitting on a gold mine.

Every day, as Sabah made his rounds in downtown, he saw construction work continuing on a massive new development. They said it was going to be a shopping mall, but it didn't look like any mall Sabah had ever seen. In fact, no one in San Diego had ever seen one like it. The idea of a shopping mall was, in itself, a relatively new idea at the time, but these sprawling temples of consumerism were always found in the outlying areas of the city. Not only was the land cheaper and more ample in the suburbs, it was where most of the consumers were, the generally white, middle-class people with higher paying jobs and more disposable income.

Even during its construction, many wondered why anyone would build a shopping mall in the middle of a deserted ghost town, but Sabah was not one of them. He saw the future coming as clearly as a train pulling into the old Santa Fe Depot.

The constant conversation among all his business neighbors in the downtown area gradually oriented Sabah to a new way of thinking. For the first time, he began to think in terms of real estate—specifically, owning real estate. Mr. Neon had been operating successfully for over five years in the same location, a turn of the century building on Sixth Avenue, just south of Broadway. By now, Victor and Fauzi, Sabah's partners in Mr. Neon, were moving on to larger projects. They were constructing a new hotel in the Old Town area of San Diego and had sold their remaining shares in Mr. Neon to Sabah for forty thousand dollars.

Sabah had kept in close touch with his brother Sam throughout the five years Sam had been living in Canada. When Sabah saw a small delicatessen for sale in the Old Town area, he knew this was just the opportunity he'd been waiting for. For less than twenty thousand dollars, Sam, who'd been working as a manager in convenience stores in Canada, could have his own business and be back in San Diego. Putting their money together, Sabah and Sam purchased the deli. Patrice, always there and always ready, would help Sam. That would have been more than enough of a contribution in itself, and consistent with who she'd always been as a wife to Sabah and a friend to his family. But now Patrice would rejoin the working world as a brand new mother. She and Sabah had just had their firstborn, a son they named Alex. Alex would be able to say, without exaggeration, that for the first year of his life he'd been raised in a deli.

Perhaps it was the fact that he hadn't been able to adequately protect and provide for his brother the first time his mother had brought him to America. Perhaps there was the slightest twinge of regret, or even guilt, in Sabah for having failed in his duties as an elder brother to Sam. Or maybe it was the fact that he was now a father for the first time. His innate need to provide safety and security to everyone he loved had grown in proportion to his age and circumstances.

The small center, which consisted of several businesses, including the deli, was for sale and Sabah knew he wanted to buy it. He wanted Sam to have an entirely new level of security. It was perfectly clear to him this was the most logical way to provide it. The purchase price was five hundred and eighty-five thousand. The down payment would be one hundred and twenty thousand. Together, Sam and Sabah had half that. The deficit seemed insurmountable, but throughout Sabah's entire life, it was precisely at moments like this that little miracles occurred.

Luck, that word again. The thing Sabah had never believed in. The idea he found annoying and irritating. Was it simply the result of opportunity meeting preparation? Was it karma, being and practicing good so good things would happen? Sometimes the men who attended church least were the men with the deepest faith. There always had been two forces at the center of Sabah's being, God and family. There was no such thing as luck, there was only reaping what you sowed.

And what had he sown? More hours working in his lifetime than a man two or three times his age. Honesty and humility, endurance and tenacity; these were the seeds of Sabah's life. If, at certain times, something like fortune intervened, like it had with that guard in an Iraqi police station so many years before, for Sabah that moment was no more than a tree bearing good fruit.

Now, here he was on July 4, a day that was quickly becoming his favorite day of the year. Sabah was celebrating with his family and friends at a park, barbecuing and waiting for the fireworks to begin. Right at that moment, his pager went off. It would have been so easy to ignore it. But Sabah didn't. He went to a pay phone and called the number. A man answered. His voice was loud, raspy, and had a thick German accent.

"This is Sabah, you paged me?"

"This is Toma? Sabah Toma?" It was more a demand than a question.

"Yes, how may I help you?"

"I'm standing across the street from your shop right now," the man said.

"Yes ..."

"I want to buy your neon."

"Okay, when would you like to do that?"

"Right now!"

"Well, you know, it's the Fourth of July ..."

"I'm leaving tomorrow for Germany," the man said.

Sabah looked over at his family and friends, laughing and enjoying themselves. He had no idea who this person was on the other end of the phone. For all he knew, it could have been some crackpot making a crank call.

So, he made a choice. His choice was to plant just one more seed in the long row he'd carefully tended every day of his life.

"Sabah, you're gonna miss the fireworks!" Patrice implored.

"Good thing I saw them last year," Sabah said, giving her a smile and a kiss on the cheek before driving the ten miles to his shop downtown.

The man's name was Klaus and he was from Germany. Within an hour of meeting Sabah, Klaus had purchased nearly the entire inventory of Mr. Neon, over ninety thousand dollars worth of neon signs. It was the largest single sale Sabah had ever made. It was the sale that allowed Sabah and Sam to purchase a little shopping mall. It was the sale that transformed Sabah, for the first time, into a real estate investor.

Leading up to this purchase, Sabah may have thought at some point, "Well, I did it for Sam, why not do it for myself?" The building Mr. Neon was in had been owned for thirty years by two Iranian brothers. They'd opened a Persian restaurant in the building in the late fifties and had been there ever since. Changes or not, golden opportunities or not, the brothers were ready to retire. Real estate prices in the Gaslamp had been slowly but steadily rising in the early eighties, preparing themselves to skyrocket off the charts by the latter half of the decade. The brothers had received an offer on the building and were ready to accept it, but Sabah had other plans.

He'd become close to the brothers over his years in business. The brothers saw Sabah inside his small shop, working before they arrived in the morning and still there after they closed for the night. The brothers had seen this day after day, week after week, year after year. In many ways, Sabah reminded them of each other. They understood what it was to arrive penniless in America with only a dream. When Sabah approached them offering to buy the building for fifty thousand dollars less than they'd already been offered, the brothers weren't confused or conflicted in any way. They accepted his offer gladly.

Now, Sabah owned the building he worked in. It wasn't long before the roles were reversed in Sabah's mentor/apprentice relationship with Victor.

Several years later, the real estate agent who had brokered Sabah's purchase from the Iranian brothers approached Sabah with another opportunity. There was a small office building for sale just off Broadway at the north end of the Gaslamp. The broker wanted to know if Sabah was interested. Sabah was and he knew exactly who he wanted to talk to.

"Victor," Sabah began again, even more urgently now. He was approaching exasperation, which was something Victor seldom, if ever, prompted in Sabah. "Listen to me. You don't know what's going on out there!"

Though Victor owned a large supermarket and several buildings in the downtown area, he continued to work as a butcher cutting meat in the windowless basement of his own market. Sabah believed, and for good reason, that Victor was completely oblivious of the apocalyptic transformation about to happen right outside his own supermarket door.

Victor rested his cleaver on a counter and looked at Sabah. "And you don't know what you're getting yourself into."

"I do!" Sabah insisted. "Look, Victor, everybody out there knows, it's not gonna last. We have a small window here. Maybe just two or three more years."

Sabah's determination to persuade Victor wasn't due to his belief in the future of the Gaslamp any more than it was due to his own ambition. Victor's loan had been the greatest gift Sabah had ever received. It would be enough to say that Sabah was a man of honor who would not rest until gifts were returned in equal measure. But that, alone, wouldn't have explained his persistence.

Sabah wasn't defined or driven by a sense of duty. He was driven by love. He respected and loved Victor, a man who had given him the most priceless gift any man can give another: the gift of freedom. Not just freedom from the law or incarceration, but freedom to experience his life and the world in an entirely new way. For Sabah, partnering in the purchase of this building was the only way he could imagine repaying Victor, or even trying to.

Victor studied his friend and business partner for another moment. Neither man said anything but Victor saw, in Sabah's eyes, everything Sabah couldn't find the words to say. Victor saw a man who would do anything for him, and was only praying for the one chance to do just that. This is a good man, Victor thought to himself. It was exactly what Sabah thought about Victor.

Still, Victor wasn't entirely persuaded. It required six more weeks of relentless insistence from Sabah for Victor to relent.

"Okay," Victor said, finally. "I'll go in half with you, but on one condition. You deal with the paperwork, the bank, real estate people, the payments, all of it. I've got enough of those headaches."

Sabah extended his hand and Victor shook it. But for Sabah, this simple gesture wasn't enough. His gratitude for so many things spilled out of him like an overflowing reservoir and he put his arms around his friend. Victor patted Sabah on the back as they embraced, and after a few moments, Sabah pulled away, smiling.

"There's gonna be a big party, Victor," Sabah said, beaming with hope and happiness.

"Where?" Victor asked.

"Everywhere. And we're gonna be right in the middle of it."

It was true, the resurrection of the Gaslamp was going to be the biggest party San Diego had ever seen, but no one, including Sabah, had any idea how big that party was going to be. Victor and Sabah had just made their first real estate purchase together. It was a new era in their partnership and another step in a beautiful friendship.

Take care of yourself first. The words had often come back to Sabah, but never more than they did now. The immigration attorney he'd seen years before, when he'd tried to help his brother get out of Syria; those were the words he'd spoken to Sabah. Now Sabah knew he'd done almost everything he was supposed to do. He'd taken care of himself in nearly every way he could. It had been over sixteen years since his arrival in America. In one more day, he would achieve his final goal. In one more day, he would be able to fulfill the mission he'd carried every day since leaving Baghdad in 1975.

In one more day he would be able to bring his parents to America.

CHAPTER FORTY-FOUR

★ ★ ★

Citizen Sabah

★ ★ ★

B alboa Park is the cultural and historic heart of San Diego and the best possible place for a Naturalization Oath Ceremony. It was 1992, six years since Sabah had received his Green Card. On this clear, crisp spring day, Sabah stood in a group of more than a thousand other immigrants, all with their own stories of determination, hope, hard work, and persistence. The group gathered in the middle of what is called the Organ Pavilion, a large amphitheater in the park. For the ceremony, the heavy metal grating covering and protecting the large pipe organ had been rolled up and fully opened. Each of the organ's shining golden cylinders stood straight and proud, an appropriate reflection of each person gathered below them, preparing to take a most solemn oath. The late morning sun shone through the graceful colonnades extending along both sides of the stage.

With his family and friends sitting close by, Sabah stood in the middle of the large group with his right hand over his heart. As he stood there, just moments away from becoming a true American citizen, he found himself thinking back to that day, years before, when he'd stood at the base of that ancient temple in Greece. The beauty and power he had only sensed in that temple, veiled by the experiences of a life yet to be lived, were now fully unsheathed. The last remnants of freedom's theoretical existence had crumbled to dust. He would never again look at that temple from the outside. He was inside now, in a place that was now his home. As he recited the words, Sabah began to cry.

"I hereby declare, on oath, that I absolutely and entirely renounce and

abjure all allegiance and fidelity to any foreign prince, potentate, state, or sovereignty of whom or which I have heretofore been a subject or citizen; that I will support and defend the Constitution and laws of the United States of America against all enemies, foreign and domestic; that I will bear true faith and allegiance to the same; that I will bear arms on behalf of the United States when required by the law; that I will perform noncombatant service in the Armed Forces of the United States when required by the law; that I will perform work of national importance under civilian direction when required by the law; and that I take this obligation freely without any mental reservation or purpose of evasion; so help me God."

And with that, Sabah drew in his first breath as a citizen of the United States.

The country he had loved for his entire life was now his own. It would be difficult to imagine another person who could cherish his country more than Sabah. If we love the most those things we pay the most for or work hardest for, then very few people, if anyone, could love America more than Sabah Toma.

But the only thing Sabah could think at the moment of his citizenship, even at his birth as an American, was that now, at last, he would be able to sponsor his parents and family. Finally, he would be able to fulfill a seventeen year mission. Now he would bring them to America and the timing could not have been more urgent.

Only weeks before the Naturalization Ceremony, Sabah had received word from his father. Sabah's mother had suffered a heart attack and a third of her heart was no longer functioning. The urgency to get his parents to America was no longer solely based in his love and longing for them, but in the medical care his mother needed and Sabah's ability to assist her once she was here. But simply being able to sponsor his family didn't eliminate all the obstacles Sabah still needed to overcome in order for his parents to migrate.

Not the least of which was that the United States had recently declared war on Iraq. The United Nations had placed travel and trade sanctions on Iraq, and Sabah would go there only at great personal risk. Going to Iraq at this time could result in a ten thousand dollar fine, a year in prison, or both. But these were the least of his concerns.

Since his mother's brief trip to America seven years before, taken in order to deliver her son Sam safely and permanently out of Iraq, all passports and visas had been denied and repealed by the Hussein regime. Very few people were getting into Iraq and even fewer were getting out. The challenge of passports would have to be dealt with if and when Sabah was able to successfully return to, and re-enter, Baghdad.

In many ways, Sabah's life was like that of a great action hero and adventurer we see in a suspense movie. Always involved in a quest, yet not knowing the exact obstacles he would need to negotiate in order to obtain his goal, he simply kept moving forward as best he could. During some periods of his life, he would progress at a much higher velocity than at others, but regardless of the pace of his progression, he kept moving.

This had been the case when he'd first left Iraq and moved to Greece. It was no less true when he finally reached America, during his trials with Faraj, his exploration into insurance sales, the creation of Mr. Neon, and even, to a certain extent, his marriage to Patrice. All these steps had been a journey in faith. His mantra and fundamental rule in life had always been, first, to take action, then to adjust to and accommodate the consequences of that action.

It wasn't surprising, then, that Sabah should have purchased a round trip ticket to Jordan before he knew how he would get into Iraq, let alone how to get his parents out. With the faith of a mustard seed, Sabah moved mountains throughout his life, yet they were not snow-covered alpine peaks. They were the self-imposed mountains many people place in their own paths, the mountains that prevent us from attaining the life and success we most dearly desire, the mountains that forever relegate and isolate some of us to a land of unfulfilled dreams. So many of us stop before we even begin, but for Sabah, the journey was eternal. It was his faith that turned the mountains in his life into fields of gold.

His life was powered and propelled by faith in life itself. It was his faith in some permanently blurred, mirage-like image always just ahead. It was a faith in something called the future. Sabah knew it would be better there, and because he knew it, it always was.

Just days before his departure to bring his parents and family to America, Sabah attended a concert with his old friend Steve. This was the same Steve who had been with him on that day, years before, when Sabah was apprehended by two I.N.S. agents and taken to jail. Despite that ugly memory, or perhaps because of it, the two had grown even closer over the years.

Steve, a lover of music just like Sabah, had come to Sabah years earlier with tickets for a local concert featuring a new Middle Eastern singer named Kazom Al Sahir. The singer was so unknown that Steve and Sabah had actually promoted and organized the concert for him, which was primarily attended by members of the San Diego Chaldean community. This had been almost ten years earlier. During each of Al Sahir's tours through San Diego over the next decade, Steve and Sabah's direct promotion waned but they remained his most ardent fans. Also during this period, something amazing had happened with this singer. Now he was returning to San Diego and performing in venues built to hold thousands of people. Since Sabah and Steve had first met Al Sahir, he had become the most famous and beloved singer in the entire Middle East.

Now, Steve and Sabah were simply fans, paying for admission like anyone else. So it was humbling and gratifying to Sabah that Al Sahir's manager actually returned Sabah's phone call. He invited Steve and Sabah to have dinner with himself and Al Sahir after the concert. It was at this dinner that, with a single name and phone number quickly handwritten on the back of business card, Sabah was given all the information he would need to get his family out of Iraq.

Sabah knew that the old saying "it's not what you know, it's who you know" had always been perfectly applicable to his home country. This had been true over the course of his entire life, but it was particularly relevant right now, in his war-ravaged and isolated homeland. He thought about that day, a lifetime before, when the wife of an Iraqi ambassador had handed him another business card with another name and number. That name had allowed him to leave Iraq. The card he was holding now would allow him to enter it.

A week later, Sabah was in Jordan, at the Iraqi border where, because of the sanctions placed on Iraq, an unusually long line of taxi drivers waited for the opportunity to transport inbound travelers along an eight hundred mile, eleven hour drive to Baghdad. Based solely on the CNN coverage of the world's first "live war," Sabah had prepared for the worst in returning to the city of his birth. What he saw, in the early morning hours after an all night drive, was a city both familiar and unfamiliar.

Certainly there were damaged buildings. The telecommunications building his brother had worked in was abandoned. Several floors in the center of the building remained gutted and blackened, the aftermath of the new American "smart bombs." At the same time, new roads and buildings, unrecognizable to Sabah, infringed on the borders of his memory. The city was an odd and unsettling mixture of the relatively new and the recently destroyed. Sabah was overrun with so many emotions it was impossible for him to know exactly what he was feeling or experiencing.

But if there was any ambiguity, conflict, or confusion in seeing Baghdad once again, it all disappeared the moment Sabah's SUV turned the corner and onto his parents' street.

There, on the street corner, Sabah saw his father standing in his familiar dishdasha. Like a faithful sentry, his father had been standing there for hours, waiting for his son to arrive. Sabah climbed out of the car and, in a silent, tearful embrace, he held his father until they were both fully convinced that they were really, truly together again.

His father's face was as strong and resolute as the day Sabah had left Baghdad, but there was a rigidity and stillness in his body that couldn't conceal an immeasurable fatigue. It was as though the life force had almost drained out of him and now, in its place, all Sabah could see was this man's unfathomable will to live. Perhaps his father had even remained alive for only one reason: to experience this day, this very moment.

Sabah and his father entered a different home than the one Sabah had left. It was small but comfortable. Sabah's father had built it with his own hands. There, in the plain, austere interior of their home, so similar to the home Sabah had shared with them half a lifetime before, his mother sat waiting. More than anything, she would have loved to walk to her son and hold him, but she only had the strength to gently gesture with her hand, beckoning Sabah to come to her. Sabah did so and knelt by her chair, putting his arms around her as she kissed his forehead.

Sabah's sisters Nadal, Wyam, and Hyatt were also there, along with Hyatt's husband, Issa. By now, the Toma family had scattered and taken whatever refuge they could from the all-consuming control of the Hussein regime. Sabah's brother George had already started his own migration to America and was now in Greece, waiting for his visa to be approved. Sabah's other sister Wifa and her husband had already come to San Diego and were well assimilated into the Chaldean community. His other brother and sister, Wally and Anna, were safely living in Canada. For the time being, Hyatt would stay behind in Iraq with her husband.

With the aid of that single business card given to Sabah by Al Sahir's manager, Sabah's parents, along with his sisters Wyam and Nadal, went through a process in one day that would have taken most Iraqis weeks or months to accomplish, if ever. The morning after Sabah's arrival, the group walked into one of those cold, colorless institutional buildings Sabah had been in prior to his own departure. Even a war hadn't changed the depressing look and atmosphere of the place, Sabah thought to himself as he looked inside the building again. By that afternoon, all of them would have passports and the next day, with whatever each of them could carry in a single suitcase, they would all leave their country forever.

Before they left, however, there was a final, bizarre excursion led by Sabah's brother-in-law. Sabah was never sure what exactly had precipitated it. It could have been Issa's own peculiar way of adding to the probability of a successful departure for the group. Though Sabah barely knew the man, he credited Hyatt with not marrying someone who would do something like this simply out of braggadocio. Sabah's confusion in this regard only enhanced his growing instinctive anxiety as Issa drove them through the narrow, winding streets at the center of Baghdad. While his parents and sisters were being processed, approved, and stamped for departure, Issa and Sabah were idling at the third barricaded checkpoint within the past mile.

Issa had passed each of these checkpoints with nothing more than a wave or tilt of the head. He would receive the same in return from dozens of uniformed soldiers, all holding military grade rifles.

"Are you scared?" Issa asked with a smile as they passed through the third checkpoint.

"Not at all," Sabah said, then added, "But it would be nice to know where we're going."

"You'll see," Issa answered.

Eventually, Issa and Sabah stood in a small office on the third floor of an office building that was otherwise unremarkable, except for that fact that it was being guarded and secured by at least a hundred soldiers.

A short, bald man with a moustache and reading glasses was seated at a desk. He wasted no time, immediately confirming Sabah's background with a few personal questions. Was Sabah an American? Was he now living in America? Was he a successful businessman there? Yes, yes, and yes. The man, either pressed by a very busy schedule or even graver matters than Sabah could only try to imagine, got straight to the point.

"Right now, I have a super tanker at our port in the Persian Gulf. It's fully loaded. Over five hundred thousand deadweight tons, crude oil. Okay?"

"Okay," Sabah said, completely at a loss as to where the man was heading.

"It's yours. I'll give it to you. I'll trade it for medical supplies. Also, Caterpillars or John Deeres."

"You mean tractors?" Sabah asked.

"Yes, tractors."

"How many tractors?" The proposal was so absurd that he had to remind himself not to smile. His inquiry was based purely in curiosity, rather than anything approaching a serious business negotiation.

"You name it," the man said. "A hundred, a thousand, whatever you can do."

So, this was what Iraq had come to, Sabah thought to himself. Isolated, starving, and so desperate that Sabah himself would be considered the subject of substantial opportunity and advantage by no one less than Iraq's Minister of Oil.

The entire situation was preposterous. Of course Sabah couldn't provide this man, or Iraq, with heavy machinery for farming. With international sanctions and an embargo in place, how would he do that, even with the proper business connections? He made a polite promise to see what he could do and left the office with Issa.

The next day, as Sabah, his parents, Wyam, and Nadal drove across the vast, empty desert toward the Jordanian border, Sabah felt the joy of knowing that, as of this moment, his parents would be with him for the rest of their lives. At the same time, he felt a sense of sorrow, a small but sharp twinge of sadness for the fate of a country he had once called home.

CHAPTER FORTY-FIVE

★ ★ ★

The Mother Lode

★ ★ ★

Sabah was confused, and slightly bewildered, as to why Mr. Toma wasn't completely enthusiastic about his personal move to America. Perhaps it was because of all the years Mr. Toma had lived in Iraq before the Baathists took power. He'd had much more time to live in a country that, though imperfect, was far from the tyrannical state Sabah had been raised in. During the few months preceding Sabah's return to Iraq and his parents preparations for departure, Sabah often spoke on the phone with his father. During these conversations, Sabah found himself in the surprising role of salesman for the United States.

"Dad, you're gonna live like a king here. The streets, the houses, the supermarkets, the people, I just can't tell you what it's like."

During the few months the family waited in Oman, Jordan for Mr. Toma's visa to be approved, Sabah repeatedly tried to describe a world better than anything Mr. Toma could imagine. But Sabah couldn't have understood. For a man his father's age, a man in his mid-sixties, home was something only time could create. As far as Mr. Toma was concerned, there weren't enough years left for him to experience two homes in his life. Even if his first home had been raped, ravaged, and stolen beyond all hope of recovery, it would probably remain the only home Mr. Toma would ever have. If there was some reluctance to leave that home or, at the very least, ambivalence, it was understandable. Only time could create this particular disposition and only time could change it.

For the first few months after their arrival in San Diego, Mr. Toma, Mrs. Toma, and Sam all lived in a small house with Patrice, Sabah, and

324

their infant son, Alex. Though she was immediately accepted by Sabah's parents, and a genuine fondness was quickly formed between them, Patrice felt that the living accommodations were just a little tighter than she would've preferred. At the same time, she knew that Sabah's happiness and comfort with their new living conditions wasn't entirely due to his renewed contact with his parents, nor to his ability to provide for them.

Patrice had a deep understanding of her husband, combined with a wisdom distilled from many years of hard work in her own life. She knew that in the congested living conditions created during the first few months of his family's arrival, Sabah was reliving the home of his own childhood. He hadn't lived with so many people in so small a space for more than twenty years, yet he was relating to the experience as though it had happened only yesterday or, perhaps, had never ended at all.

At the same time, Patrice knew that the man who had existed in Baghdad, twenty years before, did not exist today. Sabah was an American now. He'd grown accustomed to living at a certain level of comfort, created solely by work done alone and in partnership with Patrice. Sabah knew that the American Dream included the idea of a home for every husband and wife. Patrice also knew that, as far as Sabah was concerned, no husband and wife in America were more worthy of that dream than his parents.

Within a year, Sabah had purchased his parents a neat and clean three bedroom home in El Cajon, near the Chaldean church and its surrounding community. His mother would attend the church seven days a week as his father gradually began to warm up to his new country. In fact, before Mr. Toma had been in San Diego a year, he was happier than Sabah had ever seen him.

Mr. Toma was a dignified man, always well-groomed and properly dressed. Since arriving in America, he had taken to dressing in a more a western style, with suits he regularly purchased at thrift stores. He would often go with his son to the Mr. Neon office, always packing a lunch for Sabah, which was as touching as it was unnecessary. His English gradually became passable and, like Sabah, he wandered around the streets of the downtown area, though not for business purposes. Mr. Toma was simply a social person who loved people. Very soon he was known, recognized, and welcomed within the downtown area as Abu Sabah or Father Sabah.

Sabah had never felt more fulfilled or complete than he did with his father and mother once again in his world and in his life. Mr. Neon soon outgrew its small, eight hundred square foot space and Sabah relocated to another building in the downtown area. His entire building on Sixth Avenue was empty now, but he wasn't concerned about his payments. He was confident he would find a tenant soon, but he never could have guessed who that tenant would be.

Sabah had been doing sign work for some time with a company in San Diego called Deja Vu. Deja Vu was then, and still is now, part of the world's largest chain of adult dance clubs. Peter Luster was the General Manager of a club in the San Diego area and Sabah's original contact with the organization. Sabah was never concerned about the moral reputation or community standing of the clients who hired him. He would never say no to a job opportunity simply because some people, or perhaps even many people, considered his client's product or service to be unsavory or lacking in moral character.

At the same time, though, Sabah made no extra effort to socialize or become particularly close to the people of the Deja Vu community. Certainly Patrice wasn't partial to the organization. Those peculiar, but strong and distinct, religious sensibilities Sabah had cultivated throughout his entire life created a cordial but clear separation between his personal life and the world of Deja Vu. But all of this changed with one person. Through Peter, Sabah met the owner and founder of the Deja Vu empire, a man named Harry Mohney. Harry was someone Sabah understood completely, and almost at first sight.

Like Sabah, Harry was a man of integrity. He was a man of his word who approached the world and everyone in it without pretense or guile. From the moment Sabah met Harry, he found him completely honest yet without any of the arrogance one might assume would be so commonplace in a man of his standing. On the contrary, more than anything else, Sabah was impressed with Harry's politeness and humility. As Sabah's work for Deja Vu expanded and his contact with Harry increased, Harry became equally impressed with Sabah. Harry realized Sabah approached business, and the world for that matter, exactly as Harry himself did, with a fairness and decency that wasn't in the least associated with whatever his business happened to be.

Harry soon began to see Sabah as more than just an honest, fair, and reliable vendor. Soon the two men became friends. But it was Peter who first learned that Sabah had a building for lease in the Gaslamp. Peter mentioned it to Harry, who was immediately interested, though not for himself. Harry had a business partner who was looking for a location exactly like Sabah's. That partner was Larry Flynt, the same Larry Flynt who had created Hustler Magazine and the empire associated with it.

In 2000, Sabah Toma, a Chaldean immigrant from Iraq, became Larry Flynt's landlord. On behalf of his partner, Harry Mohney signed a twenty year lease at five year renewable reviews. The negotiation took a full day and was attended by attorneys for both parties. Detailed percentage increases were accounted for and discussed, associated with each five year period. Yet when the final contract was drafted, Sabah didn't fill in the final percentage amounts. Harry saw Sabah's signature and looked incredulously at the blank percentage increases.

"You fill them in," Sabah said.

"But we talked about …"

"I know, but whatever you decide is good for me. I trust you."

It was an amazing and memorable moment for Harry and, in a way, it was the beginning of a very long and close friendship. For Sabah, it was a business relationship that would change his life, certainly in financial terms. But in a less tangible though equally significant way, Sabah's notoriety among the Chaldean and downtown business communities was elevated by an ongoing mystique. After all, how many people are able to call Larry Flynt a tenant?

Mr. Flynt, an incredibly savvy businessman himself, recognized the direction and potential of the Gaslamp. The opportunity to set up a Hustler shop in that area was a case of being in exactly the right place at exactly the right time. Sabah knew this, but it had never occurred to him to make a "quick buck" off anyone, even people with pockets as deep as Larry Flynt and Harry Monhey. Sabah simply practiced the business lessons and philosophy he'd learned as far back as his first swap meet days. He would make some money for himself, but allow the person he was trading with to benefit just as much as he did.

Like all the best landlords, Sabah wasn't interested in how much his lease agreement would profit him this month or even this year. Treating a tenant fairly, keeping them happy, and developing the longest term relationship possible with that tenant was the path to something more than financial success. It was the path to prosperity in every sense. It had always been a simple formula, learned from the man who had now returned to his life and become, once again, his closest friend and counselor. His father had taught Sabah well: live honestly, treat others fairly, help when you can, and always stay away from greed.

More than anything else, Sabah always tried to do the right thing. After a lifetime of practice, he no longer needed to think about it—doing the right thing came to him as naturally as breathing.

This was why, when Harry told Sabah that Larry wasn't happy with their agreed rent increase after the third five-year lease period, Sabah called Mr. Flynt and spoke with him personally. Negotiating with Mr. Flynt directly wasn't a common practice for Sabah. Harry had been the more accessible and visible partner of the two. In fact, over the long period in which they'd been leasing from Sabah, Harry had become one of Sabah's closest personal friends. But Larry Flynt wasn't the kind of man to suppress his dissatisfaction. Mr. Flynt actually seemed to thrive on conflict and the adversarial arena of negotiation.

"Hey, Sabah, I'm getting the short end here," Larry said when Sabah called him.

"Mr. Flynt," Sabah said, "you've been here a long time, and I appreciate it very much, but rates have gone up in the Gaslamp."

In fact, since Mr. Flynt had signed the original lease ten years before, leasing rates had nearly doubled in the Gaslamp. Sabah was one of the very few landlords in the area who had not raised his rates.

"You know what, Mr. Flynt?" Sabah continued. "You've been in the building ten years and we've never just talked. I only hear from you when we have to fix something. You know Harry and I are good friends. We go golfing. We go on trips. I think maybe we should get together sometime and just talk. You know what I mean?"

"Okay, I'll tell you what," Mr. Flynt said. "I'll see you at the Four Seasons in Beverly Hills on Wednesday morning. I'll buy breakfast, but you're not getting much more than that out of me."

Sabah smiled. "I'll be there."

In the end, Sabah renewed Mr. Flynt's lease at a rate far below market value and a rate that made Mr. Flynt happy. He did this not because of the prestige value in having such a well-known tenant. Certainly it wasn't out of charity. He did it out of gratitude, not only to Mr. Flynt, but to every person in his life who had helped him along the way.

He could easily have made more money with another tenant—much more. But hadn't the Iranian brothers originally given him the building for fifty thousand less than what they'd been offered? Hadn't Victor become his closest friend and business partner because of all that Victor had first done for Sabah? Hadn't Peter Luster been kind enough to introduce Sabah to Harry and Mr. Flynt? Hadn't Patrice become the rock and foundation of his life because she had been there, every day of his life, to support him and work side by side with him to build their dreams together? Each of them, and so many others, had given Sabah more than he could ever repay. His gratitude was a verb; it always expressed itself in action.

With a simple handshake in the restaurant of the Four Seasons Hotel, Sabah achieved his purpose in meeting with Mr. Flynt. The men parted with a mutual respect and appreciation that neither had fully experienced before that moment. Perhaps because of this newly forged level of trust and confidence, Sabah felt prompted to tell Mr. Flynt something he hadn't planned on talking about.

"Mr. Flynt, I wonder what you'd think about something. I want to know, I've been thinking for a while about writing a book."

"What about?" Mr. Flynt asked, as his assistant rolled him out of the restaurant in his wheelchair.

"A book about how immigrants succeed in America. Do you think anybody would read it?"

"I don't know, Sabah. People read a lot of junk, that's for sure." Then, perhaps seeing a slight twinge of disappointment or even hurt in Sabah's eyes, Mr. Flynt amended his response. "Then again, it might be a best seller. What do I know? Poverty stricken Iraqi refugee flees tyranny and becomes millionaire in America. What's wrong with that?"

"Really? You think so?"

"Sabah, you write it and I'll see what I can do to help you publish it."

Before that moment, Sabah had never considered his journey through the world to be more important than anyone else's, or any more interesting for that matter. But if Larry Flynt thought he might have a story worth telling, then maybe it wasn't such a bad idea after all. Perhaps his life wasn't so extraordinary, but all he'd learned, the values so deeply instilled within himself, the particular path he'd taken in achieving what so many considered to be the "American Dream"—if he could help others understand how to take that journey themselves, it might be worth the effort.

Sabah thought long and hard about what success means and how one achieves whatever one considers success to be, particularly in a place he believed with all his heart to be the greatest country on Earth, the United States of America.

CHAPTER FORTY-SIX

★ ★ ★

The Circle Connects

★ ★ ★

O f all the gifts Sabah received from Patrice in their twenty-four year marriage, nothing even closely approached the birth of their two sons, Nick and Alex. Sabah's two sons were the very center of his world. Every hardship he had to pass through, he would do his best to help them avoid. Every kind of deprivation he had experienced, they would never have. They were born in America and all they would ever know would be the best part of Sabah's own life.

At the same time, they were taught, as Sabah had been taught, the all important lesson of hard work. Advantage and birth into relatively fortunate circumstances, compared to Sabah's own family, had absolutely nothing to do with working hard. For Sabah, this was the core of a man's character and, as far as he was concerned, shaping that character was the most important job he shared with Patrice.

Alex, four years older than Nick, was the first to attend college. It was 2008 and Alex had been accepted into Suffolk University in Boston. It was an interesting year for any college freshman in America. The first year of college, so marked by opportunity, a new world of learning, optimism, and hopefulness in an unlimited future. At the same, it was the year that officially marked the worst financial downturn in the American economy since the Great Depression of the 1930s.

By the time Alex graduated college four years later, America was still reeling from the effects of a financial system in collapse. The man who had sold Sabah and Sam their first shopping center years before, and had subsequently assisted Sabah and Victor in purchases of other buildings and a large shopping center in Temecula, California, had now become a successful manager at the largest commercial real estate brokerage in the country, Marcus and Millichap. He was more than happy to do what he could to assist Alex in an economically challenging time by offering him a job as an agent in training.

With income from his several commercial properties as well as profits from Mr. Neon, it had been some time since Sabah had needed to work every day, or even work at all. But there was a kind of tinkerer in Sabah. Just as some men like to build things in their home workshops or preoccupy themselves with other hobbies, Sabah was constantly imagining new business ideas, new ways of catering to the insatiable needs and desires of America.

The past few years had been a long, hard road for many Americans. In general, people were saving more and spending less, but people still wanted extra money for as many reasons as they'd always had, from fun and frivolity to debt payments and everything in between. But in such a tight economy, money wasn't so easy to come by, let alone extra money. What was the answer? Sell what you had. So, the idea of Mr. Consignment was born. It was the right time for the consignment business and Sabah decided to open his own unique version, called Mr. Consignment USA, in the Old Town area of San Diego. The business was started in a warehouse owned by Victor.

The whole enterprise was fun for Sabah. It reminded him, in so many ways, of his swap meet days in Spring Valley and the Midway area. Those days, in turn, reminded him of his youth in Baghdad where his entire world was a system of trade and barter, bickering and haggling for a deal that would always be sealed by a warm handshake and a genuine smile or laugh. It was a world that had always been in Sabah's blood and it was just the right time for many Americans to more fully appreciate the joy and substance of this world.

For months, Alex would come home after a day at Marcus and Millichap, dressed in his suit and tie, trying to be as cheerful and optimistic as he could. He had learned much from Sabah about the value of endurance and perseverance, but there were forces beyond Alex's control, beyond everyone's control, shaping the economic opportunities in America.

For years, everyone in San Diego had seen them: the large "For

Lease" signs in front of office buildings in huge commercial real estate developments. More than any other visual symbol of the economic downturn, these signs were, perhaps, the most obvious and persistent. Businesses had gone away and, for now, they weren't coming back. So what was a commercial real estate broker to do, particularly one so young in the industry, without the advantage of a long client or referral list to help him through difficult times?

What to do? What have people always done? What did Mr. and Mrs. Toma do to feed their nine children? What did Sabah do to see this day in his own life? They did whatever they needed to do and, hopefully, something other people needed to. Alex was about to learn the most important lesson Sabah could ever teach him. Alex was going to learn how to survive.

Largely due to national and global economic circumstances far beyond his control, Alex couldn't excel in Marcus and Millichap as he had hoped and planned to do. Though Alex was as much a stoic as his father, Sabah easily recognized the signs of disappointment and discouragement slowly gathering in his son. It was Sabah who first suggested that Alex might want to consider working at Mr. Consignment.

It was such a different world. Alex hadn't graduated college to work in a warehouse filled with bric-a-brac. He'd envisioned himself in the sexy, high tech offices of contemporary corporate America, having power lunches where multi-million dollar deals were consummated as quickly as glances shared with pretty waitresses. Still, Alex wasn't proud, and unlike many of his young, twenty-something American peers, he had no sense of privilege or entitlement. His father had taught him again and again that if he wanted anything in this world, he would have to earn it, and as long as he earned it honestly, it didn't matter what job he did to achieve it.

He began working at his father's new store and found that he loved it. First, there was a lot to be said for not having to put on a tie everyday. But far more than that, he loved the challenge of it. He loved, as his father did, the idea of starting something new, building and nurturing it with your own imagination and hard work. The experience became a process of self-expression and creativity unlike anything he'd encountered at Marcus and Millichap. Strange how simple it was to find work that was so fulfilling.

Or perhaps it wasn't so strange for someone as open to opportunity as Alex was.

As happy as Alex was to make the transition, Sabah was much more so. It wasn't simply because, as a father, his son's happiness made Sabah happier than anything else in the world. As he watched Alex's mind and heart become increasingly engaged in their entrepreneurial enterprise, Sabah couldn't help feeling that some vast cycle was being completed; a full circle of one life time was connecting to another. Everything Sabah had ever learned, everything of importance he'd ever achieved, was now touching something else, melding with a beginning in Alex's life. The moment created a sublime sense of meaning and purpose that he was unable to express to himself, let alone to his son.

Sabah had been gone for years from his Baghdad home by the time he was Alex's age. Sabah thought of his own father, who was gone from the world now, but gone only after he'd live the happiest ten years of his life in America. Sabah knew he had deprived his father this moment in his own life. But would his father have experienced what Sabah was experiencing now if Sabah had stayed in Baghdad? Perhaps, with or without the terrible cloud of the Hussein regime, Mr. Toma could have felt the joy Sabah was now feeling. Had Sabah stayed, perhaps Mr. Toma would have had the transcendental satisfaction of seeing his son complete some great cycle in Mr. Toma's own life.

But that was then, in another place and time, in a place called Iraq where a man named Saddam Hussein had made himself father to an entire nation and stolen that precious happiness from every other father in the land.

And this was now, in a place called America, where even in its most challenging economic times, a father could still feel hope and carefully pass that hope, like a single candle during a dark night, into the hands of his sons.

Sabah thought back to the days when he would ride on the handlebars of his father's bicycle. They would be riding toward the little café where, together, they would sell lunches prepared by Mrs. Toma. They would pedal through the expensive neighborhoods with gated houses that looked much like the house Sabah and his family lived in today. Sabah hadn't known then. How could he have known? Mr. Toma hadn't intentionally been trying to teach Sabah anything. He had simply been living his life and Sabah was a most fortunate beneficiary; he was the son of the man who had lived that life.

Though Mr. Toma hadn't been trying to teach Sabah anything, Sabah had learned everything. He'd learned that nothing would be easy, that everything must be earned. He'd learned that if he ever wanted anything, there was only one person in the world who could give it to him: himself. He'd learned to never compare himself to others who might appear more fortunate, or to envy other people in any way. And, of course, to never, ever feel sorry for himself. Sabah had learned that he could have whatever anybody else had and the only person who would ever stop him was himself.

Without ever intending to, Mr. Toma had taught Sabah all these things. Now, Sabah knew that both Alex and his younger brother Nick were becoming men and were beginning to fully grasp these fundamental truths themselves.

From Sabah's first day in America, these principles had been like the unfailing beam of a lighthouse, drawing him across storm-tossed seas toward a harbor of unimaginable tranquility. This was why he had purchased that suit in Greece so many years ago. This was why, during his first days living in that Hollywood residential hotel, the one with tenants of such questionable character, he had worn that suit every day.

America was not a place Sabah had come to to ask for anything. Even then, he had known that America, more than any other country in the world, rewarded most those who worked the hardest. From the moment of his arrival, and now, nearly forty years later, Sabah's gratitude had only deepened for the country that had given him his life.

CHAPTER FORTY-SEVEN

★ ★ ★

The Nature of Blessings

★ ★ ★

On the cusp of his sixtieth year, Sabah Toma is hardly what some would kindly refer to as a "senior citizen." He retains a full head of dark hair and a smooth, wrinkle-free olive complexion, partially the result of his culture but more a gift from his particular family genes. With regular exercise and a healthy diet, overseen and created by Patrice, Sabah has remained trim, active, and possessed with almost as much energy as that small boy playing soccer in the streets of Baghdad.

Though he has come to an end of the story of his life, his life is far from over. It can be said that, throughout Sabah's life, he has received blessings at critical moments, blessings that protected him, guided him, or strengthened and encouraged him. Blessings which, like trapeze rings, extended to him out of the darkness, allowing him to hold on and propel himself just far enough to reach the next and the next ... and the next. Above all, they are blessings for which he is eternally grateful.

Why did these blessings come to Sabah? Why did Mrs. Al-Ghamdi, a diplomat's wife and frequent client of the Tokalon Salon, offer Sabah the name of her contact in the Iraqi Embassy? Why did Mr. Moghadam offer Sabah his business card on that fateful day when Sabah was so dejected, working in his father's small sidewalk café?

Why did Mr. Naifeh, his high school vice principal, threaten to kill the student leader of the school's Baath party if he so much as looked at Sabah the wrong way? Why did a kind and merciful police officer allow Sabah and his friend their freedom when so many others, arrested and detained for similar or even lesser offenses, would spend months or years as prisoners of the Hussein regime? Why did George Tajirian, the legendary guide to Chaldean refugees, take Sabah under his wing and personally guide him across the golden border of the United States, but not do the same for Sabah's traveling companions?

Why did Lynn Goldberg accept Sabah's case when everything in his head told him it was a fool's errand? Why did Judge Shwartz, who was perhaps the only man in San Diego who could have saved Sabah, postpone his deportation only hours before it was scheduled to occur? Why had this man literally saved Sabah's life, sparing him from an almost certain execution immediately upon his return to Iraq?

Why did Victor, no more than a casual acquaintance, offer his home as collateral for Sabah's bail bond, allowing him freedom instead of languishing for an indeterminate period, perhaps even years, within a federal holding area for immigrant detainees? How was it possible that, at the very moment Judge Shwartz's ruling was being appealed by prosecutors from San Diego, President Reagan should sign the first sweeping federal immigration amnesty bill under which Sabah would be qualified, thus making the entire appeal process irrelevant?

Why did the Iranian brothers and restaurant owners sell their building to Sabah, when they could have made tens of thousands more from another buyer? Why did Klaus, the German businessman, appear and purchase almost all of Sabah's Mr. Neon inventory, allowing Sabah and his brother Issam to change and transform their lives in a way they never had before?

Why did a singer's manager write a single name on the back of a business card, connecting Sabah to a person in Iraq who would allow him to take his mother and father safely and permanently out of that country and into America?

Why?

Strangely, Sabah never asks this question himself. Certainly, more than anyone else in the world, he understands how blessed his life has been and his gratitude for all that has happened in his life is without end or limit. But that all of these things should have happened as they did, when they did, may have appeared extraordinarily coincidental to some. To someone with a faith like Sabah's, simple though profoundly mystical in its own way, everything in his life has happened for only one reason: because God allowed it to.

Sabah's gratitude is boundless. He is grateful to everyone who has ever helped him. His constant prayer is only that he might be able to repay, in some small way, each of those people who have given him his life.

He is grateful to God and prays for all those who do not have the joy of knowing God, that they might discover the vast dimensions of happiness found only through this experience.

He is grateful for his wife, Patrice, knowing that whoever he is, whatever his journey has been, however far he has come and wherever he will go from here, it could not and would not be without her.

He is grateful for his sons and the way they have taught him a new meaning of happiness. He is grateful for his many friends and the richness of those friendships, which is far greater than gold. But there is one thing more for which Sabah is grateful.

From the time he ran barefoot as a boy in the streets of Baghdad, she was his shining star. She has been his idol, his mentor, his companion, and guide. She was there with him during his darkest nights and loneliest days. She gives him hope and reinforces his will in a way that, even together, ten thousand others would fail to do. She is merciless and merciful, strict and generous, but always as constant and unwavering as that single star on which the solo traveler forever sets his course. She beckoned him as a boy, nurtured him as a youth, and blessed him as a man.

She, above all others, is his dearest and most beloved friend, because without her, he would have nothing. When Sabah prays, he thanks God for many people by name. But at the end of every prayer, her name is always the last word from his lips.

Her name is America.

AFTERWARD – In His Own Words / An Interview With Sabah